TEXAS WOMAN'S UNIVERSITY LIBRARY

D1482750

OSCAR WILDE
THE DOUBLE IMAGE

OSCAR WILDE
THE DOUBLE IMAGE

by
George Woodcock

BLACK ROSE BOOKS

Montréal - New York

Copyright © 1989
Black Rose Books

No part of this book may be reproduced or transmitted in any form by means, electronic or mechanical, including photocopying and recording, or by any information storage or retrieval system, without written permission from the publisher, except for brief passages quoted by a reviewer in a newspaper or magazine.

Black Rose Books R134
Hardcover — ISBN: 0-921689-43-8
Paperback — ISBN: 0-921689-42-X

First published 1949

Canadian Cataloguing in Publication Data

Woodcock, George, 1912-
    Oscar Wilde
 	
Previously publ. under title: The paradox of Oscar
    Wilde. London: MacMillan, 1949.
ISBN 0-921689-43-8 (bound) -
ISBN 0-921689-42-X (pbk.).
 	
    1. Wilde, Oscar, 1854-1900. I. Title. II. Title:
The paradox of Oscar Wilde.
 	
PR5823.W6 1989   828'.8'09   C89-090123-6

Cover design: ZEBRA Communications Inc.

Black Rose Books

3981, boul. St-Laurent   340 Nagel Drive
Montréal, Québec H2W 1Y5   Cheektowaga, NY 14225
Canada   USA

Printed and bound in Québec, Canada

CONTENTS

INTRODUCTION

This book was completed almost exactly forty years ago, and the long gap is one of the reasons why I present it without revision. Not only have my own attitudes to life and literature changed profoundly during that period, but so have critical views of Wilde and also our general attitude towards the kind of behaviour for which he was so cruelly and extravagantly punished. The recent decision of the United Church of Canada to allow the ordination of homosexuals as ministers projects a degree of permissiveness that did not prevail even as late as 1949, when this book first appeared; then the laws under which Wilde was imprisoned were still on the statute books and occasionally invoked. It is evident that to bring my book up to date in the sense of adapting it to the changes of four decades would mean a complete rewriting, and in the process it would lose not only its freshness of approach but also its relevance as a document in the process of critically assessing Wilde's works and his ideas.

Had *The Paradox of Oscar Wilde* been a biography, which it is not, so much new material has become available during the past four decades that I would have been obliged to present what would virtually have been a new book, but fortunately Richard Ellman made that task unnecessary by writing the excellent life, *Oscar Wilde* (1987), which brought to an end his distinguished career as a critic-cum-literary historian. Had I been concentrating on the more controversial aspects of Wilde's life I would have been obliged to chart in some detail the changes in public attitude that would have made impossible in the 1980s the kind of condemnation which Wilde endured and the even more harmful social ostracism that accompanied it. But, as will soon become evident to the reader, I was considering Wilde as a thinker and as a writer of unavowed didactic tendencies rather than as a social lion or a voluptuary; my use of biographical data, and my references to the more controversial aspects of Wilde's behaviour were always subordinate to the main argument, which was based mainly on a reconsideration of Wilde's writings to show how far he was an originative thinker whose seminal ideas eventually influenced the society that rejected him. I set out to demonstrate that when he called *The Importance of Being Earnest* "a Trivial Comedy for Serious People", he was laying claim to something far broader and more durable than a first night public.

Thus the new biographical data that makes Ellman's book so different from and so much richer than the earlier lives by writers like Hesketh Pearson, Arthur Ransome and such self-seeking figures as Frank Harris and Lord Alfred Douglas, has in no way changed the basis for my arguments in *The Paradox of Oscar Wilde*, and given this fact I believe there are advantages to allowing the text to stand and so to anchor this book within its period as one of the earliest to enter deeply into the intellectual content of Wilde's works and his life.

Books of this kind often have their special pieties, and in writing *The Paradox of Oscar Wilde* I was paying a debt. When I came of intellectual age, in a small English provincial town at the end of the 1920s, the literary influences that percolated through were not the Modernists like Eliot and Pound, Joyce and Lawrence; rather they were the turn-of-the-century generation like Bernard Shaw and H.G. Wells, who taught me that nothing was too sacred to be questioned or mocked. Shaw made me think about the social moralities; Wells taught me the vast potentialities for good or evil in human inventiveness operating on the natural world. The third of these liberators was Oscar Wilde.

My parents, quite exceptionally, were consistent defenders of Wilde, which took a certain amount of courage at a period when his very name still carried a connotation of evil in large sections of English society. Not only was Wilde anathema among pious church-and chapel-goers of all sects, but he had become a kind of monster figure in folk mythology, the hero of smutty verses and bar-room legends. Class hatred even entered into the situation and anyone rash enough to walk through a slum street in a good suit risked, as late as the 1930s, being followed and mocked by a swarm of small boys shouting, "Hey, Oscar! Oscar Wilde!" and throwing mud. My father's sound argument was that we must judge an author by the way he wrote. For him Wilde was a superb stylist, and anything else he had done was irrelevant to judging him on an artistic level. Characteristically, he was careful not to give me any hint of what the "anything else" might be when he started me off as a boy reading Wilde's fairy stories, which led inevitably to the rest of his writings.

At first it was the worst aspects of Wilde that appealed to me: his ornate prose, his facile romanticism, the perpetually adolescent aspects that caught an echo in my own sensibility as I worked my way forward as a young poet through the equally facile romanticism of the Georgians to the spare style and social concerns of the 1930s.

But very soon I found other aspects of Wilde's writings commanding my attention: his mockery of social conventions, his original insights into the relationship between creation and criticism, and his particular kind of individualism that began to draw me towards anarchism when Kropotkin was no more than a name to me and I had barely heard of Proudhon. And gradually I began to sense the peculiarly dualistic nature of Wilde's mind, balancing factor against factor and rejecting nothing, in the manner of a belated gnostic, which increasingly for me seemed to explain the complexities of his thought and which in the end would give me the structuring concept on which the present book could be based.

Most writers, if their memories survive their physical death and their works are read as much as a year after it, tend to go through a series of phases of acceptance. Sometimes, if their work has hit a particular nerve in the collective awareness, as George Orwell's last books did, their fame will go on increasing until they reach such a classic status that it is unlikely the vagaries of fashion will henceforward affect their status. Others — Orwell's friend Herbert Read is a good example — may suffer a rapid diminution of attention immediately after death, and if this trend continues they will probably be quickly forgotten, as most best-selling authors are. But sometimes, half a generation or so later, their work will begin to be seen more clearly in the perspective of its age, and interest in it will revive, until it moves into a belated acceptance and literary beatification — if not sanctification — occurs. It looks today as if Herbert Read's work is now moving into this position, twenty years after his death.

The fluctuations in the reputations of such writers depend in general on the quality of their writing, seen as a whole, and on its apparent relevance to the life and culture of their times. In Wilde's case the situation was different. After his trial the fragile edifice of acceptance he had built up around the image of the writer, considered as wit and social personage, collapsed entirely. All the fair-weather friends who had admired him when he was a figure of fashion fell away; publishers and theatre managers no longer wanted his work, for which they had recently competed; his plays disappeared from the stage, and he was forced until his death to rely, for the publication of such of his books as found their way into print, on the loyalty of that eccentric pornographer, Leonard Smithers. During the last years of his life he wrote nothing that was not in some way connected with his downfall and with the double punishment of imprisonment and social os-tracism which had followed. Through a sheer power of feeling that had not been in his works before, and through the way in which they touched the consciences of those who had shunned him in his misfortune, *The Ballad of Reading Gaol* and his two long letters on prison conditions to the *Daily Chronicle* spoke for this man who seemed to have come out of a tomb to denounce the cruelty of the prison system and by implication the inhumanity of all coercive institutions.

The only other piece that Wilde wrote after his condemnation to hard labour in 1895 was the strangely mutilated work which his Canadian friend Robert Ross published under the title, *De Profundis*. This was a highly edited version of the long letter which Wilde had occupied his last days in prison writing to his lover — and the main author of his downfall — Lord Alfred Douglas. The complete text, which was not published until 1949, was an often bitter and self-pitying account of Wilde's relations with Douglas and how they had led to his descent into shame and poverty and to Lord Alfred's going scot-free. But the part that Ross abstracted and published in 1905 concentrated mainly on Wilde's thoughts on the redemptive function of suffering. This, with the prison writings, distorted the public view of Wilde for many years after his death. He appeared either as the woeful artist self-condemned to destruction like his own Dorian Gray, or as a sacrificial victim to the hypocrisy of Victorian England, *perfide Albion*. Both views are indeed partly true, the first subjectively and the latter objectively, and there were undoubtedly times when Wilde saw himself as one of the last of the great tragic heroes. He had been fascinated with Aeschylus, and particularly with the *Prometheus*, from boyhood, and he told André Gide that he had put his genius into his life and no more than his talents into his writings.

But lives continue only in memory, and we feel their poignancy only vicariously as we feel the wretchedness of Wilde's exile permeating the final chapters of Richard Ellman's biography. It is the works that survive as they were written, and one of the unfortunate features of the general attitude to Wilde during the first four decades of the twentieth century was that a fascination with the calamity of his disgrace and the behaviour that led to it tended to hinder the redirection of attention to what he wrote. Even where his works were played or published, as they were increasingly in France and especially Germany in the early 1900s, at least one of the motives was to expose English perfidy, which led to the exaggeration of Wilde's importance as a romantic artist and to the unfortunate elevation of some of his more sensational but less able works, notably *Salome*, which, after Lugné-Poë's modest productions in Paris during the 1890s, was magnificently staged by Max Reinhardt in Berlin in 1903 before it was put into music by Richard Strauss and launched as an opera in 1905.

All this was very much the political side of literature, and the situation was complicated by the fact that so many people had to justify themselves as actors in the real life drama of Wilde's life; the stream of memoirs and personal apologiae disguised as biographies continued to appear until World War II. Lord Alfred Douglas was still at it in 1938, with a third volume of prevarications entitled *Without Apology*, and in the same year André Gide evoked Wilde as a Mephistophelian tempter in his *Oscar Wilde*. A few of these books, mostly by people who were friendly with Wilde but not emotionally involved, still evoke him with freshness, like Laurence Housman's *Echo de Paris*, Vincent O'Sullivan's *Aspects of Wilde*, Charles Ricketts' *Oscar Wilde: Recollections*. All these little books stress Wilde's good personal qualities, his likeability, his rash generosity, his marvellous kindness, but even these sympathetic accounts do not lead us far in a critical examination of his writings and the thought they embodied. It seemed indeed as though, as Wilde had thought, the quality of his personality would be remembered for good or ill, and the quality of his work be unexamined and thus unrecognized.

After World War II the situation changed considerably. Most of the people who had known Wilde were dead, and those who now wrote on him were moved by motives neither of self-justification nor of self-aggrandisement. Montgomery Hyde's publication in 1945 of the transcripts of Wilde's trials made it possible for these occasions to be seen more calmly and in their appropriate contexts. Moreover, the great relaxation of prejudices against homosexuality that led to the Wolfenden Report in 1957 and to the Sexual offences Act of 1967, eliminating the law under which Wilde had been condemned and imprisoned, had already begun, and it was much more easy to write with relative objectivity about this aspect of Wilde's life, as Hesketh Pearson's unheated biography of him in 1947 displayed.

There still remained hesitancies and inconsistencies as we moved into this freer world, and my book shows some of them. I was still — when I wrote it — an anarchist activist, more than a little touched by old-fashioned revolutionary puritanism, so that though

I was appalled by the laws that persecuted gays, I still — with an inconsistency which W.H. Auden pointed out at the time — regarded homosexuality as a malady that psychologists could investigate and cure. I did not then, as I do now, follow my anarchist beliefs to their logical conclusion and accept it as an alternative to "normal" sexuality that should be allowed to flourish without restriction so long as nobody is manifestly harmed, which of course applies to "normal" sex as well. But I leave unchanged the passages that I would now reject, since they do after all represent the viewpoint most writers would have adopted at the time *The Paradox of Oscar Wilde* was written.

The most important effect of this shift in attitudes towards the more controversial aspects of Wilde's life was to turn attention back towards his works. His comedies gained a popularity on the stage which they have never lost since then. *The Picture of Dorian Gray* settled into the role of a constantly reprinted marginal classic. But it was also becoming recognized that as a writer Wilde was much more than an entertainer; that in fact he did have a role in the development of the literature of his time and of criticism as directed to the arts and to society.

I remember well my discussions with fellow writers when I was working on *The Paradox* between 1946 and 1948. Julian Symons was indeed sceptical about the extent of serious thought in Wilde's writings, and when my book appeared he charged me with "trying to break a butterfly on the wheel." Herbert Read, on the other hand, was immediately interested in my plans, since he recognized in Wilde a predecessor in the fields of industrial design and education through art to which he devoted so much of his own attention. And George Orwell surprised me by writing that he had always been "very pro-Wilde" (which was unexpected in view of his fulminations against the "pansy poets" of the 1930s), and that he particularly liked "*Dorian Gray*, absurd as it is in a way." Shortly afterwards, in 1948, when I published an edition of *The Soul of Man under Socialism*, Wilde's anarchistic essay which had been out of print for some time, Orwell discussed it very seriously in the *Observer*, and, while he regarded Wilde as in many ways excessively Utopian, he came to a final favourable conclusion:

> But that is not to say that Wilde is altogether wrong. The trouble with transitional periods is that the harsh outlook which they generate tends to become permanent. To all appearances this is what has happened in Soviet Russia. A dictatorship supposedly established for a limited purpose has dug itself in, and socialism comes to be thought of as meaning concentration camps and secret police forces. Wilde's pamphlet and other kindred writings — News from Nowhere, for instance — consequently have their value. They may demand the impossible, and they may — since a Utopia necessarily reflects the aesthetic ideas of its own period — sometimes seem 'dated' and ridiculous, but they do at least look beyond the era of food queues and party squabbles, and remind the Socialist movement of its original half-forgotten objective of human brotherhood.

Unknown to me, another writer was at this time also striving to present Wilde as a serious influence in the development of contemporary attitudes towards art. This was Edouard Roditi, who late in 1947 published a small and very illuminating book — Oscar Wilde in the Makers of Modern Literature series that James Laughlin had launched through his avant garde house, New Directions. In those days new books were not very quickly imported into Britain from the united States, and the productions of small houses like New Directions rarely came to one's attention. Though I finished The Paradox of Oscar Wilde about a year after Roditi's book appeared in New York, I did not see his Oscar Wilde until some time in 1949 when it was too late for me even to make acknowledgement of its existence. There are parallel insights which draw our books together, but we reached them independently. All the same, I take this late opportunity of acclaiming Roditi's book and recommending it to readers whom The Paradox of Oscar Wilde may interest. It is a fine study of Wilde's relationship to the currents that led to the emergence of literary and artistic modernism during the years following his death.

Since the 1940s, views of Wilde as a writer have moved only in one direction — towards the final recognition that despite all past appearances he was no mere ephemeral harlequin of literature.

His criticisms of morals and manners have turned out to be prophetically accurate. The daring ideas of the role of criticism and of the relations between art and life that so disturbed his contemporaries have become the commonplaces of contemporary criticism, so that it is difficult to imagine how — say — a Northrop Frye could have shaped his system without Wilde's preparatory ideas. The plays stand firmly on their own stages as marvellous works of theatre and ever provocative exposures of the varieties of pretence and prejudice, while in our cruel world *The Ballad of Reading Gaol* sounds as contemporary as an Amnesty International Bulletin. And all this has been recognized without Wilde the man having been forgotten, in all his geniality and his wit. A harmonization of the personality and the work has taken place in our minds. We perceive that Wilde spoke for causes we must still defend, that he belongs as much to our century as to his own, but we still see him as an extraordinarily interesting and original human being, "so generous, so amusing and so right," as Richard Ellman says in the last words of his monumental biography.

George Woodcock
May, 1989

THE DOUBLE IMAGE

MANY books have already been written on and around Oscar Wilde, and he has been the source of long literary and personal controversies during the half-century since his death. It may therefore appear rash, and even presumptuous, for yet another writer to venture on this vexed subject. Yet it was the lack, among this mass of writing, of a really balanced judgment of Wilde's works or his significance in literature and social thought that prompted me to attempt a new evaluation.

This study does not claim to be another biography. That work has already been done well by Hesketh Pearson, whose *Oscar Wilde* gives all the necessary information about the events of Wilde's life, and conveys a very convincing portrait of his complicated personality. Pearson also deals with the story of Wilde's downfall in a relatively sympathetic and unprejudiced way, and avoids, as almost no other writers have done, the temptation to portray Wilde as a black sinner or a misunderstood saint, as a weak-willed half-wit or a "Lord of Language"—to use Wilde's own half-serious phrase. He shows us Wilde as a human being endowed with charm and generosity, and demolishes resolutely many of the legends that have made Wilde appear a more trivial and foolish character than he really was. But his book, excellent as it is, has all the limitations of a biography. Its appreciations of Wilde's works are necessarily brief, and, while Hesketh Pearson makes some lucid remarks on the ideas they represent, he does not profess to give an elaborate literary study.

The remaining books concerning Wilde—I have myself read at least forty—are for various reasons even less satisfactory. Wilde's sexual deviations and his imprisonment seem to have destroyed any possibility of an objective literary criticism by the majority of his students, while those personal friends who were sufficiently moved to write biographies or semi-biographies seem to have been provoked into a hysteria of controversy, disagreement and mutual abuse that makes their books unreliable and often distasteful.

Frank Harris wrote his *Life of Oscar Wilde* from an inaccurate memory, and in order to make a saleable book, filled in the gaps from his fruitful imagination. He gives long conversations and "confessions" in which Wilde talks like a bowdlerised Harris; he actually describes a train journey with Wilde which existing correspondence shows that Wilde made alone. Sherard, who devoted several books and pamphlets to defending Wilde, is over-anxious, even at the expense of the truth, to whitewash his former friend and to pretend the non-existence of incidents that offended his own aggressive sexual normality. Lord Alfred Douglas, in at least three badly written and childishly petulant books, sets out to clear himself with the world at Wilde's expense. Gide tells stories about Wilde which certainly have the air of fantasy rather than of reality. Between these four individuals and other friends of Wilde, such as Robert Ross, there have been violent literary battles, in which accusations of lying and caddishness have been exchanged freely, and which have thrown the unfortunate reader into a mêlée of argument where his idea of Wilde has become steadily more confused. On one occasion Douglas actually carried the controversy into the courts with a libel action against yet another writer on Wilde, Arthur Ransome; he deservedly lost the case.

The sense of guilt that drove Wilde's personal acquaintances to such confused polemics made them useless as biographers, and the best contemporary writings on Wilde are by such sane and gentle men as William Rothenstein, Charles Ricketts, Vincent O'Sullivan and Laurence Housman, who have been content to leave records of their personal impressions and have avoided the bitter controversies over Wilde's conduct. Such brief memoirs are invaluable for gaining a balanced judgment of Wilde, but they, again, do not set out to give an adequate consideration of his writing and thought.

Naturally enough, so colourful a personality attracted the attention of every kind of crank and partisan, and there are several tedious books giving theosophical or quasi-mystical explanations of his significance. Some, like the Comtesse de Bremont's *Oscar Wilde and His Mother,* were written by people who knew him personally, and contain a few authentic reminiscences; the remainder merely try to claim him as a follower of their particular creed, and are wholly useless except as literary curiosities.

There remain a few very superficial literary studies, and one or two technical volumes, such as Stuart Mason's *Bibliography of Oscar Wilde,* which has a strictly limited purpose and fulfils it admirably. But so far I have discovered only one satisfactory biography, that of Hesketh Pearson, and no satisfactory critical discussion of Wilde's work. As I have already said, it was this opinion which impelled me to commence this short study.

I have used, as will become evident, a dialectical method. This is not because I see any particular virtue in the dialectic—I am neither a Hegelian nor a Marxist—but because I think that the peculiar nature of Wilde's development renders this method most likely to be fruitful in illustrating his important characteristics as a writer. His life, writing and thought are full of apparent contradictions, and many critics have interpreted this as a sign of fundamental insincerity. I believe that Wilde was in fact a more earnest man than he or others believed, and that he was sincere in almost everything he did. The contradictions which become evident at a very early period in his writing and activities, and which continue until his death, were the result of a very deep cleft in his mental process. Two currents of feeling and thought ran through his life, and must give to any account of his work the quality of that figure of speech which was always on his lips—the paradox. It is very likely that Wilde loved the paradox because it suited the peculiar duality of his attitude towards the world. Significantly, his only novel, *The Picture of Dorian Gray*, deals with a version of the *doppelgänger* theme. In this novel Wilde has split himself into two: he is the witty cynic, Lord Henry Wootton, but his desire for a continued youth and his own attempts to gain the essence of all experience form the two essential elements of the character of Dorian Gray. Furthermore, one of his most interesting stories, *The Fisherman and His Soul*, is written around the actual parting of the two sides of a man's nature under the demands of an unfulfilled desire.

Of course, this idea of the split personality is in no way new. It has been the basis of much folklore and legend, and to-day lives on in popular novels and films. It has even been applied before, in an oblique way, to Wilde himself, and it must have become evident to many readers that Wilde's nature was of a schizoid type. But so far nobody has attempted a thorough analysis of his work on this basis.

Yet the evidence of this cleft in Wilde's emotional and mental life is so clear, and its influence on his work so strong, that any examination of his writing which does not investigate it is necessarily superficial. Unless one accepts this inner division, it is really impossible to give any satisfactory account of his work or his actions. Either he must be taken as a profound artist and a serious thinker—in which case his less responsible acts must be hidden like family skeletons, as in Sherard's biography. Or he must be regarded as a superficial poseur—in which case the serious and profound content of his work is necessarily ignored, or, at best, dismissed as insincere pastiche.

Both of these extreme attitudes are clearly wrong. Wilde clowned and posed and indulged in pathetically sordid and ridiculous debauches. He was a social snob and could play the sedulous ape to any writer whose work he admired. Nevertheless, he undoubtedly possessed a gift for presenting important ideas in a fresh and striking way, and at times such ideas showed a deep wisdom. He was capable of excellent writing (only prejudice can deny the quality of his plays), his scholarship was very extensive and thorough (in spite of his pretence of idleness), his hatred of social injustice was deep and sincere, and he seems to have been one of the great conversationalists of all time. Personally, he balanced his weaknesses with an unstinting generosity, a willingness always to be of service to his friends, and a lack of malice rare in so brilliant a talker.

Harris, reliable at least in this, since he was expressing his own thoughts, said: "I have known no more charming, no more quickening, no more delightful spirit"; and added, "I do not believe that in all the realms of death there is a more fascinating or delightful companion." The dour W. E. Henley, one of Wilde's most bitter enemies, admitted that he was "a scholar and a gentleman," while Sir Peter Chalmers Mitchell, a scientist and a very acute observer, was surprised to find that "Oscar Wilde was a man of very wide information and interests, and of commanding intelligence." Sir William Rothenstein, who knew almost all the great English and French literary figures of his day, said of him:

> He was not only a unique talker and story-teller—I have never heard anyone else tell stories as he did—but he had

an extraordinarily illuminating intellect. His description of people, his appreciation of prose and verse were a never-failing delight. He seemed to have read all books, and to have known all men and women. . . . He was remarkably free from malice. Moreover, I have met no one who made me so aware of the possibilities latent in myself.

Not only did he gain the respect of literary men, artists and scientists, but also the affection of types as varied as prison warders, working-class convicts, Norman peasants and French hotel proprietors (the devotion of Dupoirier, *patron* of the Hôtel d'Alsace where Wilde died, is an impressive example). The evidence of such varied people and the undoubted qualities of his work leave no doubt that Wilde had a personal sincerity and an intellectual capacity of extraordinary depth.

Yet the opposite qualities cannot be denied. Wilde posed continually; he had an irresponsibility of character that made him totally unable to resist the onset of wealth and fame; he often wrote artificially and shallowly, and spoilt some of his best work by self-conscious elaboration. For these reasons he remains among the nearly great—only at times reaching true greatness of achievement. Henley, in a flash of insight, called him "the sketch of a great man." But for all this he is not the less fascinating in writing, not the less amiable in personality, not the less fruitful in ideas expressed with an unparalleled epigrammatic brilliance; and a serious study can clearly succeed only by admitting and embracing both sides of his varied nature.

Such a method of examination appears all the more necessary on a closer perusal of his work. Not merely are there contradictions in his actions, personality and style of writing. The cleavage runs right through his ideas as well. Thus, there is the continual rivalry of paganism and Christianity, of the gospel of hedonism and the gospel of suffering. There is the contrast between his æsthetic clowning—which he himself admitted to be little more than posture—and the valuable critical theories expressed in his lectures and essays, and carried out in his own writing. There is the contrast between the delightful but often superficial nonsense that occupied so much of his conversation and drama, and the deep thinking on artistic, philosophical and social subjects that supported his outward brilliance. There is the contrast between the social snob, with his attitude of apparent flippancy towards the poor, and the social critic, whose ideas on political justice and attacks on existing relationships in society were of a truly subversive nature. And there is the contrast between the playboy whose antics brought about with a strange inevitability the crisis of Wilde's downfall, and the self-conscious "prophet" who emerged chastened from prison, only to be replaced again by the temporarily suppressed playboy of the last days in Paris.

In the five major essays forming the second part of this book, I shall discuss these themes of contrast, illustrating them from Wilde's writing and life and the views of his contemporaries. By this simple dialectic method I shall reach a conclusion in the final section that will attempt to unite the various conflicting strains in such a way as to give a clearer picture of Wilde's real achievements and the true nature of his work than seems possible from a merely biographical or literary study. I should make it clear that I do not claim an absolutely clear line of division between the various conflicting characteristics—or that the same kind of contrast exists in each case. But always there will appear the evident duality that existed in Wilde's personality and gave his work both its richness and its at first baffling inconsistency and irregularity. My final aim is to reach and bring into prominence those really important elements of thought which are undoubtedly present in Wilde's writing. And this can only be done by an admission of the essential conflict that at once obscured and assisted his intellectual activity.

But before beginning to discuss the actions of Wilde in that strange combination of adolescence and maturity which constituted his manhood, it is necessary to consider the two most significant periods of his formative years.

The first of these was that embracing the rich background of his childhood in Dublin, with the varying influences of his parents and, more indirectly, of his kinsman, the Gothic novelist Maturin, which determined the major aspects of his future development.

The second was during his time at Oxford, when the contrasts in his character and work were already becoming evident and clearly defined. These differing strains were developed largely under the influence of two of the dons then teaching at Oxford, Walter Pater and John Ruskin, and it is necessary, therefore, to consider these two men and their respective influences on Wilde. Naturally, I do not attribute to either of them a major responsibility for what Wilde became finally. Ruskin himself later included Wilde among the occasional subjects of his Old Testament wrath, while poor respectable Pater was very doubtful of the disciple who applied his precepts to real experience. But they crystallised and gave direction to certain tendencies already present in his character, and therefore a brief study of their curiously incompatible natures and philosophies, and the way in which they both influenced Wilde at this formative stage, is an important prelude to examining the conflicting tendencies of his later life.

MERRION SQUARE

UNDOUBTEDLY, like most impressionable men, Wilde was very much influenced by his family, which, from all the reports that have survived, seems to have been a richly eccentric one. Among other commentators, the poet W. B. Yeats, a fellow Dubliner and a moderately close friend of Wilde during the last decade of his life in England, expressed the opinion that much of Wilde's character and many of the actions of his mature years are explainable by his family life, and this writer's remarks can be taken, with reservations, as a basis for our picture of the early background, since they do represent fairly faithfully the myth of the Wilde family that has survived in Dublin and, to a lesser extent, elsewhere.

The Wilde family were clearly of the sort that fed the imagination of Charles Lever, dirty, untidy, daring, and what Charles Lever, who loved more normal activities, may not have valued so highly, very imaginative and learned. Lady Wilde longed always, perhaps, though certainly amid much self-mockery, for some impossible splendour of character and circumstance. She lived near her son in level Chelsea, but I have heard her say, 'I want to live in some high place, Primrose Hill or Highgate, because I was an eagle in my youth!' I think her son lived with no self-mockery at all an imaginary life; perpetually performed a play which was in all things the opposite of that he had known in his childhood and early youth; never put off completely his wonder at opening his eyes every morning on his own beautiful house, and in remembering that he had dined yesterday with a duchess, and that he delighted in Flaubert and Pater, read Homer in the original and not as a schoolmaster reads him from the grammar. I think, too, that because of all that half-civilised blood in his veins he could not endure the sedentary toil of creative art and so remained a man of action, exaggerating, for the sake of immediate effect, every trick, learned by him from his masters, turning their easel painting into painted scenes.

In all this I think Yeats has been somewhat unjust both to Wilde and to his parents. To take his last point, Wilde in fact seems to have regarded his own oddities with a great deal of amusement, and none knew better than he how to use a mask with calculated effect. On the other hand, his love of the classics was based on genuine scholarship rather than on the satisfaction of a fantasy, and he had a good deal more of this quality than Yeats himself showed in most of his own writings. As for the description of Wilde as a man of action, this, as we shall show later, sprang from a singular but persistent misunderstanding by Yeats of the real nature of Wilde's character.

Nor, though there is much truth in Yeats's rather malicious talk, which undoubtedly approximates closely to the contemporary gossip and surviving legends about the Wilde family, does his description convey by any means a just and accurate picture of their real importance and their undoubted virtues. Wilde himself perhaps went to the other extreme when, in an excess of contrition during his imprisonment, he said that his parents "had bequeathed me a name they had made noble and honoured, not merely in literature, art, archæology and science, but in the public history of my country, in its evolution as a nation. I had disgraced that name eternally." Whereas, in fact, if the names of Sir William and Lady Wilde are remembered to-day outside a narrow circle of specialists in medical and literary history, it is solely as the parents of Oscar, who, if he "dragged" that name "through the very mire," was to give it an adventitious immortality made all the more secure by his own sufferings.

Nevertheless, both his parents were undoubtedly people of great intellectual energy and wide interests, whose achievements in their own fields of serious activity very much compensated for the seedy Bohemianism that gave them a temporary notoriety in nineteenth-century Dublin.

Sir William Wilde may, as his enemies suggested, have looked like an ape, and his dislike of washing may have been compensated by an excessive love of alcohol (initiated by the success of an equally eccentric physician who had cured him of an apparently hopeless illness by the application of copious quantities of strong ale). But even on the physical plane, these disadvantages did not prevent him from gaining wide success with the ladies of Victorian Dublin, and he became the father of numerous natural children and the hero, or perhaps the villain, of a notorious law case in which he was accused of having seduced a professor's daughter with the help of chloroform. The lady's virtue was estimated by a Dublin jury to be worth a farthing, but the case merely added to Sir William's disrepute as an elderly rake.

On the intellectual plane the elder Wilde was a man whom most of the Dublin scoffers had more reason to envy and respect than to despise. He was one of the greatest surgeons of his time, and had been known to perform a difficult tracheotomy successfully with no better instrument available than a pair of ordinary scissors. He was an eye and ear specialist of international repute, recognised as an authority even by the advanced German medical profession. In his spare time, he became a leading student of Irish archæology, conducting many important excavations. He gave substantial scientific backing to the claims of the Irish nationalists by preparing the formidable medical report on the 1851 census, showing the inhuman results of the Irish land system, for which, ironically, he was knighted by the Viceroy. He even ventured into literature with an erudite work on *The Closing Years of Dean Swift's Life* and a volume of archæological and piscatorial reminiscences entitled *The Beauties of the Boyne and Blackwater*. For a while he enjoyed a fashionable success that touched even royalty—the office of Surgeon Oculist to the Queen in Ireland was created especially in his honour, the King of Sweden decorated him for services to medicine, Maximilian of Hapsburg paid him a visit on his way to a tragic empire in Mexico, and Napoleon III sent a special emissary to consult him. The scandals of his private life led to a diminution of this kind of success, but Sir William remained until his death in 1887 a considerable figure in Irish medicine and archæology.

So far as one can see today, there was little in common between Sir William and Oscar—though Willie, the elder son, followed closely in his father's path as a drinker, a practical opponent of over-cleanliness and a sexual acrobat. Sir William was a small man, irritable, malicious, and stirred by a perpetual and restless store of physical energy. Oscar, on the other hand, was tall, dignified even in his most childish pose, courteous in manner, kind in speech and action, and phenomenally indolent except as a talker—country walks tired him, he travelled in hansoms even for short distances whenever he had sufficient money, and once, when a humourless athlete asked about his preferences in outdoor games, he remarked that he had only played dominoes outside French cafés.

Indeed, some of Oscar's habits and inclinations seem almost to have been caused by a reaction against his father. Even in his most depressed period of poverty and social ostracism, he was always neat and scrupulously clean (in prison it was a matter of great grief that he could not polish his shoes or shave properly), and the dandyism maintained throughout his life may well have been provoked at least partly by his father's untidiness. Again, while he was a great connoisseur of intoxicants, he disliked drunkenness, and despised his brother Willie for his immoderate alcoholic addictions. Moreover, Oscar never emulated his father's feats with women. In his younger days he seems to have had few affairs, and, although on one occasion he toured the brothels of an American town and acquitted himself to the satisfaction of his young companions, heterosexual adventures figure hardly at all in his history. Towards the women he met in society he behaved with a scrupulous courtesy that was old-fashioned even in his own day, and he disliked the racy talk which men like Frank Harris practised in mixed company. Alfred Douglas says that "I never heard a coarse or indelicate allusion come out of his mouth," and many other writers have confirmed this extreme lack of vulgarity in his conversation. Willie's unconsciously humorous remark to Bernard Shaw: "Oscar was *not* a man of bad character; you could have trusted him with a woman anywhere," was literally true, even before Wilde's homosexuality manifested itself in practice. One of the reasons for his extreme popularity with women seems to have been that he could always be charming without an ulterior motive. Much of this, of course, was due to his innate homosexual tendency, but, at least in the early days of his marriage, he seems to have found pleasure in normal sexual intercourse, since Sherard tells us of the embarrassingly detailed enthusiasm with which he spoke of his early marital experiences. It was only after quite a long period of pederastic activity that he completely ceased to be attracted towards women and reached the stage where, after his famous visit with Dowson to a brothel in Dieppe, he could say, "The first these ten years—and the last. It was like cold mutton."

Oscar Wilde's homosexuality is a complicated phenomenon, and it would be foolish to explain it by any one cause, but his original disinclination towards normal sexual activity may well have been influenced by the distaste a sensitive boy, deeply attached to his mother, might feel for the antics by which his father created unhappiness within the family.

Except, therefore, for a common love of learning, Oscar had few positive debts to his father. From his mother, on the other hand, he inherited much, both good and bad, and we might begin by quoting his own tribute to Lady Wilde's good qualities, which also reveals something of the character of her relationship with her trying husband:

> She was a wonderful woman, and such a feeling as vulgar jealousy could take no hold on her. She was well aware of my father's constant infidelities, but simply ignored them. Before my father died, he lay in bed for many days. And every morning a woman dressed in black and closely veiled used to come to our house in Merrion Square, and unhindered either by my mother or anyone else used to walk straight upstairs to Sir William's bedroom and sit down at the head of his bed, and so sit there all day, without ever speaking a word or once raising her veil. She took no notice of anybody in the room, and nobody paid any attention to her. Not one woman in a thousand would have tolerated her presence, but my mother allowed it because she knew that my father loved this woman, and felt that it must be a joy and a comfort to have her there by his dying bed. And I am sure that she did right not to grudge that last happiness to a man who was about to die, and I am sure that my father understood her apparent indifference, understood that it was not because she did not love him that she permitted her rival's presence, but because she loved him very much, and died with his heart full of gratitude and affection for her.

One of Wilde's biographers has criticised him for admiring his mother's tolerance on this occasion, and has regarded it as evidence of the bad influence of the family background on his moral standards. But, from any charitable viewpoint, Lady Wilde's action seems to have been truly moral, and Christian in the purest sense of the word.

There were many points of resemblance between Oscar and his mother. Like him, she was tall and stately, and never allowed her feelings to disturb her dignity, which she combined with an impulsive generosity. She had also a richly eloquent voice, and, again like Oscar, delighted in conversation. A lady novelist who regularly visited her "At Homes" in the 1880's records:

> As for her own talk it was remarkably original, sometimes daring and always interesting. Her talent for talk was infectious; everyone talked their best. There was tea in the back room, but no one seemed to care about eating or drinking.

She delighted in epigrams, and her conversation was often sufficiently *risqué* to shock her nineteenth-century guests, as when she expressed publicly the opinion that "there has never been a woman yet in the world who wouldn't have given the top of the milk-jug to some man if she met the right one." She made no objection when Oscar, in his student days, introduced her to a friend with the words, "I want to introduce you to my mother. We have founded a society for the Suppression of Virtue." Indeed, she probably appreciated the remark as well as her son, though there is no evidence to support the conclusion Bernard Shaw drew from it, that Lady Wilde was "so strongly in reaction against Victorian prudery that she brought up her children as Immoralists."

Another side of Lady Wilde's character, which she shared with Oscar, was her love of ostentation. Like him, she was somewhat taken up with the charm of aristocratic names, and sought the acquaintance of the socially distinguished. She boasted proudly of her relationship to the celebrated terror novelist, Charles Robert Maturin (to whom we shall return), and is even said to have claimed that her maiden name of Elgee was derived from Alighieri, and that she was descended from Italian émigrés of Dante's family. In the latter claim, if she ever made it, there can have been no substance, since Oscar, whose admiration for Dante and love for famous ancestors were equally great, is never known to have repeated it.

Lady Wilde's passion for show was also expressed in a sartorial extravagance which touched on barbarity. A visitor to her salon in Merrion Square described how—

> . . . she wore that day a long crimson silk gown which swept the floor. The skirt was voluminous, underneath there must have been two crinolines, for when she walked there was a peculiar, swaying, swelling movement, like that of a vessel at sea, with the sails filled with wind. Over the crimson silk were flounces of Limerick lace, and round what had been a waist an Oriental scarf embroidered with gold was twisted. The long, massive, handsome face was plastered with powder. Over her blue-black, glossy hair was a gilt crown of laurels. Her throat was bare, so were her arms, but they were covered with quaint jewellery. On her broad chest was fastened a series of large miniature brooches, evidently family portraits. . . . This gave her the appearance of a walking family mausoleum. She wore white kid gloves, held a scent-bottle, a lace handkerchief and a fan. Lady Wilde reminded me of a tragedy queen at a suburban theatre.

Others have described her more kindly, but always the oddity and ornateness of her attire have been stressed.

All this had its parallel in Oscar's self-conscious splendours of dress, his æsthetic garb of velvet coat and breeches, his

Neronian coiffure, fur overcoats, jewelled Balzacian walking-
canes and green carnation buttonholes. The tendency, which
in the mother degenerated into an untidy showiness, in the
son developed into an over-dressed but not wholly unpleas-
ing dandyism.

Yet another characteristic which Lady Wilde transmitted
to her son was her horror of age. Time and again we are told
of the dim, pink-shaded lights and curtained windows, intended to hide the signs of age when she received her visitors, and of the pathetic aid of cosmetics by which she en-
deavoured to preserve that appearance of physical youth
which she probably felt was compatible with her continued
mental vigour. Oscar also hated to think of the approach of
age: his works are filled with tributes to youth and regrets
at its passing. One of the key passages in *The Picture of
Dorian Gray* is that in which Lord Henry Wootton praises
Dorian for his good looks, and remarks, with a feeling unusual in so cynical a character:

> You have only a few years in which to live really, per-
> fectly and fully. When your youth goes, your beauty will
> go with it, and then you will suddenly discover that there
> are no triumphs left for you, or have to content yourself
> with those mean triumphs that the memory of your past
> will make more bitter than defeats. . . . Youth! Youth!
> There is absolutely nothing in this world but youth!

Indeed, the significant theme of *Dorian Gray* is its neo-
alchemical dream of the magic preservation of youth. Wilde,
nearing the end of his forties, seems to have become extremely conscious of the pressing tread of time, and at this
period he began to speed the pace of his life to a frenzied
hunt for new experiences before it was too late to enjoy
them. A couple of years later Lord Illingworth, Wilde's *alter
ego* in *A Woman of No Importance*, was made to say, min-

gling solemnity with flippancy in a characteristically Wilde-
ian conversational gambit:

Remember that you've got on your side the most wonderful thing in the world—youth! There is nothing like
youth. The middle-aged are mortgaged to Life. The old
are in Life's lumber-room. But Youth is the Lord of Life.
Youth has a kingdom waiting for it. Everyone is born a
king, and most people die in exile, like most kings. To win
back my youth, Gerald, there is nothing I wouldn't do—
except take exercise, get up early, or be a useful member
of the community.

Oscar was ever anxious to disguise his own age, and at his
trial claimed, until challenged by Carson, to be two years
younger than he actually was. In this he resembled the society ladies he ridiculed in his plays, who ceased to grow
older when they reached thirty-five; the very fact that he
should have repeated this jest so often is evidence of his preoccupation with the problem of keeping young.

Like many middle-aged homosexuals, he chose young men
for his lovers, and undoubtedly there was a great deal of Nar-
cissism in his attitude towards them. He was clearly hypno-
tised by his own personality, and sensitive that in growing
old he was losing his physical charm.

Feeling his own youth slipping away, he tried to recover it
vicariously by contact with young men, and it is for this
reason that Lord Alfred Douglas made such a fatal appeal
to him—fatal and illusive, since in character Douglas was so
meanly unworthy an object of Wilde's admiration.

One of Wilde's favourite conversational stories, which he
liked sufficiently to turn into a written "prose poem," concerned Narcissus. Narcissus died, and the pool turned to
salt tears, but when the nymphs said that they grieved with
her for the loss of so beautiful an admirer, the pool answered,
"But I loved Narcissus because, as he lay on my banks and

looked down on me, in the mirror of his eyes I saw ever my own beauty mirrored." In the eyes of young men Wilde saw his own youth mirrored.

But, however much he may have shared his mother's reluctance to admit the loss of his youth, Oscar certainly did not follow her in using artificial aids to preserve it, and there is no reason to believe the malicious story of Carson's biographer, that during his last days in Paris Wilde used to paint his face.

However, Lady Wilde was much more than a showy eccentric who tried to keep young much longer than was dignified. She was also a poetess of minor ability, and a translator of some importance, having rendered into English, among other novels, Meinhold's terror romance, *Sidonia the Sorceress*, which was admired by Rossetti, and which Wilde himself read often and voraciously during his childhood. This book, with the works of Maturin, was no doubt largely responsible for that preoccupation with the macabre and the supernatural which occurs continually in Wilde's works, expressed with levity in *The Canterville Ghost* and *Lord Arthur Savile's Crime*, and with gravity in *The Sphinx*, *Salome* and *The Picture of Dorian Gray*.

Lady Wilde, however, was perhaps best known as the "Speranza" or "John Fanshaw Ellis" who played a flamboyant part in that movement of Irish rebellion which arose in the 1840's and reached its climax in the "year of revolutions," 1848. During 1847 she became interested in the Young Ireland movement, and began to write for *The Nation*, which was edited by Gavan Duffy. At that time the discontent produced by the great potato famine of 1847–8 had reached its height, and, encouraged by the revolutionary outbreaks on the Continent, the Irish malcontents were moving somewhat ineptly towards an activist attitude. *The Nation*, as well as its more extreme rival, John Mitchel's *The United Irishman*, began to advocate armed resistance. Smith O'Brien talked of guerrilla warfare, John Mitchel called for a violent uprising, and in the pages of both journals appeared naïve but inflammatory articles on blowing up bridges, casting bullets and the use of rifles. The Government was alarmed, suspended *Habeas Corpus,* and arrested all the leading agitators who could be found. Smith O'Brien's rising proved an abortive answer to the campaign of coercion.

The Nation was run by a skeleton staff of volunteers to replace the imprisoned editors, and appeared with a somewhat verbose and florid article by "Speranza," one of its temporary staff, entitled *Jacta Alea Est,* in which she declaimed:

The Irish nation has at length decided. England has done us one good service at least. Her recent acts have taken away the last miserable pretext for passive submission. She has justified us before the world, and ennobled the timid, humble supplication of a degraded, insulted people, into the proud demand for independence of a resolved, prepared and fearless Nation.

Now, indeed, were the men of Ireland *cowards* if this moment for retribution, combat and victory were to pass by unemployed. It finds them slaves, but it would leave them infamous.

Oh, for a hundred thousand muskets glittering brightly in the light of heaven, and the monumental barricades stretching across each of our noble streets, made desolate by England—circling round that doomed Castle, made infamous by England, where the foreign tyrant has held his council of treason and iniquity against our people and our country for seven hundred years. . . .

Gather round the standard of your chiefs; who dares to say he will not follow, when O'Brien leads? Or who amongst you is so abject that he will grovel in the squalid misery of his hut, or be content to be flung from the ditch side into the living tomb of the poor-house, rather than charge proudly like brave men and free men, with that glorious young Meagher at their head, upon the hired mercenaries of their enemies? One bold, one decisive move. One instant to take breath, and then a rising; a rush, a charge from North, South, East and West upon the English garrison, and *the land is ours.* . . .

To-day this sounds little more than rather flatulent ranting, well in keeping with the tawdry medallions of a later decade. But it made a sensation in its day, and was undoubtedly moved by a sincere feeling of defiance that had caught the young poetess into the whirl of a revolutionary movement. The British authorities evidently saw danger in it, for they immediately suppressed this issue of *The Nation,* and charged Duffy with sedition. At the trial a sensational scene was enacted, when, after the Attorney-General had demanded Duffy's conviction, "Speranza" rose in the court and shouted: "I am the culprit. I wrote the offending article." The trial petered out and Duffy was saved from the transportation imposed on his comrades, Smith O'Brien, Meagher, Mitchel and others. Eventually he made his peace with the conquerors and finished his life comfortably on the Riviera, decorated with a British knighthood.

Like Duffy, "Speranza" also rested on the laurels of this single victory. Her achievement brought the admiration of the simian Don Juan who became her husband, and she sailed into the quiet waters of literature and conversation, taking no further active part in the Irish political movement, and making no protest when Sir William, like Duffy, accepted a title from the hands of the alien rulers. Yet she remembered her old achievements with a certain pride, which led her to talk of having been "an eagle" in her youth, and when Oscar was brought to trial her head was still sufficiently filled with sentimental nationalism to see him, with singular inaptness, as a symbol of Ireland standing out against English oppression.

But her importance in the Irish revival was not wholly of

a political nature, for Yeats, arch-priest of Celtic Twilight literature, has acknowledged that her *Ancient Irish Legends* had a real influence in awakening the Irish to their native literary tradition. He said of her book:

> We have here the innermost heart of the Celt in the moments he has grown to love through years of persecution, when, cushioning himself about with dreams, and hearing fairy-songs in the twilight, he ponders on the soul and on the dead. Here is the Celt, only it is the Celt dreaming.

Speranza's Irish consciousness had gone inward, and taken to less obtrusive channels, but it may well be that with such books as this she did more to assist the germination of a spirit of national cohesion than by all her windy patriotic articles and poems.

Oscar was never a very outspoken or extreme Irish Nationalist. His ideas and tastes were too cosmopolitan to be bounded by any parochial creed. Sherard tells us:

> He had a strong aversion for what was local in interest, for what was *outré* and self-assertive, and in all these ways his Irish Christian names offended his taste. For the rest Oscar Wilde never willingly placed himself on the losing side in any division of men. Irishmen and Irish matters have always been unpopular in the London society to which he aspired, as they are in lower sections of the Anglo-Saxon mob; and although Oscar Wilde never denied his nationality, he took particular care not to let it transpire.

Sherard's remarks are true in so far as Wilde certainly never gave himself to crude nationalism of any kind, and had much too deep a consciousness of the international character of civilisation and culture to be led away into any patently foolish propaganda for the superiority of Irish art. The eclectic admirer of Dante and Flaubert, of Shakespeare and

Theocritus, of Chuang Tzu and Kropotkin, was hardly likely
to be greatly impressed by the kind of Dublin parochialism
which at that time attempted to elevate Celtic literature into
a major position in the world of writing. He knew well that
Ireland owed her greatest contributions, not to any one race,
but more than many another country to the mixing of races
and cultures; the great Irish writers, like Swift, Goldsmith,
Congreve, Sheridan, Maturin, and, in Wilde's own day, Shaw
and George Moore, as well as Wilde himself, were products
of the mixture of English, Scottish and native Irish blood
and ideas, and their work stands or falls as part of a varied
pattern of Anglo-Saxon-Celtic literature. They brought to it
a Celtic vitality and good-humour, but to narrow this down
to an Irish localism would have been to deny the peculiar
significance of their contribution.

But Sherard's suggestion that Wilde never liked to be on
the losing side is patently untrue. In some of his review articles we find both condemnation of British policy in Ireland
and support for rebels, like Wilfred Scawen Blunt, who had
been imprisoned for the cause. As we shall show in a later
chapter, Wilde always showed an interest in minorities, and
would give his moral support to unpopular causes and ideas
with much disinterestedness. Clearly, he must have known
that *The Soul of Man Under Socialism* would not increase
his popularity with the upper-class salons of London, while
in his comedies of social life he was certainly not over-careful
about his jests at the aristocracy.

Thus, if Oscar did not share the extremity of Irish nationalism which had brought his mother notoriety in her youth,
he certainly shared amply that same strain of rebelliousness
which provoked her actions in those early days of '48. He
also shared, unfortunately, her inconsistent weakness for the
glamour of social prestige.

Between Oscar and his mother there seems to have been a
deep and constant affection; undoubtedly her influence on

his development was great and, in many ways, decisive. Some authors have, in fact, tried to fasten on her the whole blame for his later homosexuality, but their arguments are clearly too simplified to explain that complex phenomenon. Their contentions are based mostly on the story that Lady Wilde, after having borne one son, was very anxious for a daughter, and consequently disappointed to have another boy. In compensation, it is said, she dressed and treated Oscar as a girl for the first few years of his life. One contemporary writer talks of Oscar being so decorated with trinkets that he looked like a little Hindu idol. But, even if this did have any effect on Wilde's later tastes, it can only have been a contributory one, and this possibility is countered by the fact that in his homosexual love-affairs he seems, from what evidence exists, to have played a masculine rôle. Certainly the legend of his effeminacy has been amply exploded by the accounts of his prowess as a fighter when provoked beyond endurance, and his powers of out-drinking tough American alcoholics, a faculty which created such an impression that years after Wilde's lecture tour to America, Sir Frank Benson was told by a South-Western cowboy, "That fellow is some art guy, but he can drink any of us under the table and afterwards carry us home two at a time," while the Californian miners decided that he was "a bully boy with no glass eye." We can reasonably accept the opinions of such experts that Wilde was sufficiently manly in his attitude and achievements not to have been greatly harmed by the eccentric dresses his mother put on him in childhood!

A more likely factor in his homosexuality was his close emotional relationship towards his mother, amounting almost to an acknowledgment of her domination. He was the "model son," always attentive to her needs. In emotional mother-son relationships of this kind it often seems difficult for the son to achieve any complete relationship with other women. Hence the large number of homosexuals, particu-

larly among the middle-classes, who have suffered from dominant mothers in their youth.

Lady Wilde appears to have petted and spoilt Oscar as a
child, and to have taken great pride in his achievements in
manhood. Even at the time of his trial, as we have seen, she
stood by him, but her support on this occasion seems to have
done more harm than good, for she is said to have remarked:
"If you stay, even if you go to prison, you will always be my
son; it will make no difference to my affection; but if you go
I shall never speak to you again." It was largely as a result
of this maternal pressure, supported by his brother's idiotic
fulminations about the duties of an Irish gentleman, that
Oscar decided to disregard the advice of Harris, Sherard and
his other friends to flee the country before his trial, and
instead stayed to "face the music."

Nevertheless, Wilde, with his sense of humour, could never
take his mother completely seriously, and her eccentricities
certainly amused him as much as other people. In the version
of *The Picture of Dorian Gray* which appeared in *Lippin-
cott's Magazine* he portrays her satirically and recognisably
as Lady Brandon. Lord Henry Wootton, after describing Lady Brandon's eccentric manner of introducing people
with a rapid summary of their attributes, says:

> I like to find out people for myself. But poor Lady Bran-
> don treats her guests exactly as an auctioneer treats his
> goods. She either explains them entirely away, or tells one
> everything about them except what one wants to know.

Perhaps the portrait appeared too obvious, and it may have
hurt Speranza's feelings, for it was cut considerably when
Dorian Gray finally appeared in book form. On the whole,
while Oscar was too honest a judge of human character not
to see his mother's weaknesses, his attitude towards her seems
to have been one of consistent devotion.

Apart from the direct influences—very deep in themselves

—which his mother exercised over Oscar Wilde, the atmosphere of the home at Merrion Square, with its easy-going life and its reverence for learning, was bound to have its influence on any boy of more than ordinary sensitivity. Thus, when Oscar went to Portora Royal School, and afterwards to Trinity College, Dublin, his home life had already given him a self-sufficiency that left little room for these institutions to affect him in any decisive way. At both places he learnt only what he wanted to learn. Mathematics did not attract him, so he did not trouble to make himself proficient in this subject; Greek studies, on the other hand, he absorbed eagerly, and rapidly became one of the best classical scholars of his time, winning the Berkeley Gold Medal at Trinity, which, if he had no greater value for it, stood him in good stead as a pawnbroker's pledge during various periods of poverty, right down to his last hard days in Paris. But, apart from fostering his interest in the achievements of classical and pagan antiquity, his early educational environments can have added little to what he had already learnt in the untidy household at Merrion Square. The narrow Irish Protestantism of Portora Royal School perhaps helped to create his later sympathy for the Roman Church, but his youthful attitude towards religion was hardly a reverent one, for one of his favourite amusements was entertaining his schoolfellows with burlesque representations of saints on stained-glass windows. Harris's story that Wilde's first encounter with homosexual behaviour took place at Portora can be taken as apocryphal for lack of real corroborative evidence.

The one really important incident during his years at Trinity College, Dublin, was his meeting with the Rev. John Pentland Mahaffy. This very unclerical clergyman was Professor of Ancient History, and in many respects he showed predilections which Oscar himself was already beginning to develop. He was fond of festivities and aristocrats. He practised the studied art of conversation and actually wrote a handbook on the subject, which Wilde reviewed during his journalistic period (he found it characterised by "pedantry" and an "arid and jejune" style). But all these things Wilde did not acquire originally from Mahaffy: he had already gained them from his home background, and Mahaffy merely encouraged actively the potentialities he found in a willing and receptive pupil. His deepest influence over Wilde, though it was by no means so decisive as that of Pater or Ruskin on the later stages of his career, came from encouraging his love for Greek antiquity. Oscar's holiday with Mahaffy in Greece was a turning-point in his life, but it was, after all, what he saw rather than the man he accompanied that made this such a significant and fruitful interlude.

THE WANDERER

BEFORE terminating this study of the early roots of the various tendencies in Wilde's life and writing, it is necessary to return to his family, and to note a strange genius who, while not actually an ancestor, certainly wielded a great influence on Wilde's ideas because of the fact that, in Oscar's youth, his name was highly respected in the house at Merrion Square and his books were read there with much attention and pride.

This was his great-uncle, Charles Robert Maturin, a Dublin Protestant clergyman of Huguenot descent, who became one of the most celebrated and certainly the most able of the early nineteenth-century Gothic novelists. In Maturin's hands the terror novel, and the kind of theatrical melodrama associated with it, achieved a genuine literary quality and imaginative power which raised them above the pinchbeck Gothicism of Horace Walpole, the rather sentimental sensationalism of Mrs. Radcliffe and the crude horror of Gregory Lewis. Some of Maturin's novels are still good reading, which is more than can be said for *The Castle of Otranto* or *The Monk*, and they combine a fine atmosphere of suspense with considerable originality of thought and incident. *Melmoth the Wanderer,* the story of a man who accepts a new lease of life for selling his soul to the devil, and wanders over the earth trying in vain to get some unfortunate individual to take his burden, is to my mind the best of the English Gothic novels, superior even to Godwin's *St. Leon,* by which Maturin was much influenced—particularly in his description of the terrors of the Inquisition.

Maturin, although his literary career was not wholly successful, gained the respect of such contemporaries as Scott and Byron, who were responsible for bringing his plays before the public at Drury Lane; one of these tragedies, *Bertram,* was, as Byron put it, a "well-merited public success," while Scott called it "grand and powerful." Byron also referred on several occasions to Maturin as a "very clever fellow," although he also remarked that "he has talent, but not much taste." Coleridge apparently came to the rather wrongheaded conclusion that Maturin had neither taste nor talent, for he devoted a long passage in *Biographia Literaria* to an attack on *Bertram,* on Maturin for writing it, and on the Drury Lane Theatre for producing it.

But, despite Coleridge's disapproval, Maturin gained a very wide reputation by his major works, which included, besides *Melmoth,* another terror romance called *The Fatal Revenge, or the Family of Montorio,* and a very powerful historical novel, *The Albigenses.* His repute, and, what is more important, his influence on literary expression and content, extended over many decades of the nineteenth century, and affected writers, not only in England, but also in France and Germany, and even as far away as Russia. The greatest of all terror writers, Edgar Allan Poe, was much influenced by him and acknowledged his genius, while neither Scott nor Victor Hugo was above borrowing from him. The French Romantics as a whole regarded him with enthusiasm; Villiers de l'Isle Adam and Baudelaire were among his disciples, and the latter talked of "the celebrated wanderer, Melmoth, that great Satanic creation of Maturin. What could be greater, what more powerful in relation to poor humanity than this

pale and wearied Melmoth?" Balzac was even more profoundly influenced by Maturin. In *L'Elixir de longue vie*,
he names Maturin with Goethe, Molière and Byron among
the greatest geniuses of European letters, and his own story,
Peau de Chagrin, reproduces Maturin's plot of a man who
has made the devil's bargain, while a number of incidents in
this book, for all its more contemporary and "realistic" setting of France under the July monarchy, resemble very
closely some of the scenes in *Melmoth the Wanderer*. But
Balzac went even farther than this in his tribute to Maturin's
influence, since he actually wrote a semi-humorous sequel to
the original romance, which he called *Melmoth Reconcilié*.
This story tells how Melmoth finally gets rid of his curse to
an embezzling cashier, whom he has detected in fraud. In the
diabolic atmosphere of the Paris Bourse, the cashier easily
finds an equally desperate prey, and so for a whole day the
devil's bargain passes from hand to hand among the frenzied
speculators. Finally, it is left with a careless gambler, who
spends a gay fortnight and then, not having been provident
enough to pass on the curse, dies in damnation, taking his
evil burden with him. It was one of Balzac's less able stories,
and he was more successful when he adapted it and created
Peau de Chagrin.

Maturin also influenced the school of German terror novelists, and in Russia he was read admiringly by the belated
romantics of the 1840's. His influence is even to be detected
here and there in Dostoevsky; Murin, in *The Landlady*, with
his "fiery, feverishly glowing eyes," is very much of a Maturin
creation, and the eyes of Melmoth are once again reproduced
in the terrifying glare of Rogojin, in *The Idiot*, a character
whose morbidity and cruelty have much in common with the
kind of beings created by the English Gothicists.

Among English writers of the Victorian age, Maturin's
prestige was not so great as among their French contemporaries. Yet even here we find men like Stevenson and

Rossetti fascinated by his writing, while Thackeray talked of the terror which the character of Melmoth had aroused in him as a boy. To complete the picture, only a few months ago I found evidence of Maturin's lingering or reviving in-fluence, in an English Surrealist miscellany which included a long quotation from *Melmoth the Wanderer*!

Maturin was an unhappy figure. Although a good preacher, he fitted poorly into the church, whose duties he found a great impediment to his literary activities. He seems to have suffered from a mild form of paranoia, and was always complaining querulously of ill-fortune, even in times of apparent prosperity and success, while criticism would prompt him to hasty and fatal replies, like an ill-advised attack on Coleridge which drew a gentle reproof from Scott.

He dressed eccentrically, and even, in his younger days, ostentatiously, although in later years he seems to have been more like the traditional absent-minded scholar, for Clarence Mangan tells of seeing the old novelist walking in the street with a boot on one foot and a shoe on the other. In his youth he is said to have liked writing with people sitting and even conversing in his room; he also acted in amateur theatricals, with a preference for the more ranting and horrific plays of Nathaniel Lee and Otway, whose influence is evident in his own dramatic works. But as he grew older he became more lonely and unsociable. He would stick a wafer on his brow while at work, to warn those who entered his study not to disturb him, and Mangan records that, in old age:

> An inhabitant of one of the stars dropped upon our planet could hardly feel more bewildered than Maturin habitually felt in his consociation with the beings around him. He had no friend, companion, brother; he and the "Lonely Man of Shiraz" might have shaken hands and then —parted. He—in his own dark way—understood many people; but nobody understood him in any way.

Maturin was a man of strong views and prejudices. As an Irish Protestant, he had a boundless hatred for the Catholic Church. A large section of *Melmoth the Wanderer* is dedicated to an exposure of the Inquisition, while Maturin's one historical novel is a strongly tendentious defence of the Albigensian heretics and a denunciation of their Catholic exterminators. Since his own religious convictions do not seem to have been particularly strong (although accusations of apostasy seem without evident foundation), it is probable that his dislike for the Catholic Church was based less on doctrinal points than on its great institutional tyranny over the individual conscience. In politics he seems to have been, like most Irish Protestants of his class, nominally Tory, but here and there in his books, and particularly in *Melmoth,* he shows the influence of the doctrines of man's natural nobility put forward by the philosophers of the Enlightenment.

Throughout his life Wilde was proud of his connection with Maturin; as a boy he enjoyed the terrors of *Melmoth the Wanderer,* and its continued place in his esteem is shown by the fact that, when he left prison and went into exile, he chose to assume the name of Maturin's unhappy hero, and went to live in France as Sebastian Melmoth. He too saw himself as a man condemned to wander, for having in his own way made the devil's bargain, which must be expiated in his sufferings.

Undoubtedly the element of Satanism in Maturin's work found a responsive chord in Wilde's nature. Throughout the latter part of his successful literary life, Wilde was closely preoccupied with the question of sin, and seems to have regarded himself as a man in touch with the forces of evil. In this Baudelaire, Balzac and his other masters had their influence, but undoubtedly, as his later adoption of the name of Melmoth shows, he often identified himself in imagination with the wanderer of Maturin's masterpiece.

This feeling of playing with Satanic powers, with beings

who themselves had made terms with evil, is shown in a
passage from *De Profundis,* written when Wilde was in
prison, contemplating and mentally dramatising the events
that had preceded his downfall:

> People thought it dreadful of me to have entertained at
> dinner the evil things of life, and to have found pleasure
> in their company. But then, from the point of view
> through which I, as an artist in life, approach them they
> were delightfully suggestive and stimulating. It was like
> feasting with panthers; the danger was half the excitement.
> . . . They were to me the brightest of gilded snakes, their
> poison was part of their perfection. I did not know that
> when they were to strike at me it was to be at another's
> piping and in another's pay.

In this way Wilde had always dramatised the sordid things
of life, the seedy little manifestations of evil or of mere dirti-
ness, and given them a Satanic magnificence. Parisian
apaches had always been to him veritable kings of sin; he
could talk for hours to wholly degenerate characters of the
Quartier Latin like Bibi-la-Purée, and the corrupt nancy-
boys who went simpering into the witness-box to betray him
became in his eyes like beautiful beasts of prey. In the same
way, in an earlier part of his career, he had talked with
barely concealed hero-worship of what he called the "strange
sin" of Wainwright the poisoner.

But it was in *The Picture of Dorian Gray* that Maturin's
influence was most clearly shown, both in the general atmosphere of Satanism that pervades the book—the Satanism
of an agnostic, as Wilde's was also the Christianity of an agnostic—and in the plot as well. Many critics have suggested
that Wilde borrowed *The Picture of Dorian Gray* from Balzac's *Peau de Chagrin.* In fact, while the influence of *Peau
de Chagrin* and also that of Huysmans' *A Rebours* is evident,
Wilde's novel contains a number of elements which neither

of these books possesses, but which it is clear he borrowed directly from *Melmoth the Wanderer*.

Dorian Gray, like Melmoth, wishes for a prolonged youth, and, while the bargain with the Devil is not explicit, as it could hardly be in a book so permeated with scepticism, it is implied in Dorian's wish and in his perpetual alliance with depersonalised evil. Like Melmoth, he has a "strange and dangerous charm"; like him, he draws others to their destruction, and his sinister reputation as well as his uncannily prolonged youth makes him shunned by the world in which he seeks to make his home and find his prey. He is human, but not wholly mortal, and so walks apart in the haunts of men. Like Melmoth, he gathers all experience into his grasp, and his continual youth gives him the power of attracting things and persons towards him; he has almost the Midas touch as well as the secret of halting the advance of age.

Finally, when the hour of reckoning comes and Dorian must surrender the youth he has unnaturally retained, the other self that has been growing old and depraved beside him suddenly enters his body, and brings an instant disintegration into the collapsing rot of age. In the same way all the years that Melmoth has lived, but failed to pay for, descend abruptly on him and precipitate a senescence so rapid that it is evident to those who are watching him. The youth that both Dorian and Melmoth were given had, for different reasons, become burdensome to them. Already Melmoth had tried many times to persuade others to take the bargain from him so that he could sink into the sleep of common death. And Dorian, feeling the burden of his sins about him, thinks to rid himself of them by destroying the painting that has carried their ageing record. There are disparities in detail and style, but the means of precipitating the final end are essentially similar.

Wilde's dabblings in the occult, unlike those of Maturin, had usually a touch of the burlesque, for an element of flippancy garnished his most earnest expressions of belief. In *Lord Arthur Savile's Crime*, great fun is made out of the young man who, since a palmist has prophesied that he will commit a murder, ranges far and wide, again rather like Melmoth, vainly seeking for a victim to complete his destiny, until a foggy night finds him standing on the Embankment behind Mr. Podgers, the unwitting palmist, whom he tips into the river, so that his own fate may be appeased and allow him to wed with an easy heart the girl he loves so passionately that he dare not soil their marriage with the shadow of an uncommitted murder. In *The Canterville Ghost*, elementary but delightful amusement is made out of the subject of ghosts, while in *The Fisherman and His Soul* the *doppelgänger* theme is worked out more explicitly than in *The Picture of Dorian Gray*, by an actual division between the man and his spirit.

In this last story there is an even more direct echo of Maturin, for the agent of the devil who attends the Sabbath, at which the Fisherman dances with the young witch, has a Melmothian appearance, and his eyes, like Melmoth's, are so compelling that throughout the Festival the Fisherman is acutely conscious of their persistent gaze.

Wilde was much interested in magic, as were many of the young English and French poets of his time. He often introduced fragments of magical learning into his conversation, and references to the art occur continually in his writings. He was particularly interested in the magic qualities of jewels, which are discussed at length in *The Picture of Dorian Gray*, and also in *Salome*.

In his daily life Wilde was addicted to superstitious observances. He refused to drive in a cab with a white horse, and at dinner he would object if there were mauve flowers on the table. These observances may have contained an element of affectation, but a story told by Vincent O'Sullivan seems to show fairly convincingly that Wilde took his omens much in earnest:

In Naples he pointed out to me in the street an old woman. "Unless that old woman asks you for money, do not offer it to her. But if she asks you, be sure not to refuse." Some days later we were sitting in a restaurant when the witch came by. She paused a moment, looked at us both steadfastly, and then went her way. Wilde was very much disturbed. "Did you see that? She has looked in at the window. Some great misfortune is going to happen to us."

Indeed, Wilde had such a constant interest in the occult that I find it difficult to accept O'Sullivan's opinion that "he shuns the mysterious; and in himself he was not mysterious, nor had he the aura of mystery and its attractions. It is not in the desert that his Sphinx propounds her riddles, but in a room—a room in an hotel."

This is clearly not wholly true, for Wilde, besides his minor superstitions and his rather boyish delight in the mysterious for its romantic elements, had a curiously strong sense of fatality in life. This appears in the careers of some of his characters, such as Dorian Gray, Lord Arthur Savile, even Salome, whose destinies are worked out as if at the bidding of some compulsive external pattern. And he seems to have had that feeling about himself as well—a feeling of which the fates of his characters were only a reflection in fancy. Sensational failures always appealed to him; as a child he saw himself the defendant in a celebrated law-suit, and only a year or so before his own downfall, in his play, *An Ideal Husband*, a public figure threatened with scandal goes through the preliminary stages of apprehension and anxiety that Wilde himself was to experience a few months later when his own folly had brought him into the hands of the law. One of the characters in this play, Mrs. Cheveley, while threatening the hero, actually presages with amazing accuracy one prominent feature of Wilde's downfall, when she says:

> Sir Robert, you know what your English newspapers are like. Suppose that when I leave this house I drive to some newspaper office, and give them this scandal and the proofs of it! Think of their loathsome joy, of the delight they would have in dragging you down, of the mud and mire they would plunge you in. Think of the hypocrite with his greasy smile penning his leading article and arranging the foulness of the public placard.

This semi-prophecy need not be taken, as I think some writers have done, to indicate Wilde's possession of any kind of occult prescience, although there is some evidence, for what it is worth, that he had a certain telepathic sensitivity, since he claimed that on the night of his mother's death he knew what had happened, as she appeared to him, clad for walking out, when he was sitting in his prison cell. At the time when *An Ideal Husband* was written, it was clear that he had the feeling of a great fate hanging over him—it was part of his personal myth; and months before it happened he believed in the reality of his own downfall, in his destiny to become one of the great failures and sufferers of the world, as, indeed, he did become. Gide, who met him in Algiers when the scandal against him was moving to a climax, and when it already seemed clear to many of his friends that he was riding for a fall, describes him as being resigned to and even longing for the precipitation of his fate; he said, "My friends are extraordinary; they beg me to be careful. Careful? But can I be careful? That would be a backward step. I must go on as far as possible. I cannot go much farther. Something is bound to happen."

As a boy, he thought he heard the banshee calling before the death of a member of his family; he certainly heard the banshee that announced his own doom. When Gide again met him after his imprisonment and asked whether, when he was in Algiers, he had really anticipated what was in store for him, he answered: "Oh, naturally, of course I knew there would be a catastrophe, either that or something else: I was expecting it . . . to go any farther would have been impossible, and that state of things could not last . . . there had to be some end to it. . . ."

This myth of his own destiny was naturally magnified after Wilde left prison, when he talked continually of the great men doomed to be failures, particularly Napoleon and Christ, and when he took upon himself the name of Maturin's formidable and unhappy hero. But the very fact of his writing such stories as *The Picture of Dorian Gray* and *Lord Arthur Savile's Crime* shows that the same feeling of fatality was in his mind even before that time. In the years previous to his trial he acted like a man who had sold his soul for enjoyment, and must make the most of his time while it was left to him. His head was full of the stories of men who had both lived dangerously and suffered for their daring; later, after imprisonment, he identified himself with them, saying: "When I was a boy my two favourite characters were Lucien de Rubempré and Julien Sorel. Lucien hanged himself, Julien died on the scaffold, and I died in prison." But undoubtedly the strongest imaginative influence on his boyhood was that of Maturin and his haunting novel, and one may suggest that the part of his mind which was always preoccupied with romances and romantic heroes and destinies may well have absorbed the book and the fate of its hero to such an extent that it influenced his life as well as his only novel, which it is doubly significant should itself have been modelled on Maturin's masterpiece. Besides common blood, there were clearly a good many tendencies and ideas which Wilde shared with his eccentric and talented kinsman, and which, refined by Wilde's more fastidious and sceptical mind, contributed much both to his literary style and to his philosophical ideas.

CHAPTER

4

THE GEM-LIKE FLAME

WILDE went to Oxford in 1874. A year earlier Walter Pater, one of the most retiring of the dons at that University, had published a book, *Studies in the History of the Renaissance,* which caused a minor flutter in academic and literary circles over certain expressions of a hedonistic and "dangerously" amoral philosophy, and which was later, to Pater's own evident embarrassment, to become the bible of a whole generation of English intellectual youth, who combined it with the teachings of Baudelaire and the French decadents to form the basis of England's own decadence of the eighteen-eighties and nineties.

The offending book was a meticulously written work of self-conscious prose, a masterpiece of artificial writing in the best sense. It contained some very delicately conceived studies of Renaissance painters and poets, and of such philosophers as Pico della Mirandola and Winckelmann. Apart from the quality of the prose in which they were written, there was nothing very startling in these scholarly little essays. But a tinge of heresy crept into the preface with Pater's hedonistic and egoistic definition of the function of criticism:

What is this song or picture, this engaging personality presented in life or in a book, to *me?* What effect does it really produce on me? Does it give me pleasure? and if so, what sort or degree of pleasure? How is my nature modified by its presence and under its influence? The answers to all these questions are the original facts with which the æsthetic critic has to do; and, as in the study of light, or morals, or number, one must realise such primary data for one's self, or not at all. And he who experiences these impressions strongly, and drives directly at the discrimination and analysis of them, has no need to trouble himself with the abstract question what beauty is in itself, or what its exact relation to truth or experience—metaphysical questions, as unprofitable as metaphysical questions elsewhere. He may pass them all by as being, answerable or not, of no interest to him.

But it was in the *Conclusion* that Pater, gathering his courage after contemplating these fine spirits of the past, emitted that pronouncement which was taken by the young as a vindication of immorality, and which made Pater unwillingly notorious as a rebel against the moral conventions of Victorian England. To-day what he says may seem almost a commonplace of radical thought, but still his phrases spring from the page with an impressive and sonorous richness:

To burn always with this hard, gemlike flame, to maintain this ecstasy, is success in life. In a sense it might even be said that our failure is to form habits: for, after all, habit is relative to a stereotyped world, and meantime it is only the roughness of the eye that makes any two persons, things, situations, seem alike. While all melts under our feet, we may well grasp at any exquisite passion, or any contribution to knowledge that seems by a lifted horizon to set the spirit free for a moment, or any stirring of the senses, strange dyes, strange colours, and curious odours, or work of the artist's hands, or the face of one's friend. Not to discriminate every moment some passionate attitude in those about us, and in the very brilliancy of their gifts some

tragic dividing of forces on their ways, is, on this short day
of frost and sun, to sleep before evening. With this sense of
the splendour of our experience and of its awful brevity,
gathering all we are into one desperate effort to see and
touch, we shall hardly have time to make theories about
the things we see and touch. What we have to do is to be
for ever curiously testing new opinions and courting new
impressions, never acquiescing in a facile orthodoxy of
Comte, or of Hegel, or of our own. Philosophical theories
or ideas, as points of view, instruments of criticism, may
help us to gather up what might otherwise pass unregarded
by us. "Philosophy is the microscope of thought." The theory or idea or system which requires of us the sacrifice of
any part of this experience, in consideration of some interest into which we cannot enter, or some abstract theory we
have not identified with ourselves, or of what is only conventional, has no real claim upon us.

Finally, after enlisting Rousseau, Voltaire and Victor Hugo
on his side, Pater concludes with an open declaration of the
amoral nature of art and of the need to live passionately,
regardless of outside criteria.

Great passions may give us this quickened sense of life,
ecstasy and sorrow of love, the various forms of enthusiastic
activity, disinterested or otherwise, which come naturally
to many of us. Only be sure it is passion—that it does yield
you this fruit of a quickened, multiplied consciousness. Of
such wisdom, the poetic passion, the desire of beauty, the
love of art for its own sake, has most. For art comes to you,
proposing frankly to give nothing but the highest quality
to your moments as they pass.

Of course, there was nothing intrinsically degenerate in
these lines, nor was there anything in them new to philosophy
or moral ideas. The need to realise one's self, to judge experience subjectively, to form one's own standard of conduct
voluntarily and in such a way as to gain the maximum self-

development and appreciation of life, had been recognised by responsible philosophers from Epicurus down to William Godwin at the beginning of Pater's century and Kropotkin in his own day. A similar philosophy was implicit in the great works of the continental Renaissance, of the English Elizabethan, Restoration and Romantic cultures; it was present alike in the poetry of Keats, Baudelaire and Whitman, in the prophetic utterances of Blake, in Emerson's essays, and the novels of Herman Melville.

Yet the fact remains that Pater did expound, and define in precise and self-conscious terms, a philosophy which the Victorians hated and chose to ignore when it was not placed so obviously before them. But there was no mistaking the contradiction of current moral ideas contained in Pater's arguments. The conventional were shocked into a truly Victorian indignation, and Pater was subjected to the disapprobation of some of his colleagues and acquired a dangerous but wholly unearned reputation among the ladies of Oxford as a subversive character. To many of the students, however, when they came to read and ponder his book, it was not merely a revelation of beautiful prose, but also a document of liberation. It was a strange and exciting event when one of their own dons recommended them to taste experience to the full, and, naturally enough, they took this to mean the tasting of experiences forbidden and therefore trebly attractive. It is impossible now to say whether, as his contemporaries alleged, Pater was the cause of the moral destruction of many young men. The probability is that those who broke the current moral code would have done so in any case, but that Pater had given them a philosophy that they could use to justify themselves.

It would be extremely unjust to Pater to suggest that he actually recommended sexual debauchery, alcoholic indulgence, or the practice of anything that the young men of the time self-consciously called "sin." Like Epicurus, whose philosophy he interpreted more fully in his later books and whose faithful adherent he always remained, he was wholly guiltless—at least consciously—of the tendencies of which he was accused. A mild, unattractive little man, he lurked in his Spartan college quarters, hiding his weak mouth beneath a drooping moustache, and avoiding shyly any too open contact with his fellow human beings. His relationships with others were in fact always the reverse of passionate, and in personal discourse he showed none of the cultured enthusiasm that inspired his writing. Wilde epitomised Pater's social behaviour very aptly in one of those conversational vignettes in which he unmaliciously exposed the weaknesses of his contemporaries and even of those whom, like Pater, he almost worshipped:

> So you are going to see Pater! That will be delightful. But I must tell you one thing about him to save you from disappointment. You must not expect him to talk about his prose. Of course, no true artist ever does that. But Pater never talks about anything that interests him. He will not breathe one golden word about the Renaissance. No! he will probably say something like this: "So you wear cork soles in your shoes? Is that really true? And do you find them comfortable? . . . How very interesting!"

Pater may not have gone so far in the simplicity of living as Epicurus himself, who declared, "I am thrilled with pleasure in the body, when I live on bread and water, and I spit on luxurious pleasures, not for their own sakes, but because of the inconveniences that follow them." Nevertheless, he lived an unostentatious and relatively austere life, and had certainly no desire to lead others into excess.

Yet, if he did give to some young men an excuse for sowing their wild oats with an easier conscience, modern psychology will admit that he may have unwittingly done them a service, since, foolish as debauchery may be, its chief psychological harm, and, indeed, its chief motivation, comes from the sense of guilt with which it is performed by those who have not shaken themselves free of conventional morality. A more rational attitude towards behaviour and experience will not only deprive indulgence of its dangers, but also lessen its attractions, and lead the impulses which become exaggerated in debauchery into their natural place in a life of balanced experience. In so far as Pater helped to bring about the less exaggerated attitude of to-day, his rôle was eminently useful. At his own time it was inevitable that the respectable should hate him and the young find in him an excuse for their own outbreaks from moral discipline.

Pater himself was very disturbed by the reception of his book; he desired neither the disapprobation of his donnish acquaintances nor what he must have regarded as the very compromising support of the wilder spirits among the young literary students. In his agitation he made an unnecessary retreat by eliminating the offending *Conclusion* from the second edition of his book, but he replaced it, slightly altered, in later editions, with the following cautious footnote:

> This brief "Conclusion" was omitted in the second edition of this book, as I conceived it might possibly mislead some of those young men into whose hands it might fall. On the whole, I have thought it best to reprint it here, with some slight changes which bring it closer to my original meaning. I have dealt more fully in *Marius the Epicurean* with the thoughts expressed in it.

Nevertheless, this famous chapter continued to have an exciting and liberating effect on a whole generation of literary young men.

Wilde did not encounter Pater or his work immediately on his arrival at Oxford. At first he occupied himself with writing a vast amount of capable, but imitative, verse, which bore the obvious influence of Matthew Arnold, Swinburne and

Rossetti. Here and there were poems sufficiently original or well-written to be worth more praise than they have received from most critics since, who have chosen somewhat unjustly to regard all Wilde's poetry as mere plagiarism. Nevertheless, the general level of his verse was such as to give little promise of his becoming an important poet in an age still overshadowed by the work of Tennyson, Arnold, Swinburne and Browning.

It was at the height of his prolific period of poetry writing that Wilde met Pater, whose work he had not yet read, and he was somewhat bewildered when Pater said: "Why do you always write poetry? Why do you not write prose? Prose is so much more difficult."

Wilde continues, in one of his periodical reviews:

> It was not till I had carefully studied his beautiful and suggestive essays on the Renaissance that I fully realised what a wonderful self-conscious art the art of English prose-writing really is, or may be made to be. . . . Mr. Pater's essays became to me "the golden book of spirit and sense, the holy writ of beauty." They are still this to me.

This was written in 1890, but years earlier, in conversation with Yeats, Wilde had said of the *Studies in the Renaissance,* "It is my golden book; I never travel anywhere without it; it is the very flower of decadence; the last trumpet should have sounded the moment it was written." Such extravagant expression covered a genuine admiration for Pater which lasted all Wilde's life, and which left a deep and consistent influence on his work and ideas.

The first aspect of this influence was stylistic. When Wilde took to prose, he naturally modelled himself on Pater, and attempted to reproduce in his own writing the same self-conscious mastery which Pater had attained. But Wilde never gained Pater's lapidary skill; he always lacked that most important element of Pater's self-consciousness, the power of restraint; he could never resist a temptation to let his prose flower into an artificial exuberance which Pater would not have owned. If Pater's prose was golden, Wilde's never went beyond good silver-gilt.

Indeed, Pater's influence was perhaps more faithfully reproduced in Wilde's conversation, where he could not so easily fall into the over-elaboration to which he so often succumbed when writing prose, and in this sphere he undoubtedly achieved an eloquent but perfectly disciplined self-consciousness which was analogous to Pater's command over written prose. Consequently, Wilde wrote best when he was more or less reproducing his conversation, as in the critical dialogues, the plays, or parts of *The Picture of Dorian Gray*, or else when he had some specific idea to express in straightforward terms, as in *The Soul of Man Under Socialism* or his letters about prison conditions. But where he allowed himself to elaborate, his prose became loaded with ornament and ostentation. If we read some of his stories as they are remembered by people who heard him tell them verbally, we see that they have much of the restrained compactness of Pater's best prose. But if we read them as Wilde finally committed them to print, we see that he has spoilt them through a frantic desire to be over-perfect. In a later chapter I shall give examples to illustrate this fact.

But, for the present, I will be content to compare a quotation from Wilde's only novel, *The Picture of Dorian Gray*, whose style was influenced by Pater as much as its plot was influenced by Balzac and Maturin, with one from Pater's *Marius the Epicurean*. The passages are similar in so far as both set out to describe a scene within a room; the differences will become apparent on reading.

Wilde: From the corner of the divan of Persian saddlebags on which he was lying, smoking, as was his custom, innumerable cigarettes, Lord Henry Wootton could just catch the gleam of the honey-sweet and honey-coloured blossoms of a laburnum, whose tremulous branches seemed hardly able to bear the burden of a beauty so flame-like as theirs; and now and then the fantastic shadows of birds in flight flitted across the long tussore-silk curtains that were stretched in front of the huge window, producing a kind of momentary Japanese effect, and making him think of those pallid jade-faced painters of Tokyo who, through the medium of an art necessarily immobile, seek to convey the sense of swiftness and motion.

Pater: At the farther end of this bland apartment, fragrant with the rare woods of the old inlaid panelling, the falling of aromatic oil from the ready-lighted lamps, the iris-root clinging to the dresses of guests, as with odours from the altars of the gods, the supper-table was spread, in all the daintiness characteristic of the agreeable *petit-maître,* who entertained. . . . The opulent sunset, blending pleasantly with artificial light, fell across the quiet ancestral effigies of old consular dignitaries, along the wide floor strewn with sawdust of sandal-wood, and lost itself in the heap of cool coronels, lying ready for the foreheads of the guests on a sideboard of old citron. The crystal vessels darkened with old wine, the hues of the early autumn fruit —mulberries, pomegranates, and grapes that had long been hanging under careful protection upon the vines, were almost as much a feast for the eye as the dusky fires of the rare twelve-petalled roses. A favourite animal, white as snow, brought by one of the visitors, purred its way gracefully among the wine-cups, coaxed onward from place to place by those at table, as they reclined easily on their cushions of German eider-down, spread over the long-legged, carved couches.

The differences are clear, and all to Wilde's disadvantage. Pater's prose is more severe and restrained, yet at the same time more evocative; within his space he tells us much more than Wilde does. We have a detailed picture of the Roman feast, but of Basil Hallward's studio there is the merest sketch in heavy chalks. Pater has an accuracy in words which Wilde lacks—it is, for instance, a pointless exaggeration to describe Lord Henry as smoking "innumerable" cigarettes. Moreover, every word Pater writes has its place, whereas Wilde is continually using redundant adjectives like "tremulous" and "pallid." He also mixes his metaphors—there is a typically Wildean incompatibility in the sentence where he describes the laburnum as "honey-sweet" and then as "flame-like." Some of Wilde's phrases have become clichés, even if they were not in his day, while Pater's sentences still read with great freshness. Moreover, Wilde uses continually the habitual words of literary fashion in contexts where they are hardly appropriate—the shadow of a bird in flight is too usual and natural a phenomenon to be labelled by the typically 'nineties adjective "fantastic." Pater's prose has none of these elementary faults. Both passages are written in a mannered style; Pater's manners are good. Wilde's are almost bad.

I admit that I have quoted a particularly slipshod piece of prose which shows Wilde at his worst. He could write much more ably, although his prose is usually marred by inaccurate phrasing and superfluous words. But the very fact that he should be capable of such lapses shows his inferiority to Pater. Pater may at times have written dully; he never wrote carelessly or inaccurately.

Wilde himself was painfully aware of his failure to approach Pater's ability, and on one occasion he admitted:

> If imaginative prose be really the special art of this century, Mr. Pater must rank amongst our century's most characteristic artists. In certain things he stands almost alone. The age has produced wonderful prose styles, turbid with individualism, and violent with excess of rhetoric. But in Mr. Pater, as in Cardinal Newman, we find the union of personality with perfection. He has no rival in his own sphere, and he has escaped disciples. And this, not because he has not been imitated, but because in art so fine as his there is something that, in its essence, is inimitable.

Incidentally, it should be observed how much better prose Wilde himself wrote when, as in this paragraph, he had some functional rather than fictional purpose.

The second way in which Pater influenced Wilde was in his ethical views. Wilde adopted Pater's Epicureanism with great alacrity, and absorbed it into his curiously eclectic mixture of philosophical ideas. The individualism, even anarchism, implicit in Pater's attitude became the basis of Wilde's social theories, and his scheme of personal life was undoubtedly aimed at the fulfilment of Pater's object, "to burn with a hard, gem-like flame." With a characteristic gusto, Wilde expressed his version of the Paterian philosophy through the mouth of his *alter ego,* Lord Henry Wootton, in *The Picture of Dorian Gray:*

> The aim of life is self-development. To realise one's nature perfectly—that is what each of us is here for. . . . I believe that if one man were to live out his life fully and completely, were to give form to every feeling, expression to every thought, reality to every dream—I believe that the world would gain such a fresh impulse of joy that we would forget all the maladies of mediævalism, and return to the Hellenic ideal—to something finer, richer, than the Hellenic ideal of life, it may be. . . . Every impulse that we strive to strangle broods in the mind and poisons us.

Pater, perhaps not unnaturally, looked on such a disciple as Wilde with distrust, as, indeed, he looked on all the young men who seemed to regard his own pronouncements as having any practical relevance to life. He took the opportunity, in a review of *The Picture of Dorian Gray* which appeared in *The Bookman* of October 1891, to define his attitude towards Wilde, whom he had previously remarked to Rothenstein as having a "phrase for everything," and whose ebullient good humour seems to have disconcerted his own retiring personality. He began by praising Wilde's critical dialogues and essays, *Intentions,* which contain the best of Wilde's prose, and the nearest to Pater's in purity and good style.

There is always something of an excellent talker about the writing of Mr. Oscar Wilde; and in his hands, as happens so rarely with those who practise it, the form of dialogue is justified by its being alive. His genial, laughter-loving sense of life and its enjoyable intercourse, goes far to obviate any crudity there may be in the paradox, with which, as with the bright and shining truth which often underlies it, Mr. Wilde, startling his "countrymen," carries on, more perhaps than any other writer, the brilliant critical work of Matthew Arnold. "The Decay of Lying," for instance, is all but unique in its half-humorous, yet wholly convinced, presentment of certain valuable truths of criticism.

It was certainly generous praise to compare Wilde as a critic with Matthew Arnold, but when Pater came to discuss *The Picture of Dorian Gray*, it seemed that he may have given lavish commendation to the essays in order better to dissociate himself from the philosophy of the novel, without adopting an attitude that might be interpreted as hostile.

He began by pointing out how the novel did not wholly carry out the æsthetic principles of *Intentions*, where Wilde declared that influential art "has never taken its cue from actual life." Pater commented:

There is a certain amount of the intrusion of real life and its sordid aspects—the low theatre, the pleasures and griefs, the faces of some unrefined people, managed, of course, cleverly enough. The interlude of Jim Vane, his half-sullen but wholly faithful care for his sister's honour, is as good as perhaps anything of the kind, marked by a homely but real pathos, sufficiently proving a versatility in the writer's talent, which should make his book popular.

One wonders how far the promise of popularity can be taken as praise in such a studious avoider of that asset as Pater. However, it was not the stylistic attributes of *The Picture of Dorian Gray* that really interested Pater.

He was more concerned to show that Wilde's hedonism was not the same as that true Epicureanism of which he found himself the apostle in England at that period. He made his objection in these terms:

Clever always, this book, however, seems intended to set forth anything but a homely philosophy of life for the middle-class—a kind of dainty Epicurean theory, rather— yet fails, to some degree, in this; and one can see why. A true Epicureanism aims at a complete though harmonious development of man's entire organism. To lose the moral sense, therefore, for instance, the sense of sin and right- eousness, as Mr. Wilde's hero—his heroes are bent on doing as fast as they can—is to lose, or lower, organisation, to be- come less complex, to pass from a higher to a lower degree of development. As a story, however, a partly supernatural story, it is first-rate in artistic management; these Epi- curean niceties only adding to the decorative colour of its central figure, like so many exotic flowers, like the charm- ing scenery and the perpetual, epigrammatic, surprising, yet so natural conversations, like an atmosphere all about it.

A little later, he returned to the same theme by talking of *Dorian* as "certainly a quite unsuccessful experiment in Epi- cureanism, in life as a fine art."

Pater was not anxious, however, to labour the point and, having demonstrated to his own satisfaction the fundamental difference between the philosophy of Lord Henry (and, by implication, of Wilde) and that which he himself had put forward in *The Renaissance*, he proceeded to accord a gen- eral praise to which the book is not wholly entitled, and to credit Wilde with a moral intention which he might well have repudiated.

But his story is also a vivid, though carefully considered, exposure of the corruption of a soul, with a very plain moral, pushed home, to the effect that vice and crime make people coarse and ugly. General readers, nevertheless, will probably care less for the moral, less for the fine, varied, largely appreciative culture of the writer, in evidence from page to page, than for the story itself, with its adroitly managed supernatural incidents, its almost equally wonderful applications of natural science; impossible, surely, but plausible enough in fiction. . . . We need only emphasise once more the skill, the real subtlety of art, the ease and fluidity withal of one telling a story by word of mouth, with which the consciousness of the supernatural is introduced into, and maintained amid, the elaborately conventional, sophisticated, disabused world Mr. Wilde depicts so cleverly, so mercilessly. The special fascination of the piece is, of course, just there—at that point of contrast. Mr. Wilde's work may fairly claim to go with that of Edgar Poe, and with some good French work of the same kind, done, probably, in more or less conscious imitation of it.

To those who to-day read *The Picture of Dorian Gray*, these praises seem too profuse. Wilde was certainly not such a master of the supernatural as Poe, nor, at any rate in *The Picture of Dorian Gray*, did he ever approach Pater himself as a prose writer. As for his conscious moral intentions, he had set them out in the so-called preface to the book, which had previously appeared in the *Fortnightly Review* as "Phrases and Philosophies for the Use of the Young," and which was later used against him by Carson during the Queensberry trial. In this he said:

The moral life of man forms part of the subject-matter of the artist, but the morality of art consists in the perfect use of an imperfect medium. No artist seeks to prove anything. . . .

No artist has ethical sympathies. An ethical sympathy in an artist is an unpardonable mannerism of style.

Wilde would doubtless have contended that *The Picture of Dorian Gray* was a scientific study (he loved the word "scientific" in all contexts) of the way in which a certain course of action has certain results, but he would almost certainly have denied any intention to pass judgment or to "push home" a moral. It is true that Wilde's attitude of the non-participation of the artist in ethical controversy had limitations in practice; there is much of a certain type of social ethics in *The Soul of Man Under Socialism,* in *The Ballad of Reading Gaol,* and even in the plays. But there is certainly no evidence of any moral intent in *The Picture of Dorian Gray* (which Wilde is said to have written for a bet), and a much more interesting aspect of the book is the way in which the personal degeneration of Dorian Gray after a life of continued vice was repeated in Wilde's life during the next three years, until his downfall in 1895. It might almost be taken as a vindication of his own theory of life imitating art!

To an extent Pater was right in disowning Wilde's interpretation of the Epicureanism which had been advocated in *The Renaissance.* Pater did not carry his theories to the same logical extremes as Wilde. Nevertheless, the fact remains that Wilde's doctrines of individualism and of the rightness of giving way to temptation were not wholly irrational conclusions from what Pater had said in his famous *Conclusion.*

It is a commonplace in the history of new philosophies that the master in his frightened latter days will disown the disciples who insist on applying his doctrines with thoroughness to real life. But, whether or not Pater disowned Wilde as a follower, he remained one of the two really important influences on his later development. With him can be linked many of the best aspects of Wilde's work, and some of the worst. The younger man's preoccupation with a self-conscious prose style, and also, by derivation, his more successful attempt to form a self-conscious and artistically perfect art of conversation, spring from Pater. Pater shared with Mahaffy the responsibility for that preoccupation with pagan and classical values which was a constant thread in Wilde's life. The desire to gain varied knowledge and experience, to live fully and even dangerously, that inspired the Renaissance figures admired by Pater, had its echo in Wilde, as did also that ostentation which, in his days of prosperity, he carried off with less grace than his Italian models. And, to the end of his days, Wilde was never to escape from that injunction to "burn with a hard, gem-like flame." Always, he tried to make his life as self-conscious as his prose, to live artistically, to taste experience to the full. He believed, like Pater and the Renaissance humanists, that the individual man was more important than moral laws and social usages, and that only through the experience of individuals could true knowledge be attained. To this belief can be attributed the arrogance and the peculiar sense of self-importance that led him to pursue his own tragedy with such apparent carelessness, and the lack of a sense of proportion that made so many of his acts merely trivial in their selfishness. But to it also can be attributed, at least in part, the finer sides of his individualism —the libertarian philosophy of a free socialism which he expanded in *The Soul of Man,* the anger at infringements of human dignity that made him praise the rebellious poor and protest against the death sentence and the foul conditions of prisons, the respect for human freedom that made him oppose its enemies and support those who defended it, and the contempt for the false values of that corrupt society which he pilloried in his comedies.

Yet in these better aspects of his attitude towards society Wilde was not influenced by Pater alone, in so far as he was influenced at all. The logical extension of Pater's ideas would hardly have produced in Wilde those most un-Paterian ideas of Christianity and social responsibility which undoubtedly were a very important element in the strange amalgam of his character as a writer and thinker; for these he was largely indebted to another Oxford don, John Ruskin, then Slade Professor of Fine Arts at Oxford.

CHAPTER

5

THE ROADMAKERS

ONE can hardly imagine two men less similar in temperament or in their outlook on life than Pater and Ruskin. All the qualities of scholarly restraint, of self-discipline, of gentle pagan Epicureanism, that characterised Pater, were reversed in his fellow don.

Ruskin was possessed by something very akin to a prophetic urge. He had a violent conscience that tortured him with the sight of social injustice, and a truly Old Testament intolerance of ideas and people he considered evil or merely wrong. For him art and morality, social doctrines and æsthetic canons, were mixed inextricably. He could not lecture on any painter without bringing in a host of religious, ethical and political ideas; his conversation, writing and public addresses were characterised by an enthusiasm that robbed them of internal discipline and turned them into eruptions in which impressions, thoughts, exhortations and brilliant theories followed each other pell-mell. Nobody who went to a lecture by Ruskin knew what he would have heard by the end of it; the titles of Ruskin's addresses had no relation to their contents, nor did he ever let any subject keep him from following the changing patterns of his thought. He was once announced to lecture on *Crystallography*, and then, on making his appearance, told his audience that he would talk on

Cistercian Architecture, adding that it did not matter what the title was, "For if I had begun to speak about Cistercian Abbeys, I should have been sure to get on Crystals presently; and if I had begun upon Crystals, I should have soon drifted into Architecture!"

Ruskin, in spite of his own chaotic manner of expression, was disgusted by the ill-ordered society in which he had to live, by its ugliness, cruelty and injustice. He felt impelled to fight for its change, to become the prophet of a new idea of life that would be based on humane values and honest work; yet at the same time he realised his own total inadequacy to the task. In 1875, the year after Wilde's arrival at Oxford, his agony was expressed poignantly in *For Clavigera*:

> What am I to claim leadership, infirm and old? But I have found no other man in England, none in Europe, ready to receive it. Such as I am, to my own amazement, I stand—so far as I can discern—alone in conviction, in hope and in resolution, in the wilderness of this modern world. Bred in luxury, which I perceive to have been unjust to others, and destructive to myself, vacillating, foolish and miserably failing in all my own conduct of life—and blown about helplessly by storms of passion—I, a man clothed in soft raiment, I a reed shaken with the wind, have yet this message to all men again entrusted to me. Behold, the axe is laid to the root of the tree. Whatsoever tree bringeth not forth good fruit, shall be hewn down and cast into the fire.

This passage tells much of Ruskin's character. Beneath all his concern—genuine and passionate—for the sufferings of the poor, he was a vast egotist. Resembling in this his great Russian contemporary, Tolstoy, he was inclined to see himself as the sole Atlas bearing the suffering world. His insistence on the need for his own leadership is significant; a less egotistical man would have wished merely to awaken others to know their responsibility. And there is a strange self-aggrandisement in the idea of himself as the only man fighting for a better world, at a time when William Morris and hundreds of English socialists were at the beginning of their struggles, when the conspiratorial groups in Russia were fighting against Tsarism, when anarchism was spreading among the downtrodden Spanish peasants its gospel of a regenerated world of free and independent men; when Europe was filled with heroic and disinterested men and women struggling for human liberation. Again, in the very self-condemnation there is a note of pride. It is the mortification of a man who has not lived up to a vast idea of his own importance.

Lastly, the two final sentences of this complaint are typical of Ruskin, of his vagueness when it came to the consideration of what should in fact be done in the world. A couple of Biblical phrases, in the suitable denunciatory style, serve to condemn a society that could only be exposed by the thorough analysis of its faults. His indignation was emotional rather than intellectual; he was a man moved by passions of rage and enthusiasm to great heights, but with little capacity for logical thought, or for considering just how the world should be changed.

Ruskin was not, indeed, always so imprecise in his statements, and, if one is patient enough to search the many volumes of his writings, it is possible to perceive the outlines of a theory of practical action, simple in nature, but usually hidden under a growth of denunciatory verbiage.

His clearest social writing is to be found in *Unto This Last,* a strong attack on the current theories of political economy and a denunciation of society based on money. It is here that Ruskin was most successful, because the systems of the political economists are weak precisely in those simple moral values which Ruskin defended. He saw with clarity when, for instance, he said: "Riches is essentially power over men," and when he declared that the essence of becoming rich is to keep your neighbour poor. Occasionally his exuberant eloquence really hit home, as in such a remark as "that which seems to be wealth may in verity be only the gilded index of far-reaching ruin, a wrecker's handful of coin gleaned from the beach to which he has beguiled an argosy." In one brief passage he exposed all the illogicality of the current "philosophy" of the political economists:

Buy in the cheapest market?—yes; but what made your market cheap? Charcoal may be cheap among your roof timbers after a fire, and bricks may be cheap in your streets after an earthquake; but fire and earthquakes may not therefore be national benefits. Sell in the dearest?—yes, truly; but what made your market dear? You sold your bread well to-day; was it to a dying man who gave his last coin for it, and will never need bread more; or to a rich man who to-morrow will buy your farm over your head; or to a soldier on his way to pillage the bank in which you have put your fortune?

He realised clearly the moral insecurity of a society based on such economic ideas:

In a community regulated only by laws of demand and supply, but protected from open violence, the persons who become rich are, generally speaking, industrious, resolute, proud, covetous, prompt, methodical, sensible, unimaginative, insensitive and ignorant. The persons who remain poor are the entirely foolish, the entirely wise, the idle, the reckless, the humble, the thoughtful, the dull, the imaginative, the sensitive, the well-informed, the improvident, the irregularly and impulsively wicked, the clumsy knave, the open thief, and the entirely merciful, just and godly person.

He concluded that:

There is no wealth but Life—Life, including all its powers of love, of joy and of admiration. That country is the richest which nourishes the greatest number of noble and happy human beings.

So far as it went, this was good criticism, and Ruskin reinforced it by his attacks on the ignobility of work in a capitalist society and "the reckless luxury, the deforming mecha-
nism and the squalid misery of modern cities."

But it was when he began to consider schemes for social
reconstruction that his autocratic nature came to the surface,
and he conceived a society as authoritarian as Plato's *Republic*, Thomas More's *Utopia* or the present Russian oligarchy.
Unlike Morris, for instance, his ideas of the dignity of work
did not make him wish to vest the control of industry in the
hands of industrial workers or that of the land in the peasants
or farm labourers. On the contrary, he spoke of an industrial
system of "just and benignant mastership," in which "the
master, as a minor king or governor, is held responsible for
the conduct as well as the comfort of those under his rule."
A revivified aristocracy would flourish, the land being en-
trusted in perpetuity to the great old families, who would be
paid salaries by the State. An intensive supervision over all
individuals by the State would be organised; each family
would be called on to submit a written statement of its activities every year to an officer of the State, and for each hundred
families an overseer would be appointed to see that duties to
the State were carried out. Marriages would be contracted
only with State permission, but men and women allowed to
marry would receive a State pension for seven years after
marriage. All industries would be controlled by trade guilds,
which would regulate prices. In everything the interests of
society, embodied in the State, would be considered before
those of the individual.

As more general aims, Ruskin proclaimed the health and
happiness of the individual and the distribution of produce
in such a way that no one would be without satisfaction of
his or her elementary needs. And, while we can speculate
how far such claims are in fact compatible with the kind of
restrictive society he envisaged, they and his desire to give a

new meaning and integrity to work, through the return to an intimate connection between the worker and real craftsmanship, remain the most important elements in his social philosophy.

With his enthusiasm and the autocracy which emerged in his public statements, Ruskin combined, as is often the case in such individuals, a great personal charm and friendliness. Frederic Harrison, who knew him well, said:

> He was the very mirror of courtesy, of an indescribable charm of spontaneous lovingness. It was neither the old-world graciousness of Mr. Gladstone, nor the stately simplicity of Tourgenieff—to name some eminent masters of courteous demeanour: it was simply the irresistible bubbling up of a bright nature full to the brim with enthusiasm, chivalry and affection. No boy could blurt out all that he enjoyed with more artless freedom; no girl could be more humble, modest and unassuming. His ideas, his admiration and his fears seemed to flash out of his spirit and escape his control. But (in private life) it was always what he loved, not what he hated, that roused his interest. Now all this was extraordinary in one who, in writing, treated what he hated and scorned with really savage violence, who used such bitter words even in letters to his best friends, who is usually charged with inordinate arrogance and conceit. The world must judge his writings as they stand. I can only say that, in personal intercourse, I have never known him, in full health, betrayed into a harsh word, or an ungracious phrase, or an unkind judgment, or a trace of egotism. Face to face, he was the humblest, most willing and patient of listeners, always deferring to the judgment of others in things wherein he did not profess to be a student, and anxious only to learn.

This personal charm helped to gain him the friendship of the students; his lectures aroused their enthusiasm. The attendances were so great that the Sheldonian Theatre had to be used, and this popularity continued throughout the thirteen years of his professorship. He was a fascinating lecturer, not merely because of the unconventional nature of his talks, with their unexpected items of knowledge, their fierce denunciations and their wholly undisciplined structure, but also because of his way of speaking. One of his old students said that the published lectures "convey to the reader but a faint echo of the fascination they exercised over the hearer," and another remembered that his "singular voice . . . would often hold all the theatre breathless."

But Ruskin did not confine his activities at Oxford to lecturing. He founded a museum, organised a school of draughtsmanship, formed working and travelling parties of undergraduates, and tried to attain a direct relationship with his students. It was the inspiration of this personal contact that made him such an influence over a generation of Oxfordians. He had little real standing among artists, because he intellectualised too much about art, but he was a formative influence on many important literary men, including Arnold Toynbee, W. G. Collingwood and, of course, Wilde, who became a devoted disciple of Ruskin almost from their first meeting, and was a regular attendant at the breakfast parties where Ruskin discoursed intimately with his favourite followers.

Wilde was immediately fascinated by Ruskin's character and his eloquent rhetoric. He began to take a much greater interest in art, and to consider its relationship to life. It was also probably under the influence of Ruskin's Old Testament phrases and mediæval Christianity that he began to take that interest in Biblical language which was later so evident in his prose, and to adopt that concern for Christian mythology and ethics which appeared throughout his career as a counter-balance to his paganism.

Wilde was also led to take part in at least one of those unselfish but useless social experiments which Ruskin occasion-

ally initiated—this time the never finished road across Hinksey Marsh. Wilde told this story in an exaggerated version
during one of his American lectures on *Art and the Handicraftsman.*

> One summer afternoon in Oxford . . . we were coming
> down the street—a troop of young men, some of them like
> myself only nineteen, going to river or tennis-court or
> cricket-field—when Ruskin going up to lecture in cap and
> gown met us. He seemed troubled and prayed us to go back
> with him to his lecture, which a few of us did, and there he
> spoke to us not on art this time but on life, saying . . . that
> we should be working at something that would do good to
> other people, at something by which we might show that in
> all labour there was something noble. Well, we were a good
> deal moved, and said we would do anything he wished. So
> he went out round Oxford, and found two villages, Upper
> and Lower Hinksey, and between them there lay a great
> swamp, so that the villagers could not pass from one to other
> without many miles of a round. And when we came back in
> winter he asked us to help him make a road across this
> morass for these village people to use. So out we went, day
> after day, and learned how to lay levels and to break stones,
> and to wheel barrows along a plank—a very difficult thing
> to do.

Wilde's story was rather fanciful, since, although he did
join the later stages of the roadmaking experiment, he was
not at Oxford when the plan was first mooted by Ruskin.
However, the very fact that he should have considered the incident important enough to elaborate in this way showed that
in his younger days he was sufficiently impressed by Ruskin
to wish to appear one of his close disciples. But in later years,
while he retained the interest in social matters and the hatred
of injustice and misery which he shared with Ruskin, he by
no means continued to share Ruskin's idea that sporadic attempts to do good would be effective in changing society. In-

deed, he attacked the philanthropic schemes of Ruskin's more orthodox disciples, such as Toynbee, and showed that palliative measures, aimed at making poverty tolerable, would be of no use whatever in solving the problems of social injustice. He even went so far as to denounce altruism as a socially harmful quality, and showed his superior understanding by indicating the eventual futility of all reformist measures and the need for a revolutionary change to a libertarian and property-less socialist society. Perhaps this also was due, at least in a negative manner, to the influence of Ruskin, since the fiasco of the Hinksey road must have impressed Wilde with the silliness of such social tinkering. It also left him with a deep dislike of laborious manual work, for years later, in *The Soul of Man Under Socialism*, he attacked the idea of the dignity of manual toil, and he was doubtless thinking of his own roadmaking efforts when he said: "Man is made for something better than disturbing dirt. All work of that kind should be done by a machine."

As Ruskin aroused Wilde's interest in social reform, so he awakened him to a realisation of the social function of art. The fact that Wilde should have started his career as an exponent of "æsthetics" was almost wholly due to the direct influence of Ruskin's conversations and lectures, and the theories which Wilde put forward during his early lecture tour in America were those of Ruskin expressed in a less rhetorical manner and pruned of some of their strange extravagances and lapses of taste. The ideas of the function of design in work, and of the importance of the æsthetic element in education, which Wilde continually impressed on his listeners, were derived mostly from Ruskin. On the other hand, Wilde combined with Ruskin's ideas his own classical and late Renaissance predilections, which Ruskin was very far from sharing. He also avoided some of Ruskin's worst errors of taste; he never followed his gross over-estimation of Reynolds and, for all his later quarrels with Whistler, never supported Ruskin in his ridiculous abuse of that painter's work.

Perhaps it was not unnatural, when one considers the extravagance and sensationalism of Wilde's æsthetic campaigns, that Ruskin should have been displeased with an apostle who spread through the lecture halls of England and America a very Oscarised Ruskinism, combined with an eccentric but studied cult of dress reform and a flair for catching the public eye. Yet there is no doubt that in his campaign Wilde actually improved on Ruskin's method of conveying his ideas to the public, and had some success in persuading people to adopt the rational ideas of design suggested by Ruskin.

However, at this time there was no open breach between the two men. During his æsthetic period Wilde took Lily Langtry, then one of his closest friends, to meet Ruskin; later, when he had settled in London as an established writer, Ruskin was among the visitors to his Chelsea home.

Wilde continued to admire Ruskin as a personality and a writer of rhetorical prose, and to appreciate the contribution he had made to the theory of art. Ruskin maintained towards Wilde a guarded neutrality which turned into hostility after Wilde's imprisonment. Ruskin was one of those rebels who cannot understand revolts in which they do not participate, one of those Christians who measure their charity towards the sinner according to the nature of his sin. Yet Wilde spoke well of Ruskin afterwards, as he did of others who failed him when he needed them most.

Ruskin, then, was the formative influence on much of that part of Wilde's personality which leaned towards religion, which saw the need for social change, which acknowledged the importance of art in every-day life. On the other hand, he was perhaps responsible for a great deal of the inaccuracy of phrasing, the tendency to rhetorical purple passages, and the somewhat uncritical imitation of Biblical English, which made Wilde so much less a writer of good prose than Pater.

But Wilde had always the advantage over Ruskin, that he recognised the human individual as being more important than society. This fact, with his personal tolerance, made him a much more humane but also a much more accurate social critic. His relatively greater effectiveness can be seen by comparing, as criticisms of social corruption, *An Ideal Husband* with *Unto This Last*. Wilde's play is more telling, not merely for a greater intellectual grasp of the concrete problem, but also for its much more acute psychology.

In the last two chapters I have sought to portray the two men who had the most profound influence over Wilde's literary and intellectual development. I do not say that either of them made Wilde what he was. They merely helped him to realise tendencies already present in himself, but a study of their ideas and the way they actually influenced him is, I think, necessary for an understanding of the duality of Wilde's personality and outlook, and will assist us in the consideration of the various ways in which this duality later manifested itself in his career and his works.

6

PAGANISM AND CHRISTIANITY

I HAVE already mentioned that the pagan Greeks had a great influence over Wilde's philosophy; he imbibed their worship of beauty, their love of thought, their Epicurean ideals of a balanced life, both as interpreted in their own works and also in the writings of his immediate masters like Pater. Time and again, both in his æsthetic youth and in his years of maturity, he praised the Greek ideal of life and Greek concepts of art. The Greeks, he said, made their great contribution to civilisation by giving to mankind the critical spirit.

And this spirit, which they exercised on questions of religion and science, of ethics and metaphysics, of politics and education, they exercised on questions of art also, and, indeed, of the two supreme and highest arts, they have left us the most flawless system of criticism that the world had ever seen.

These two "supreme and highest arts" he defined as "Life and Literature, life and the perfect expression of life." The Greek principles of life, he contended, could no longer be realised "in an age so marred by false ideals as our own." But in literature all the vital principles of criticism we retained were invented by the Greeks. "Whatever, in fact, is modern in our life we owe to the Greeks."

For the greater part of his manhood, Wilde tried to live in accordance with the Greek view of life, or what he conceived to be the Greek view of life. Too often, indeed, he took the Greek ideal of complete living to mean self-indulgence, and confused Epicurus with his perverted disciples of the Roman decadence. But the fact remains that he accepted the pagan attitude, considered himself most of his life a pagan, and frequently, in spite of occasional lapses into mystical language, proclaimed himself a devotee of the visible world and a worshipper of man. In his early poem, *Humanitad*, he says, "That which is purely human, that is Godlike, that is God," and this humanism, typical of the best of Greek and Renaissance neo-Greek philosophy, he united with a somewhat vague pantheism of the kind also to be found in many of his Greek masters, notably the followers of Pythagoras. A rather naïve example of this exists in his poem *Panthea*, where he says:

> . . . *We shall be*
> *Part of the mighty universal whole,*
> *And though all æons mix and mingle in the Cosmic Soul,*
> *We shall be notes in that great Symphony*
> *Whose cadence circles through the rhythmic spheres,*
> *And all the live World's throbbing heart shall be*
> *One with our heart; the stealthy creeping years*
> *Have lost their terrors now, we shall not die,*
> *The Universe itself shall be our Immortality.*

So complete, indeed, was Wilde's recognition of the constructive rôle played by the Greeks in forming social values, of the nobility of their ideal of life, of the beauty of their literature and art, that some of his chroniclers have claimed that he was wholly taken up with pagan values, to the virtual exclusion of any other kind of thought. Sherard, indeed, went so far as to attribute Wilde's homosexuality to his absorption in classical literature, but we can dismiss this as a psychologically inadequate explanation. Wilde, having already homosexual tendencies, may have found justification for them in Plato's *Symposium* or the works of Petronius Arbiter, but that is about as far as the influence went. It can hardly have originated his tendencies.

More serious statements regarding his essential paganism have been made by such personal friends as Frank Harris, André Gide and Vincent O'Sullivan. Harris, for instance, in his *Life and Confessions of Oscar Wilde,* expressed the opinion that—

> . . . no one will understand Oscar Wilde who for a moment loses sight of the fact that he was a pagan born: as Gautier says, "One for whom the visible world exists," endowed with all the Greek sensuousness and love of plastic beauty; a pagan, like Nietzsche and Gautier, wholly out of sympathy with Christianity, one of "the Confraternity of the faithless who *cannot* believe" to whom a sense of sin and repentance are signs of weakness and disease. . . .

> Oscar Wilde stopped where the religion of Goethe began; he was far more a pagan and individualist than the great German; he lived for the beautiful and extraordinary, but not for the Good and still less for the whole; he acknowledged no moral obligation; *in commune bonis* was an ideal which never said anything to him; he cared nothing for the common weal; he held himself above the mass of the people with an Englishman's extravagant insularity and excessive pride. He held the position Goethe had abandoned in youth. . . .

Gide went even farther, in suggesting that Wilde's paganism actually involved him in an active hatred of Christianity. "The gospel disquieted the pagan Wilde. He did not forgive its miracles. Pagan miracles, these were works of art; Christianity robbed him of these."

And O'Sullivan, one of the most reliable and unbiased commentators on Wilde, deprecated in very strong terms his preoccupations with Christianity, and dismissed his attitude towards religion as little more than another æsthetic pose.

No doubt, O'Sullivan admitted, Wilde was influenced by the enthusiasm of converted friends like Ross. "But if he died in the Church, he did not live in it." He was motivated primarily by an "æsthetic sympathy with Catholicism, with its pageantry and historical side." He was also moved by a revulsion from the ugliness of Protestant religion. But he had no part, O'Sullivan points out, in the real Catholic revival among the intellectuals of his time.

> How could he? His philosophy is pagan. The practical side of Catholicism, with its obligation to a certain order of life and to certain devotions, would have bored him. Before the Catholic devotion and its images—the stabbed, bleeding and excruciated figure, the heart dripping blood, the woman's heart with a knife in it, he would have felt as strange and disconcerted as one of the young woodland gods who haunted the sacred groves of Thessaly. He knew little about theology, and the theological mind he abhorred. All he had retained out of Newman was the passage about the snapdragon under the walls of Trinity. He never with me, and, I should think, not with anybody, discussed Christianity as a devotional exercise or as a means of saving one's soul alive. All that lay outside the circle of his interest. When he spoke of Christianity as an historical revelation he became "sketchy," and even sometimes took a burlesque attitude.

Here we have three opinions claiming that Wilde was a pagan and in no real sense Christian. Another acquaintance, E. F. Benson, went further in contending that he was not even a good pagan:

> He took his own Dorian Gray as a model, and saw in himself the exemplar of the truly delectable life, denying himself no pleasure, full of wit and laughter, rejoicing in heedless extravagance, even adopting the ancient kings of

Ireland as his ancestors to give birthright to this regal sumptuousness, and by some strange lack of just perception believing that he was realising for a drab world the ancient Greek ideal of the joy and beauty of life. Nothing could have been less like what he was doing, for the Greek genius for exquisite living was founded on physical fitness and moderation in all things, while he based it on the un-bridled gratification of animal appetites.

There is some truth in all these statements. That of Harris, as usual, is the least reliable. He lifts quotations from *De Pro-fundis* without giving the context—quotations which are in fact embedded in a text that shows a very deep and not wholly æsthetic preoccupation with the personality of Christ and the doctrine of redemption through suffering that has been associated with his life.

Similarly, both Gide and O'Sullivan fall into the error of believing that, since Wilde was not closely concerned with the theological side of Christian doctrine, his interest in Christianity was necessarily "æsthetic" and superficial. This idea, as we shall see, is itself superficial, since it disregards much important evidence in Wilde's life and writing that more than one aspect of Christianity, or perhaps rather of Christ, played an important part in the development of his philosophy.

E. F. Benson's point has perhaps more substance. Wilde certainly never lived wholly according to the ideals of the great Greek philosophers. Pythagoras, Epicurus, Socrates alike would have condemned the kind of life he led at the dizzy height of his career, just as Pater, a truer Epicurean than Wilde, condemned the mock-Epicureanism of Dorian Gray. Nevertheless, the influences of Greek art, Greek phi-losophy and Greek literature are so closely woven into his work that it is impossible to conceive what Wilde would have been had he not fallen so deeply under the influence of the

Greek writers, whom in his youth he studied with so much enthusiasm as to make him one of the best classical scholars of his day.

Wilde's initial interest in Christianity perhaps came from the fact that he was greatly moved and æsthetically excited by the beauty of the Catholic ritual, and it was undoubtedly this interest in ceremonial and liturgy, aided by the pressure of his friends, that was most influential in forming his perennial preoccupation with entering the Roman Catholic Church. In considering this fact, it is worth remembering that, beneath all his flippancy, Wilde was a sentimentalist as well as a sensationalist.

His first burst of Catholic enthusiasm took place at Oxford, where he became associated with a number of students who, with all the zeal of converts, set about assiduously to add him to their number. One of his closest friends in these days was David Hunter Blair, later to become a priest, who induced Wilde to attend the Catholic Church in Oxford, in the hope of gaining a speedy conversion. The officiating priest, however, was perhaps more shrewd than Oscar's young friends, for he seems quickly to have perceived the superficiality of Wilde's Catholic enthusiasm, and decided that he was not yet "ripe for conversion." Nevertheless, Wilde persisted in his Catholic pursuits, while making the best of both worlds by becoming a Freemason. In 1875 he made a short trip to Italy, and, his impressionable senses surrounded by the beautiful trappings of the Roman religion, experienced his most violent Catholic enthusiasm. On his return to Oxford, he replaced the engravings of naked young women, which had adorned his rooms, with photographs of Catholic dignitaries, and a contemporary memoirist who met him at this period remarked that "his long-haired head" was "full of nonsense regarding the Church of Rome." On a second journey to Italy, in 1876, Wilde was blessed by the Pope and

produced a crop of sonnets and songs dedicated to the
Church. In one of them he sang:

O joy to see before I die
The only God-anointed King,
And hear the silver trumpets ring
A triumph as he passes by!

Or, at the altar of the shrine
Holds high the mystic sacrifice,
And shows a God to human eyes
Beneath the veil of bread and wine.

In addition to the titillation of his emotions and æsthetic
senses by Catholic pomp and glory in the Holy City, Wilde
enjoyed some of the minor pleasures of martyrdom, for the
publication of one of his pro-Catholic sonnets in a Dublin
magazine resulted in his losing an expected legacy from an
Irish Protestant relative. Even this suffering for the faith did
not, however, drive him completely over the threshold, and
by 1877, the devil, in the shape of his old tutor Mahaffy, succeeded in winning him, if not back into the Irish Protestant
fold, at least safely away from Catholicism.

Wilde and Mahaffy, as we have seen, had in common a vast
enthusiasm for classical learning, and Mahaffy combined this
with a considerable knowledge of Hellenic archæology. In
1877 he made a trip to see the recent excavations in Greece,
and invited Wilde to accompany him. "I am going to make
an honest pagan out of you," he said, and was as good as his
word. Oscar was delighted with Greece. The country, the
architecture, the people, all showed him that Rome and the
Catholic Church had no greater beauty to offer than the relics
of the old pagan culture, even in its decay. His classical en-
thusiasms, given a concrete and physical background, were
revivified, and he became dominated again by that ideal of
the balanced Greek life which all his days he strove, vainly

and at times ludicrously, to realise. For the time being he was lost to the Catholics, and in Genoa he said:

> *Ah, God! ah, God! those dear Hellenic hours*
> *·Had drowned all memory of Thy bitter pain,*
> *The Cross, the Crown, the Soldiers and the Spear.*

At the same time he began to build up that conception of the human Christ which was to become such an important feature in his later work and thought: even at this time he seemed to recognise the incompatibility of the man Christ with Catholic dogmas and practice, for there is another sonnet in which he contrasts the pomp of Papal liturgy with the poverty of the wandering prophet.

> *The silver trumpets rang across the Dome:*
> *The people knelt upon the ground in awe:*
> *And borne upon the necks of men I saw*
> *Like some great God, the Holy Lord of Rome. . . .*
> *My heart stole back across wide wastes of years*
> *To one who wandered by a lonely sea,*
> *And sought in vain for any place of rest:*
> *"Foxes have holes, and every bird its nest.*
> *I, only I, must wander wearily,*
> *And bruise my feet, and drink wine salt with tears."*

For the time being, and, in fact, for almost the whole of his remaining life, Wilde was won back to paganism. It is true that he continued to flirt with Rome. When he left Oxford for London, his first act was to make a zealous confession at Brompton Oratory, but his devotions never went beyond these occasional pleasurable indulgences in ceremonial, and the nature of his attitude towards religion in these years can be seen in one of those passages describing the development of Dorian Gray which are most clearly autobiographical.

It was rumoured of him once that he was about to join the Roman Catholic communion; and certainly the Roman

ritual had always a great attraction for him. The daily sacrifice, more awful really than all the sacrifices of the antique world, stirred him as much by its superb rejection of
the evidence of the senses as by the primitive simplicity of
its elements and the eternal pathos of the human tragedy
that it sought to symbolise. . . .

But he never fell into the error of arresting his intellectual development by any formal acceptance of creed or
system. . . . He felt keenly conscious of how barren all intellectual speculation is when separated from action and
experiment. He knew that the senses, no less than the soul,
have their spiritual mysteries to reveal.

This passage, I think, fairly represents Wilde's own attitude towards religion during most of his life. He had an
æsthetic interest in liturgy, such as is frequently found among
homosexuals, and an intellectual interest in certain religious
and irreligious doctrines, but it is quite evident that he enjoyed no deep spiritual experience, and that the doctrines,
either of the Church or the mystics, meant comparatively
little to him.

In general his attitude remained hedonistic; he thought
that through the medium of the senses must be realised the
deeper mysteries of life, and, if his researches in this direction perhaps went astray through his own personal inability
to control a voracious appetite for sensation, this should not
be allowed to invalidate the fact that his ideas have since
been given much basic support by the contentions of modern
psychologists, particularly Freud and radical post-Freudians
like Wilhelm Reich, or that his theories, as distinct from his
somewhat immoderate practice of them, had been anticipated
by many philosophers, from Epicurus onwards. Because of
this attitude, which represented one side of paganism (it has
actually less relation to the Platonic doctrines than Wilde
liked to believe), he always condemned the ascetic manifestations of Christianity, and his attitude towards living is aptly

illustrated in another passage from *The Picture of Dorian Gray*, further illustrating Dorian's intellectual development.

> Yes, there was to be, as Lord Henry had prophesied, a new hedonism that was to recreate life, and to save it from that harsh, uncomely puritanism that is having, in our own day, its curious revival. It was to have its service of the intellect, certainly; yet, it was never to accept any theory or system that would involve the sacrifice of any mode of passionate experience. Its aim, indeed, was to be experience itself, and not the fruits of experience, sweet or bitter as they might be. Of the asceticism that deadened the senses, as of the vulgar profligacy that dulls them, it was to know nothing. But it was to teach man to concentrate himself on the moments of a life that is itself but a moment.

Here we have more than a little of Pater, much of Baudelaire and of those Renaissance thinkers who so brilliantly revived the Greek learning and spread it widely over Europe. But of the more orthodox currents of Christianity there is very little.

As he himself realised later, Wilde in his period of prosperity betrayed his own Epicureanism by degrading it to triviality and by indulging in that very "vulgar profligacy" which he had condemned.

> Desire, in the end, was a malady, or a madness, or both. I grew careless of the lives of others. I took pleasure where it pleased me, and passed on. . . . I ceased to be lord over myself. I was no longer the captain of my soul, and did not know it. I allowed pleasure to dominate me. I ended in horrible disgrace.

Yet at the same time he did not change his basic philosophy. He did not consider that his mistaken practices could affect that, nor did he admit that even his follies were intrinsically wrong. He maintained, and, I think, rightly, that—

> to regret one's own experiences is to arrest one's own development. To deny one's own experience is to put a lie

into the lips of one's own life. It is no less than a denial of the soul.

Nevertheless, he admits that, "While I see that there is nothing wrong in what one does, I see that there is something wrong in what one becomes." A significant advance, indeed, in experience, but not inconsistent with the original theory.

In spite of his idea of the validity and justifiability of all experience, Wilde had always a lively idea of the significance and importance of sin. Indeed, like Dostoevsky and some of the Christian heretics of the Eastern Church, and also like some modern psychologists (although he used a different and more sensational language) he was acutely conscious of the purifying and liberating effect of sin. This, although an unorthodox attitude, is not wholly incompatible with Christian beliefs. Christ, after all, claimed that he came to call sinners and not the righteous to repentance, and his whole attitude towards sin seems to have been relative, rather than absolute, since he once said of the adulteress, "Her sins are forgiven her, because she loved much."

A similar theory seems to have been held by the mediæval alchemists, whose ideas Wilde may well have encountered through the then famous treatises on magic of Eliphas Levi. Alchemical ideas were much in the air at that time, particularly in France; Rimbaud drew deeply on alchemical imagery for his poems and actually believed quite literally in some of the more far-fetched statements of the contemporary magicians; for instance, he became keyed up to an almost hysterical expectation during 1879, because of Eliphas Levi's prophecy, calculated from hints in the writings of the mediæval hermeticists, that in that year would be established a world empire of peace and order, centred on France.

The alchemists had a whole system of philosophy linked to the symbolism of their art; indeed, there are some students who contend that the idea of the hunt for gold was itself

merely a device to disguise a heretical philosophy of regeneration, and this theory is supported by the fact that, even in
the exoteric theory of alchemy, the gold sought was not ordinary metal gold, but philosopher's gold, the *aurum potabile*
which was also the elixir of long life. The esoteric meaning
of this was probably that by the search for virtue and for
mystic communion with God, the alchemist attained a spiritual life in an inner and ever-present eternity.

The alchemists had a whole range of mystic colours, linked
to the vowels of the alphabet, which symbolised the process
of regeneration. There was, firstly, black, signifying the
process of putrefaction, dissolution, degeneration. When he
saw this colour, the alchemist became filled with hope, because it was the first sign of regeneration, and in the alchemical imagery of seasons, the period when the mixture in the
crucible turned black was called "The Golden Age." To the
black process of putrefaction succeeded a stage when the matter in the crucible turned white; this was the age of purifica-
tion. Thence, if the process were going well, there followed a
stage when the material turned red. Then the alchemist
could hope to see the philosophical gold appearing. If it did
not materialise at red, and the experiment were carried on
satisfactorily, the colour would change to green, and finally
to blue, symbolised also by the sacred letter O, standing for
Omega and meaning God. Here again the philosopher's gold
might appear. But, once having passed through the black
process of dissolution, the alchemist had to avoid carefully
any return to that colour, which would be fatal to the success
of his experiment.

Thus we have a whole heretical and partly pagan philosophy in which the process of degeneration, and therefore, presumably, the giving way to man's natural instincts, the surrender to what the poets of the 'nineties would call "sin,"
was an essential part of the regenerative process. It should
further be added that in hermetic philosophy, as in the pagan

Orphic mysteries, the descent into Hell plays an important part, and is to be taken as meaning a man's descent into his self, into his subconscious, generally regarded as a process fraught with terrible dangers.

The age of the romantic revival, of Maturin and Goethe, was accompanied by a revival of interest in the mediæval hermetic and magic philosophers, a revival which was strong in Germany, France and England alike, and in which many of the really important writers took part. Among the milder spirits of English literature, the influence of Evangelical religion was in general too great for them to follow their romantic inclinations literally, and the "decadent" tendency to see value in "sinful" experiments found its expression indirectly in the Gothic novel, and only burst out, in a delayed manner, among Wilde and his contemporaries in the 1890's. But in France, such great poets as Gerard de Nerval, Baudelaire, Verlaine and Rimbaud were very strongly influenced by this idea of the spiritual necessity of sin, which was sometimes retained in its purely magical form and at other times was somewhat inconsistently linked with Catholic mysticism.

Because of his connection with the English Gothicists through Maturin and with their German counterparts through his mother's translations of Meinhold, and also because of his own direct links with the occult influence in French romantic literature through his admiration for such poets as Baudelaire and Gerard de Nerval, as well as his intrinsically romantic attitude of being impressed by anything that was odd or outlandish, Wilde was bound to be influenced by such conceptions, and we can fairly regard his already noticed concern with magic as an important part of the foundation of his attitude towards sin.

Wilde's preoccupation with sin appears quite early in such works as *The Sphinx* and his essay on Wainwright, the poisoner, in which he says: "One can fancy an intense personality being created out of sin." In *Intentions* he amplifies this by contending:

> What is termed Sin is an essential element in progress.
> . . . Without it the world would stagnate, or grow old, or become colourless. By its curiosity Sin increases the experience of the race. Through its intensified assertion of individualism, it saves us from monotony of type. In its rejection of the current notions about morality it is one with the higher ethics.

By the time he wrote *The Picture of Dorian Gray* he had developed his idea into a theory of considerable psychological and moral validity. Lord Henry Wootton talks to Dorian Gray during their first meeting in the studio of Basil Hallward, who is painting the fateful picture which forms the subject of the novel. After condemning any attempt to influence other people and declaring that the chief aim of life is self-realisation, he goes on:

> The body sins once, and has done with its sin, for action is a mode of perfection. Nothing remains then but the recollection of a pleasure or the luxury of a regret. The only way to get rid of a temptation is to yield to it. Resist it, and your soul grows sick with longing for the things it has forbidden to itself, with desire for what its monstrous laws have made monstrous and unlawful.

It is a fact not sufficiently recognised, that men and women who adopt an attitude of this kind, which robs "sin," or whatever else one may call an infringement of the customary morality, of its attraction as a forbidden fruit and at the same time of the frustration caused by an inability to commit it, generally do less harm in the world than the virtuous who resist "sin" and have to make up for their repressions by "legitimate" forms of compensation. All the great inquisitors have been men of exemplary virtue. Dervishes and religious fanatics, men of eminently "pure" lives, have whipped up their followers to fantastic holy wars and massacres. Dictators, like Lenin, have often been men of blameless private lives, but this has not prevented them from initiating and condoning the cruelties and treacheries of their regimes. Some of the most bloodthirsty men of the French Revolutionary terror were secular ascetics of the highest order. The last example brings us to a significant point of comparison, for these men of fanatical selflessness, who murdered thousands in the name of their cause, had as an associate a rebellious nobleman whose name has since become a by-word for cruelty. This was the unfortunate Marquis de Sade, who, as a logical and thorough revolutionary, acknowledged the right of every man to do whatever he liked, even to the extent of torture and murder, if he himself found it necessary. Yet, placed in a position where he could perform almost unlimited murders and cruelties with apparent legality, the Marquis acted with extreme mildness, and for his leniency became involved in serious trouble with his Jacobin associates. Having acknowledged his own right to kill and torture, the Marquis was able to satisfy his desires by writing about them and flogging an occasional prostitute. On the other hand, his moralistic associates, who would have raised their hands in horror at the idea of killing or cruelty for their personal satisfaction, carried the desire frustrated within them and, when they found a legitimate channel through which to satisfy it, in the name of a holy cause, in the name of revolutionary expediency, their sadism came gushing out in an orgy of political murder. Ascetics in their personal lives, they became voluptuaries of the most appalling kind under the mask of serving their ideals, and in this wholly overshadowed the mild peccadilloes of their maligned associate.

In the same way, Oscar Wilde, who likewise acknowledged the right of every man to act according to his desires, to follow where the temptation led, who could look on Wainwright's murders with a dispassionate eye, had at the same time a genial and generous attitude towards his fellow men in his actual relationships with them. Except for his unfortunate wife, who was bewildered by all that went on at the time of Oscar's downfall, he injured very few people in a material way. On the other hand, he was generous almost to excess, always attending to those in need of assistance, whether it was a cold or starving beggar (he once gave away his overcoat on a winter evening) or a young author who desired an introduction, a subsidy, or a word of friendly support. The instances when his brilliant conversation fell into malice are so rare as to be engraved on the minds of his hearers by the astonishment they caused. And he was, as we shall see, singularly free from resentment towards those who harmed him.

It seems evident that Wilde's attitude of surrendering to temptation and thus preventing his desires from rankling within him actually did have a beneficial effect on his own being and on his general attitude towards people around him. Certainly he did less harm than most of the celebrated religious fanatics. Beside him, a Calvin or a John Knox, a St. Dominic or a Savonarola seem veritable monsters of physical and mental destructiveness. And Wilde himself, in his own peculiar kind of wisdom, understood the vastly harmful effect of most moral teaching. He always spoke of the stultifying effects of "the seven deadly virtues," and he once declared: "I never came across anyone in whom the moral sense was dominant who was not heartless, cruel, vindictive, log-stupid, and entirely lacking in the smallest sense of humanity. Moral people, as they are termed, are simple beasts. I would sooner have fifty unnatural vices than one unnatural virtue." When one remembers the cruelty with which the virtuous fell upon Wilde in the hour of his weakness, how they tore at a defeated and fallen man like a pack of sorry hounds tearing at a wounded stag, it is impossible to deny the truth of this statement, which Wilde made from the depth of his experience.

What he objected to mostly among the moralists and the saints was their way of interfering with the lives of others. "Do-gooders" were anathema to him, and of their activities and the so-called virtues that prompted them he had little good to say:

> What are the virtues? . . . Self-denial is simply a method by which man arrests his progress, and self-sacrifice is a survival of the mutilation of the savage, part of that old worship of pain which is so terrible a factor in the history of the world, and which even now makes its victims day by day and has its altars in the land. Virtues! who knows what the virtues are? Not you, not I, not anyone. It is well for our vanity that we slay the criminal, for if we suffered him to live he might show us what we had gained by his crime. It is well for his peace that the saint goes to his martyrdom. He is spared the sight of the horror of his harvest.

Philanthropists and others who tried to ease their consciences by "Christian" activity among the poor, while still retaining their own social advantages, he perpetually satirised in his plays and stories. Missionaries he likened to commercial travellers, and once shocked his wife, who to his ironic amusement had become enrolled in the ranks of evangelical religious activity, by remarking that they "are the divinely provided food for the destitute and under-fed cannibals. Whenever they are on the brink of starvation, Heaven, in its infinite mercy, sends them a nice plump missionary." Nevertheless, even to the detested "do-gooder," Oscar the satirist always preserved his good humour and friendly courtesy. Yeats tells an amusing story to illustrate this:

> I found Wilde with smock frocks in various colours spread out upon the floor in front of him, while a missionary explained that he did not object to the heathen going

naked upon weekdays, but insisted upon clothes in church. He had brought the smock frocks in a cab that the only art-critic whose fame had reached Central Africa might select a colour; so Wilde sat there weighing all with a conscious ecclesiastic solemnity.

In his dislike for the saints and their deeds, Wilde even went so far as to exonerate Nero for his persecution of the Christians. Nero, along with the other decadent Roman Emperors, had always been one of his favourite historical figures, and when, having had his coiffure modelled on a certain bust in the Louvre, he discovered that the head was Nero's, he was greatly delighted. On one occasion he remarked to Vincent O'Sullivan:

You know, Nero was obliged to do something. They were making him ridiculous. What he thought was: "Here everything is going on very well, when one day two ridiculous creatures arrive from somewhere in the provinces. They are called Peter and Paul, or some unheard-of names like that. Since they are here, life in Rome has become impossible. They collect crowds and block the traffic with their miracles. It is really intolerable. I, the Emperor, have no peace. When I get up in the morning and look out of the window, the first thing I see is a miracle going on in the back garden."

And, indeed, one cannot help agreeing with Wilde that, from his own point of view, Nero was right, and furthermore, that the world would have been a better, or at least could not have been a worse, place, if Peter and Paul had not appeared on the scene with their moralistic perversion of Christianity, and its heritage of mental and physical persecution and repression.

Wilde was strongly fascinated by the personality of the man Jesus, almost to the extent of trying to identify himself with him. But even to Christ he did not concede in his condemnation of interference in the lives of others, except where it might help them in gaining their own conscious ends. He said once that he would not presume to interfere with a man who was attempting to commit suicide, and of Christ and his "philanthropic" activities he told a bitter little parable, called "The Doer of Good," in which Christ visits a city and there finds those whom he has cured of leprosy or blindness, whose sins he has forgiven or whom he has raised from the dead, engaged, some in drinking, some in lechery, some in weeping. And as he speaks to them, they return his reproach each by reminding him of his own "good deed," and showing that their own acts are a natural consequence. (A spoken version of this story is quoted fully in Chapter IX.)

The intention of this parable was not, I think, to teach that one should not help people, since Wilde himself was ready to help anyone who asked it of him, but that one should not help them with any moral end in view, but merely aid them to fulfil their own wishes, and expect nothing of them.

Here it is interesting to note his curious theory that the attempt to convert people to different ways of behaviour is fruitless, since, as soon as one has succeeded in bringing another person to one's own attitude, one's original conviction disappears. This is an over-simplification based on a quite valid psychological observation; something of the kind frequently happens among fairly normal people, but such a change is less frequent among fanatics motivated by the desire to gain power by conversion, although even here we have the historical examples of great opponents and persecutors of new ideas, like St. Paul, who later become their equally fanatical advocates. Wilde embodied this idea in a play, La Sainte Courtisane, in which a young princess from Alexandria goes into the Thebaid with the intention of tempting a famous anchorite to exchange his religious contemplation for the gay life of the city. The hermit, however, sets about to convert her, with such complete success, that she decides to remain in the desert and share his holy retreat.

But, having achieved his end, the saint's own convictions are weakened; he suddenly appreciates the woman's beauty, and is tempted by the visions of an awakened lust, until finally he can endure the temptations no longer, surrenders like a good Wildean, and begs the young woman to accompany him back to the life she once asked him to adopt. But for her alike the success of her persuasions is Dead Sea fruit; she no longer wants a life of amorous gaiety, and elects to remain in the desert, in the very cave the hermit is vacating. As Wilde would remark, when he told the story to his friends, "She, I regret to say, died of starvation. He, I fear, died of debauchery. That is what comes of trying to convert people." Unfortunately, the manuscript of this play was stolen in the selling of Wilde's belongings by his creditors after he had been arrested and it was never recovered; as Wilde put it, "The robbers have buried her white body and carried away her jewels. . . ." It was, incidentally, a brilliant adaptation of a tedious novel by Anatole France, called *Thaïs,* which had appeared in 1891.

Wilde's own moral philosophy was Oriental rather than Christian. Chinese writing had been fashionable in France since the 1860's, when Gautier's sister published an anthology of translations from Chinese poets, and a little later Oriental art began to arouse interest once again in England, under the influence of Whistler. Wilde read the Taoist philosophers with great interest, finding much in common with them, and he actually wrote a long and very enthusiastic review of a selection from the writings of Chuang Tzu which was published in London during the 1880's. In a later chapter we shall recur to the libertarian social sentiments which Wilde expressed in this essay. Here it is sufficient to indicate his evident approval of Chuang Tzu's attacks on moralism and self-conscious charity, expressed in his own epigrammatic paraphrase of the philosopher's ideas.

There is nothing of the sentimentalist in him. He pities the rich more than the poor, if he ever pities at all, and prosperity seems to him as tragic a thing as suffering . . . as for active sympathy, which has become the profession of so many worthy people in our own day, he thinks that try- ing to make others good is as silly an occupation as "beat- ing a drum in a forest in order to find a fugitive. . . ."

Morality . . . went out of fashion, says Chuang Tzu, when people began to moralise. Men ceased then to be spontaneous and to act on intuition. They became priggish and artificial, and were so blind as to have a definite pur- pose in life. . . .

Perhaps even more significant, in that it gives us some idea of Wilde's basic philosophy of living, is his version of Chuang Tzu's idea of "the perfect man."

The perfect man does nothing beyond gazing at the uni- verse. He adopts no absolute position. . . . He lets ex- ternals take care of themselves. Nothing material injures him; nothing spiritual punishes him. His mental equili- brium gives him the empire of the world. He is never the slave of objective existences. He knows that, "just as the best language is that which is never spoken, so the best action is that which is never done." He is passive, and ac- cepts the laws of life. He rests in inactivity, and sees the world become virtuous of itself. . . . He is not troubled by moral distinctions. He knows that things are what they are, and that their consequences will be what they will be. His mind is the "speculum of creation," and he is ever at peace.

Wilde clearly saw himself as aspiring towards this ideal, and, indeed, there are many ways in which his plan of life ran parallel to that envisaged by Chuang Tzu. In his one political tract, *The Soul of Man Under Socialism,* he puts forward the idea that a desirable state of society can only come naturally from within men, without moralistic talk or interfering charity. It is useless to try to force men to be good: "people are good when they are let alone."

This, of course, is very little different from the essential social and moral doctrines of the Taoists, as put forward by Lao-tzu himself in his famous rebuke to the Confucians:

> Mosquitoes will keep a man awake all night with their biting, and just in the same way this talk of charity and duty to one's neighbour drives us nearly crazy. Sirs, strive to keep the world in its own original simplicity, and, as the wind bloweth where it listeth, so let Virtue establish itself.

In his own relations towards others, Wilde followed a policy of non-interference. Sherard tells how he brought a drug-crazed poet to see Wilde, in the rather naïve hope that Oscar might exert some influence to persuade the man to give up his habit. Oscar, however, refused to interfere, and shocked the Calvinistic Sherard by watching the poet's ravings with an interested detachment.

In his own life he tended towards inaction, even apart from his physical laziness. Writing itself he often found repugnant, and he gained most pleasure from talking and thinking. After his imprisonment this side of his nature became predominant, and he allowed himself to drift without much resistance down the remaining months of his life. In this way, avoiding resentment and bitterness, he was neither so broken-down nor so miserable as many another man would have been. Out of this quietism he undoubtedly gained much that will never be recorded, for all the friends who continued to see him in those days tell us that his talk had become even more eloquent than before, and much more profound in its philosophy, as certainly seems to be shown by the fragments preserved by such authors as Laurence Housman and Vincent O'Sullivan.

These tendencies towards Oriental quietism have also their

connection with Wilde's paganism. In spite of critics like E. F. Benson, he did not see merely the meretricious glitter of the Greek and Roman decadence—though even Petronius Arbiter and Lucius Apuleius have their due part in the pagan tradition. One side of his character turned towards those more profound and rational Greek philosophies, such as Stoicism and Epicureanism, in which are found, not merely the doctrines of philosophical anarchism and responsible individualism of which Wilde was an advocate, but also that sense of detachment from activity and interference which he had derived partly from the Taoists. The Stoics, like the Taoists, held that co-operation in public life must not be actuated by any desire to benefit mankind, since it can never be known whether the benefits conferred are true ones. Each man, according to them, must be concerned with the development of *his own* virtue, a doctrine which differs only in externals from Wilde's own fundamental attitude.

As we have seen, there are many important aspects in which Wilde differed from the commonly accepted idea of Christianity, and even from the doctrines of Christ himself. Nevertheless, he was certainly fascinated, for years before his imprisonment and also during and after that experience, by the personality of Jesus. His prison experience also taught him the value of the Christian doctrines of pity and of redemption by suffering.

For the most part, he thought of Christ as a man, a kind of quintessence of human virtue. I have been unable to discover just how far he accepted the divinity of Christ during his more acute periods of attraction towards Catholicism, but I imagine that even at these times he remained basically sceptical on this point. After his release from prison he tried to persuade the Roman Catholic Church to admit him to a retreat, but received a definite refusal, and a conversation with Stewart Headlam just before this application rather explains its failure, since he remarked to Headlam that he looked on all religions as colleges in a great university and that Roman Catholicism was merely the greatest and most romantic. It is not surprising that the priests at Farm Street were not impressed by the "ripeness" of such a prospective convert.

Indeed, at the times when he was most under the influence of the personality and the myth of Christ, Wilde admitted that he retained his religious doubts. In *De Profundis,* which is the most strongly and consciously Christian of all his writings, he remarked:

> Religion does not help me. The faith that others give to what is unseen, I give to what one can touch, and look at. My gods dwell in temples made with hands; and within the circle of actual experience is my creed made perfect and complete. . . . When I think about religion at all, I feel as if I would like to found an order for those who *cannot* believe. . . . Everything to be true must become a religion. And agnosticism should have its ritual no less than faith. . . . But whether it be faith or agnosticism, it must be nothing external to me. Its symbols must be of my own creating. Only that is spiritual which makes its own form. If I may not find its secret within myself, I shall not find it: if I have not got it already, it will never come to me.

Later, in Paris, Laurence Housman represents him again as the sceptic, and makes him say: ". . . Try as we may, we cannot get behind the appearance of things to the reality. And the terrible reason may be that there is no reality in things apart from their appearance."

In all Wilde's Christian parables, both before and after his imprisonment, Christ appears as human, never as divine. There is the pleasant little tale he told to Yeats, saying that he had invented a new Christian heresy. Christ did not die ˙on the cross, but merely swooned, and recovered after he was placed in the tomb, from which he escaped alive. For many years he lived among men, plying his trade as a carpenter— the one man on earth who knew that what was preached abroad as Christianity was a falsehood. One day St. Paul came to his town, and all the craftsmen except Christ went to hear the evangelist. After this, the other carpenters noticed that he always kept his hands covered. On another occasion he told the story of how, after Christ's death, Joseph of Arimathea came upon a young man weeping, and said to him, "I know how great thy grief must be, for surely he was a just man." But the young man answered: "I am not weeping for him but for myself. For I too have wrought miracles; I have turned water into wine, healed the sick, given sight to the blind, fed the multitude, cast out devils, caused the barren fig-tree to wither, and raised the dead. And yet they have not crucified me." Perhaps Wilde saw himself as this young man who had wrought miracles and yet had not been crucified. His turn was to come, and when it did he identified himself more fully than ever with Christ.

The Christian attitude first becomes evident in Wilde's writing in such stories as *The Young King* and *The Star Child,* in which young men, brought up by poor parents, but of royal blood, attain to kingship and, as a result of visions or revelations, renounce the pomp and privilege of their positions and govern their people with a sense of brotherhood towards the poor and oppressed.

Then, in *The Soul of Man Under Socialism,* Christ is brought in as the prophet of individualism, and Wilde argues that the kernel of Christ's message is that each man must realise his own potentialities as a person.

While the ancients asked that a man should *know* himself. Christ exhorted him to *be* himself. The human personality was to him the important thing, and he condemned wealth. not on any ascetic grounds, but because it diverted man's efforts from the real riches of the spirit. Life should be shaped so that external things can do no harm, and one should try to get rid of personal property, because "it involves sordid preoccupation, endless industry, continual wrong," and hinders individual development in every way. "What Jesus does say is that man reaches his perfection, not through what he has, not even through what he does, but entirely through what he is."

He tells his disciples to fulfil themselves, and not to be concerned with external things:

> What do other things matter? Man is complete in himself. When they go into the world, the world will disagree with them. That is inevitable. The world hates Individualism. But that is not to trouble them. They are to be calm and self-centred. . . .
>
> Even if people employ actual violence, they are not to be violent in turn. That would be to fall to the same low level. After all, even in prison, a man can be quite free. His personality can be untroubled. He can be at peace. And, above all things, they are not to interfere with other people or judge them in any way. Personality is a very mysterious thing. A man cannot always be estimated by what he does. He may keep the law, and yet be worthless. He may break the law, and yet be fine. He may be bad, without ever doing anything bad. He may commit a sin against society, and yet realise through that sin his true perfection.

After this original and in many ways revealing interpretation of the Christian doctrine, with its final adroit turning back to his own favourite heresy of the purifying rôle of sin, Wilde goes on to demonstrate, through the story of the woman taken in adultery, that Jesus regarded intense love as of more consequence than mere sin, and, from the story of Mary and the box of precious ointment, he draws the conclusion that "in one divine moment, and by selecting its own mode of expression, a personality might make itself perfect." Further, Wilde shows that Christ denounced the family as a hindrance to real self-expression, and concludes that for a man to be Christ-like he has to be "absolutely himself," to realise "the perfection that is within him." This cannot be gained by imitation or by trying to make men fit one mould.

There are as many perfections as there are imperfect men. And while to the claims of charity a man may yield and yet be free, to the claims of conformity no man may yield and remain free at all.

From this conception of Christ as the great individualist Wilde proceeds in *De Profundis* to his conception of Christ as the great artist. It is in this last book that his identification of himself, as a man of sorrows, with Christ, *the* man of sorrows, becomes most complete. He sees Christ as a kind of romantic figure, the hero of a poetic drama of his own devising, but he also sees into the deeper sides of Christian teaching, and enunciates very clearly those doctrines of the value of suffering, of humility, of pity, which are essential to the understanding of Christianity. Undoubtedly there is a great deal of self-pity in the passages in which he talks of these things; he dramatises his own misfortunes, but I do not think that justifies us in imagining any insincerity in his protestations of having discovered a new attitude towards life. Indeed, his last years of life show that he had absorbed fully the teachings expressed in *De Profundis*.

In this book he tells of the despair and grief, the rage and bitterness, the scorn and misery, above all, the "sorrow that was dumb" which he experienced in his years of imprisonment. "I have passed through every mode of suffering," he says, and describes how he found their value:

> But there were times when I rejoiced in the idea that my sufferings were to be endless. I could not bear them to be without meaning. Now I find hidden somewhere away in my nature something that tells me that nothing in the whole world is meaningless, and suffering least of all. That something hidden away in my nature, like a treasure in a field, is Humility.

Sorrow, he says, is the great motive in art and in personal development. It is "the supreme emotion of which man is capable"; it is "at once the type and test of all great art." Sorrow is the highest, perhaps the only, truth. Suffering is the secret of life, and "is hidden behind everything." Wilde, who in his days of prosperity had held that the existence of suffering was a proof of the lack of a loving spirit in the universe, now maintains the opposite.

Now it seems to me that love of some kind is the only possible explanation of the extraordinary amount of suffering that there is in the world. I cannot conceive of any other explanation. I am convinced that there is no other, and that if the world has indeed, as I have said, been built of sorrow, it has been built by the hands of love, because in no other way could the soul of man, for whom the world was made, reach the full stature of its perfection.

He talks of this as a "new mode of self-realisation," and contends that to have accepted it has enhanced his individuality. He sees that "the first thing that I have got to do is to free myself from any possible bitterness of feeling against the world"; for him to face life again adequately after his release from prison it is necessary to be "free from all resentment, hardness and scorn."

There is a flavour of self-consciousness, of affectation in all this. But one must remember two things: firstly, that Wilde was always a mannered writer and that his style does not detract from the essential earnestness of his nature; and, secondly, that he was writing in prison, where all his feelings, because of isolation in an unfriendly world, tended to take on exaggerated and dramatic forms. I am certain that Wilde meant what he said, and the evidence of his life in prison and his attitude after he was set free show that he really had acquired a new attitude towards life and towards the world. The old arrogance was completely gone when he emerged from Reading Gaol, and it was not merely that it had been crushed out, that he was a spiritually broken man. On the contrary, he showed a genuinely philosophical resignation which sprang from a quite sincere change in his attitude, a real acknowledgment of the value of suffering, of the need for humility and pity and understanding in order to achieve a full life. He may have been mistaken; he was certainly in earnest.

The evidence for this is decisive, if we consider the statements of those who knew him during and after his imprisonment. Sherard, who saw Wilde frequently during the years after his release from prison, testifies to his extreme forbearance:

> During his career he was often attacked and ridiculed, but I never heard him speak of those who had sought to cause him pain except in condonation. He had never a bitter word for the many friends who betrayed him. This admirable quality reached to heroism in his tragic days. In the abyss into which he was plunged, never once did a word of recrimination pass his lips. He sought to devolve on no one any fragment of his responsibility, he blamed no one for the horror of his fate, he essayed nowise to lessen the crushing fardel of his infamy, by shifting on to other shoulders any portion of its burden.

Laurence Housman, who met him in Paris during the last years, but who did not know him well, was greatly impressed by "the quiet, uncomplaining courage with which he accepted an ostracism against which, in his lifetime, there could be no appeal." Vincent O'Sullivan, one of the friends who saw him most frequently after his release, commented on the real sanctity of his attitude in these final years:

> If terrible sufferings courageously borne, the enduring of dire injustice and reviling without complaint, be matter of saintliness, then Wilde was a saint. What says the prayer

of Islam? "O God, make not man endure *all* that he can
bear." In Wilde's case this prayer was not heard. It is hard
to imagine *moral* suffering, at any rate, which went to a
farther extreme. For it must always be borne in mind that
he had the sense of an injustice committed. Nobody to-day
doubts that his punishment was out of proportion to the
fault—not only the technical punishment, but its sequel in
social persecution.

Even Harris, who liked to portray Wilde as a weak figure
falling back into his old ways and failing to practise the good
resolutions he had made in prison, had to admit that—

. . . in reality the high thoughts he had lived with were
not lost; his lips had seen the world-wonder of sympathy,
pity and love, and strangely enough, this higher vision
helped, as we shall soon see, to shake his individuality
from its centre, and thus destroyed his power of work and
completed his soul-ruin.

Harris's final conclusion, like much that Harris said about
Wilde, can be disputed. Wilde, after all, produced a small
amount of very significant work after he left prison, and the
fact that he no longer found it easy to express himself in
writing does not mean necessarily that his personality was at
all disintegrated. He seemed, perhaps, to drift with the current that was set towards his death, but for a steadfast apostle
of non-action this was merely a logical outcome of his personal philosophy. The little he wrote showed a heightened
social and personal consciousness; his talk, as all witnesses
testify, had an enhanced profundity and wisdom; and the
Stoic, jesting on his death-bed, whom we see in his last days,
certainly does not seem a man whose personality had been
destroyed or whose spirit ruined.

That Wilde continued to think in terms of suffering and
pity is shown in both his conversation and writings of these
years. Gide, for instance, reports a talk at Berneval in which
Wilde remarked:

I have learned now that pity is the greatest and most beautiful thing in the world, and that is why I cannot bear ill-will towards those who caused my suffering and those who condemned me; no, nor to anyone, because without them I should not have known all that.

Pity for his fellow victims inspired him to write his letters on prison conditions to the *Daily Chronicle*. It was also the motive of *The Ballad of Reading Gaol*, that great protest against man's inhumanity towards man, in which Wilde proclaimed his belief in the infinite worth of the suffering and broken heart.

> *Ah! happy they whose hearts can break*
> *And peace of pardon win!*
> *How else may man make straight his plan*
> *And cleanse his soul from sin?*
> *How else but through a broken heart*
> *Can Lord Christ enter in.*

Wilde's discovery of the value of suffering and his appreciation of the element of pity in Christ's teaching find an interesting parallel in the career of another writer who spent years of his life in prison. Like Wilde, Dostoevsky learnt to bear no resentment towards his persecutors, and to realise the function of sorrow in the development of personality. In an article written as early as 1887, reviewing Dostoevsky's *Injury and Insult,* and praising its literary qualities, Wilde anticipated in an interesting manner the views which he later developed more fully through his own bitter experiences:

> Goethe once had to delay the completion of one of his novels till experience had furnished him with new situations, but almost before he arrived at manhood Dostoevsky knew life in its most real forms; poverty and suffering, pain and misery, prison, exile and love were soon familiar to him, and by the lips of Vania he has told his own story. . . . Pitiless, too, though Dostoevsky is in his method as an

artist, as a man he is full of human pity for all, for those
who do evil as well as for those who suffer it, for the selfish no less than for those whose lives are wrecked for
others and whose sacrifice is in vain.

Yet Wilde, I think, rose more nobly above his sufferings
than did Dostoevsky. The latter, while he forgave his persecutors, could rarely pardon his benefactors, and developed a
pathological hatred towards those with whom he had suffered
and their spiritual descendants, the nihilists and Russian liberals. Wilde showed none of the petty bickering and animosity
that marred Dostoevsky's mature years; nothing in his history has the monumental futility of Dostoevsky's squabble
with Turgenev, and, except for a time in prison when he
expressed intemperately a passing resentment against Alfred
Douglas (in the unpublished section of *De Profundis*), Wilde
did not turn against his accomplices in the course that had
led him to prison. He could even speak forgivingly of the
mercenary creatures who had witnessed against him in the
pay of his enemies. Altogether, the forbearance and courage
of his last years make a far better impression than the really
unpleasant characteristics which came to the surface in Dostoevsky's character after *his* release from prison and exile.

Wilde's new cult of suffering was combined with an enhanced idea of Christ as a person, as a romantic figure in
history, above all as an artist in life and an inspirer of art.
Nothing in Christ could not be "transferred immediately
into the sphere of Art and there find its complete fulfilment."
It was not merely that Christ's personality touched so nearly
to perfection; his nature also was basically that of the artist,
since he was possessed of "an intense and flame-like imagination."

> He realised in the entire sphere of human relations that
> imaginative sympathy which in the sphere of Art is the sole
> secret of creation. He understood the leprosy of the leper,

the darkness of the blind, the fierce misery of those who
live for pleasure, the strange poverty of the rich. . . .
    Christ's place indeed is with the poets. His whole con-
ception of Humanity sprang right out of the imagination
and can only be realised by it. What God was to the pan-
theist, man was to him. He was the first to conceive the
divided races as a unity. . . .

Not only are Christ's ideas poetical, Wilde goes on to say,
but his life also is "the most wonderful of poems," both for
its tragedy and for its idyllic quality. To this imaginative and
in itself pleasantly heretical version of Christ, Wilde adds an
unorthodox belief in the natural explanation of the stories of
his miracles; the charm of Christ's personality, he suggests,
was such that his presence would bring relief to those in
sorrow and make them forget their pain. He opened men's
eyes to the things of the spirit and their ears to the voice of
love, expelled evil passions, and gave life to men whose existence had the monotony of death.

    For all his discovery of the value of suffering and humility,
Wilde retained his belief in individualism and regarded
Christ as its prophet, as, indeed "the most supreme of in-
dividualists." Humility, indeed, can be itself a true manifestation of individualism, the realisation of one's soul by "getting rid of all alien passions, all acquired culture, and all
external possessions."

    He reiterated the interpretations of Christ's opposition to
wealth which had already been advanced in *The Soul of Man
Under Socialism,* and then went on to prove that Christ did
not demand *altruism for its own sake.*

    To live for others as a definite self-conscious aim was not
    his creed. It was not the basis of his creed. When he said,
    "Forgive your enemies," it is not for the sake of the enemy,
    but for one's own sake that he says so, and because love is
    more beautiful than hate.

This interpretation of Christ's teaching is, of course, that of the mystics, who claim that salvation can be achieved only through a man's own soul and that individual perfection is what is to be sought from religion. But Wilde also realised that Christ combined his teaching of individual perfection with a belief in the unity and brotherhood of all men. "Since his coming, the history of each separate individual is, or can be made, the history of the world." Indeed, Christ realised himself by realising the sufferings and hopes and defeats of others. He spoke for those in pain, and "his desire was to be to the myriads who had found no utterance a very trumpet through which they might call to heaven."

Finally, Wilde pointed to the elemental sympathy which underlies Christ's attitude towards people and which forms the basis of his moral outlook. Christ's morality is "all sympathy," "his justice is all poetic justice," "for him there were no laws; there were exceptions merely, as if anybody, or anything, for that matter, was like aught else in the world!"

This version of Christian morality Wilde links to his heretical theory of the purifying rôle of sin, claiming that Christ—

. . . regarded sin and suffering as being in themselves beautiful holy things and modes of perfection. . . .

Of course the sinner must repent. But why? Simply because otherwise he would be unable to realise what he had done. The moment of repentance is the moment of initiation. More than that: it is the means by which one alters one's past.

This is an original view of Christ's teaching; like all Wilde's theories, it is full of paradoxes; nevertheless, it contains a great deal of truth about Christ which the orthodox theologians and historians have missed. It should not, after all, be forgotten that Christ himself often talked in paradox, and seemed to delight in the dangerous idea that would shock his hearers into consciousness.

Wilde's interest in Christ coincided with an intensification of his romantic tendencies; throughout *De Profundis* the adjective most often applied to Christ is "romantic." After his downfall the feeling of fatality which had dogged him in the past crystallised into a preoccupation with doom, with failure, with death. In these days his conversation was filled with the discussion of this subject. His contention was that all really great men were bound to be failures, and that failure in itself was a noble destiny, a prelude to the romantic apotheosis of death. Years before he had said of the Irish, "We are a nation of failures," and elsewhere he had spoken with feeling of the vulgarity of success. After his imprisonment Laurence Housman records him as having said (the passage is admittedly a free adaptation of Wilde's words):

The artist's mission is to live the complete life; success as an episode (which is all it can be), failure as the real, the final, end. Death, analysed to its resultant atoms—what is it but the vindication of failure: the getting rid for ever of powers, desires, appetites, which have been a lifelong embarrassment? The poet's noblest verse, the dramatist's greatest scene deal always with death; because the highest function of the artist is to make perceived the beauty of failure.

Wilde saw Christ and (strange companion) Napoleon as the great failures of history—Christ who on the cross cried out in agony, "My God, my God, why hast thou forsaken me?" and whose name has been used for twenty centuries to justify deeds he himself would never have countenanced, and Napoleon, not for his military victories (Wilde had the non-actionist's dislike for war and the history of battles), but because his great ambition was balanced by greater failure. In this cult of failure there was, of course, much self-justification and self-consolation; Wilde sought to glorify himself in this great company. But can we deny one who had suffered so much this small gratification? For, as in all his theories, there is a core of truth in this. Seen honestly and from within, all lives are failures, for the greater our ambitions and hopes may be, so much the less completely are they realised. And clearly, in Wilde's case, if his life had not produced so dramatic a failure, he would never have occupied such a position in the history of literature and would not have written his two most significant books, *De Profundis* and *The Ballad of Reading Gaol.*

Wilde's turning towards Christianity during his imprisonment was marked by a corresponding retreat from Hellenism. *De Profundis* gives a great deal more attention to the art and literature of Christianity than to those of Greece, and at times Wilde seems almost to reject his pagan heritage, for, comparing Christ with the Greek gods, he says of him that—

. . . feeling, with the artistic nature of one to whom suffering and sorrow were modes through which he could realise his conception of the beautiful, that an idea is of no value till it comes incarnate and is made an image, he made of himself the image of the Man of Sorrows, and as such has fascinated and dominated art as no Greek god ever succeeded in doing. . . .

and describes him as "a personality infinitely greater than any made by myth and legend."

Yet at the same time as he declared the supersession of Greek religion by the personality of Christ, he still retained a lingering desire to fuse them together, for on a later page he expressed the theory, with a pious hope in its truth, that Christ spoke in the Greek tongue, and could have held converse with Charmides, Socrates and Plato.

In fact, there was much more identity between certain currents of pagan Greek thought and Wilde's interpretation of Christianity than he seems to have realised. From reading his classical references, we gain the impression that his Greek scholarship, although extremely thorough in its own spheres, was limited in scope. He knew the Greek historians well, as is shown in the excellent essay written at Oxford on *The Rise of Historical Criticism,* which, for some unknown reason, the university authorities did not consider worthy of a prize. He also knew the poets, and such philosophers of literary bent as Aristotle and Plato; the last he misinterpreted, like most classical scholars, by failing fully to realise the sinister slant towards authoritarianism implicit in his ideas.

But with the great mass of Greek philosophy Wilde seems to have been unfamiliar, and the limited knowledge of Greek thought which he brought from Oxford is shown by a remark in one of his American lectures:

> The metaphysical mind of Asia will create for itself the monstrous, many-breasted idol of Ephesus, but to the Greek, pure artist, that work is most instinct with spiritual life which conforms most clearly to the perfect facts of physical life.

This, of course, is a wholly unreal view of Greek thought, which was already influenced by Asiatic ideas, by the metaphysics of the East, and which in the Orphic and the Eleusinian cults and the Pythagorean philosophies showed a mystical conception by no means based on the visible and physically proximate world alone. This one-sided attitude towards Greek thought, produced by reading only the poets and a few selected philosophers and historians, persists throughout Wilde's writing. He does not seem at any time to have spread far beyond the limited circle of knowledge which he already enjoyed in his undergraduate days, and a change in his own philosophy, an absorption and adaptation of certain elements of Oriental and Christian thought, made him think he had moved away from Greek philosophy. In fact, he had merely moved from a superficial and "poetic" paganism in the direction of philosophers who were much more radical and individualistic than Plato or Aristotle.

One of these was Epicurus. Wilde thought, no doubt, that in *The Picture of Dorian Gray* he was putting forward an Epicurean philosophy; as Pater pointed out, he was mistaken, like many who talk of Epicureanism without attempting to discover what Epicurus taught or how he lived. As I have already shown, Epicurus taught no philosophy of indiscriminate self-indulgence; on the contrary, his life and teachings had a real austerity, since he held that *true* pleasure could be gained only in the pursuit of virtue, and he was also the first man to teach that it was possible for a philosopher who had reached a true attitude towards life to welcome misfortune and be happy on the rack. We must seek the development of our individual happiness, our personal fulfilment, Epicurus taught, but in doing this we must be selective in our experiences, having always in view the sum of life. Even our sufferings can be useful and lead to good ends if we regard them in the right light. A man must limit his desires and be content with little, so as to avoid disappointment. Resignation and humility were therefore part of the doctrines of Epicurus, and he placed the greatest emphasis on friendship and brotherhood, not for any altruistic motive, but for the good and pleasure they bring. Society is instituted, he taught, wholly for the good of individuals, who find their interests best served by mutual agreement and reciprocity. Towards the gods, Epicurus was a sceptic; if the *De Rerum Natura* of Lucretius is to be taken as a true example of Epicurean teaching, the founder of this philosophy also, like Chuang Tzu, anticipated the nineteenth century by postulating an evolutionary theory of the descent of man.

It will be seen how far Wilde's own ideas, as expressed in such works as *De Profundis* and *The Soul of Man,* actually approximated to those of Epicurus.

But if Wilde's eventual philosophy in some ways resembled

closely that of Epicurus, it had also much in common with Stoicism. The Stoics taught that men should live, not in accordance with man-made laws, but naturally, and that each man should seek his own individual perfection. They held in contempt all laws, institutions and property alike, and declared that a man must govern his own destiny by making himself independent of the things he cannot command. The similarity between these ideas and some of Wilde's theories is clear. Nor were the Stoics and the Epicureans the only philosophers who maintained the attitude Wilde had taken to be Christian. The outlines of it can also be found in the Pythagoreans, while the whole doctrine of redemption through sin and suffering had its anticipations in the underlying concepts of the ancient Greek mysteries.

Thus we see that, while at times in his career Christianity and paganism seemed to represent two opposing sides of Wilde's nature, two utterly conflicting currents of his thought, in fact they were joined in a common stem. Eventually, after suffering and experience, after years of trifling with knowledge and danger, he produced a philosophy which, while justly his own, since it represented his own nature, also represented an intuitively apprehended synthesis of those common elements of Greek, Oriental and Christian thought which a man who was at once romantic and sceptic could accept as a basic philosopy of life. That Wilde was sincere in his doctrine of individualism, with its later acceptance of sin, suffering and redemption, there is no doubt; only from a philosophy, earnestly maintained, could such philosophical patience as Wilde showed during his last yea₁₃ have arisen. Inevitably, he sometimes lapsed from his ideals; the surprising thing is that, given the misery he had to endure in those years, he did not lapse entirely. According to his lights, he ended his life as a good Christian and an equally good pagan, humble in his banishment and jesting like an antique philosopher when he knew his death was near.

CHAPTER

7

THE ÆSTHETIC CLOWN
AND THE CREATIVE CRITIC

Too often we are inclined to take the legend of a man for the truth about him, and in the particular case of Wilde this is complicated by the fact that he himself, with a theatrical instinct, co-operated enthusiastically in the creation and perpetuation of the legend, which, because it contained so much of his invention, has at least an element of subjective truth.

One aspect of the Wilde legend is that of the æsthetic clown, the genial buffoon satirised by Gilbert and Sullivan in *Patience* as Bunthorne, who sang:

> *Though the Philistines may jostle, you will rank as an apostle in the high æsthetic band*
> *If you walk down Piccadilly with a poppy or a lily in your mediæval hand.*

Indeed, so much was the myth of Wilde the æsthete fostered, by Wilde's enemies and with equally enthusiastic diligence by many of his friends and above all by himself, that for years he was generally believed to have really committed in his youth all the extravagances attributed to him by popular songwriters and the jesters of *Punch*.

In fact, however, a good part of the legend is pure fantasy; the story of the symbolic walk down Piccadilly is apocryphal and many other tales contain only a fragment of truth. Nevertheless, in his æsthetic period, Wilde certainly acted in a very extravagant way and, while there was much naïve exhibitionism in all this, there was also a great deal of calculated showmanship and bravado, as is shown by Wilde's own later remark about the Piccadilly pilgrimage. After denying the truth of the story, he remarked: "Anyone could have done that. The great and difficult thing was what I achieved to make the whole world believe that I had done it."

Actually, in making "the whole world" believe that he had really performed this and other eccentricities, some of which he had and some of which he had not committed, in making society in general accept the half-humorous masquerade for the real, or rather the whole, man, Wilde did himself a great disservice; and, while he may have gained in this way a certain public notoriety and an *entrée* on the same level as a conjurer into high society, he also made the majority of people regard him as a superficial *flâneur* and neglect the real scholarship, the high and versatile intelligence and genuine literary genius that are all to be found in his work.

There were plenty of people ready to see Wilde's æsthetic posturings as the signs of madness, and these were not always the stupid Philistines, the Tartuffes and Calibans of English commercial life. Max Nordau, for instance, who, however one may dislike his general attitude, was by no means a fool, devoted much space to a hostile study of Wilde the "æsthete" as a social phenomenon, of which I reproduce a few paragraphs as an illustration of the kind of reaction which Wilde aroused against himself among many comparatively intelligent people:

> The ego-mania of decadentalism, its love of the artificial, its aversion from nature, and from all forms of activity and movement, its megalomaniacal contempt for men, and its exaggeration of the importance of art, has found its Eng-

lish representatives among the "Æsthetes," the chief of whom is Oscar Wilde.

Wilde has done more by his personal eccentricities than by his work. . . . He pretends to have abandoned the dress of the present time because it offends his sense of the beautiful; but this is only a pretext in which probably he himself does *not* believe. What really determines his actions is the hysterical craving to be noticed, to occupy the attention of the world with himself, to get talked about. . . .

The predilection for a strange costume is a pathological aberration of the racial instinct. The adornment of the exterior has its origin in the strong desire to be admired by others—primarily by the opposite sex—to be recognised by them as especially well-shaped, handsome, youthful, or rich and powerful, or as pre-eminent through rank and merit. It is practised, then, with the object of producing a favourable impression on others, and is a result of thought about others, of preoccupation with the race. If, now, this adornment be, not through misjudgment but purposely, of a character to cause irritation to others, to lend itself to ridicule—in other words, if it excites disapproval instead of approbation—it then runs exactly counter to the object of the art of dress, and evinces a perversion of the idea of vanity.

The pretense of a sense of beauty is the excuse of consciousness for a crank of the conscious. The fool who masquerades in Pall Mall does not see himself, and therefore does not enjoy the beautiful appearance which is supposed to be an æsthetic necessity to him. There would be some sense in his conduct if it had for its object an endeavour to cause others to dress in accordance with his taste; for them he sees, and they can scandalise him with the ugliness, and charm with the beauty, of their costume. But to take the initiative in a new artistic style of dress brings the innovator not one hair's-breadth nearer his assumed goal of æsthetic satisfaction.

When, therefore, an Oscar Wilde goes about in "æsthetic

costume" among gazing Philistines, exciting either their ridicule or their wrath, it is no indication of independence of character, but rather from a purely anti-social, egomaniacal recklessness and hysterical longing to make a sensation, justified by no exalted aim; nor is it from a strong desire of beauty, but from a malevolent mania for contradiction.

This statement might at first sight seem more interesting as a study of the malevolence of Nordau himself, as an illustration of typical Philistine anger when goaded by an exhibition of dissent from current sartorial standards. After all, every kind of æsthetic or intellectual originality is a form of attack on the standards of the common man, and might be classed as a manifestation of a "malevolent mania for contradiction." Besides, it is evident that there is no incompatibility between sartorial exhibitionism and genuine intellectual or artistic ability. Balzac, Disraeli, Byron, Baudelaire, Gautier, d'Aurevilly, and many other great writers deliberately dressed in such a way as to make themselves appear different from the multitude, and even Bernard Shaw, with his public wearing of the unfortunate Jaeger one-piece suit, can be included in the same category. A necessary artistic or intellectual rebellion is more often than not combined with a defiance of the accepted conventions of living, including the conventions of dress. But, as the few examples that we have quoted show, this does not mean that the defiant are necessarily psychopathic—in fact, they often manifest a healthy individual reaction from a generally pathological condition.

Yet, in Wilde's particular case, we cannot wholly dismiss the criticisms of his enemies, though Nordau's opinions, based as they are on legend (he readily accepted the story of the mythical walk down Piccadilly), are not wholly justifiable, particularly as, contrary to his view, Wilde's oddities did not create wholesale hostility. Indeed, one of the main bases of Nordau's argument is invalidated by facts, for during his æsthetic period, and afterwards, Wilde was always popular among women, particularly Americans, and, while men were less favourable and often dismissed him as "that bloody fool, Oscar Wilde," this reaction can be attributed largely to jealousy of the ease with which he gained the friendship (almost invariably platonic) of the other sex.

Nevertheless, when we come to examine the motives that underlay Oscar's æsthetic activities, it must be conceded that his eccentricities seem to have been at least partly the result of calculation, and used self-consciously to publicise his talents. But it should also be remembered that he had an inherited love of flamboyant dress and action which, long after he had given up his æsthetic garb and pretensions, led him to continue an ostentation of dress and behaviour that frequently aroused hostility. There was also in Wilde, even in his most calculating moments, a certain naïve theatrical sense which made him enter into the part he had chosen with a zest that carried it to extremes. Thus, in sheer adolescent good humour, he made himself ridiculous where a more cunning figure, like Whistler, contrived to be irritating without appearing foolish.

Another disadvantage of Wilde's "æsthetic" follies was that he used his technique of self-advertisement prematurely. At the time of his most noticeable eccentricities, he had published only a volume of imitative poems, and a poor play which gave little promise of original literary talent. The intellectual public therefore classed him readily as an insincere showman and plagiarist, whose work was all sham and whose talk empty froth. Once formed, their opinion tended to remain constant in its hostility, and when Wilde produced really good works or said really profound things, many people rejected them out of hand as the further follies of an empty poseur. They were wrong, but Wilde himself had given their excuse.

Yet even his "æsthetic" activities must not be dismissed entirely as superficial folly. They had a basis in genuine admiration for the ideas of Ruskin and the pre-Raphaelites, and, while Oscar was not exactly the kind of showman whom Ruskin and Rossetti would have appreciated, he did spread their doctrines, and by this means wielded a perceptible influence on public habits and, to an even greater extent, on domestic decoration in Britain and America.

His "æstheticism" began as a kind of post-graduate extension of university eccentricities. Wilde, like many geniuses, remained, in his love of stunts, a perpetual student. He really believed in the ideas he had learnt from Ruskin and Morris, and at no period of his life ceased to carry on propaganda for better æsthetic standards in the everyday domestic environment. But he combined his sincerely held theories with a cynical eye to the main chance, and, after presenting himself at a ball dressed in Cavalier costume, came to London as a dress reformer and a "professor of æsthetics." An already existing acquaintanceship with the Duchess of Westminster, the sister of a college friend, gave him entry into the London drawing-rooms, where he appeared in velvet jackets, knee breeches, buckled shoes and flowing cravats, with long hair falling over his shoulders and an affected manner of speech and gesture. Already he was beginning to develop the art of conversation, and he combined his charming or startling phrases and æsthetic propaganda with a genial and well-timed insolence, as when he would draw attention to himself by arriving late and turning aside the reproaches of his hostess with some deliberately egoistic remark. He combined self-advertisement in Mayfair with the publication of his poems, which sold reasonably well among his acquaintances, although the five editions of which he boasted were more or less nominal, consisting only of 200 copies each!

The æsthetic movement, of which he claimed to be the high-priest, had little real existence outside his imagination.

There was, indeed, an æsthetic *tendency* among craftsmen and artists, who were trying to put into practice the theories of Ruskin and Morris and to introduce better standards of workmanship into ordinary domestic articles. But the oddly dressed young men who imitated Wilde, and the ladies in shapeless green tea-gowns who were caricatured by *Punch* and W. S. Gilbert, and who represented the movement in the popular eye, were for the most part fellow travellers who were not craftsmen or artists themselves and who merely brought undeserved ridicule on a number of conscientious workers. It was the kind of fashionable exploitation of a genuine movement of artistic change, of which we have seen so many examples in our own day.

Wilde, by playing carefully to the gallery, soon made himself the most notorious of the æsthetes. He was caricatured by George du Maurier and became the prototype of the queer poets and poseurs of Gilbert and Sullivan's popular comic opera, *Patience*. When D'Oyly Carte, the impresario of Gilbert and Sullivan, decided to boost his own productions by taking an original æsthete to America, Wilde was chosen for the part, accepted willingly, and for some years earned a living by appearing as a sensationally advertised freak lecturer in England as well as in America and Ireland.

How far Wilde believed the legend that he created by these activities it is hard to determine. He certainly suffered, in a relatively minor degree, from a typically schizoid tendency to live his fantasies in the mind, and found difficulty in establishing the border-line between fact and fancy. This is shown in the claims of a completely non-existent movement under his own leadership which he publicised rather too freely in his lectures to American audiences. In his lecture on *Art and the Handicraftsman*, for instance, he said:

> Well, let me tell you how it first came to me at all to create an artistic movement in England, a movement to

show the rich what beautiful things they might enjoy and the poor what beautiful things they might create.

There follows the semi-apocryphal story of Ruskin's rallying the students to work on Hinksey Marsh, and then Wilde proceeds:

> And I felt that if there was enough spirit amongst the young men to go out to such work as road-making for the sake of a noble ideal of life, I could from them create an artistic movement that might change, as it has changed, the face of England. So I sought them out—leader they would call me—but there was no leader: we were all searchers only, and we were bound to each other by noble friendship and by noble art.

Wilde was never over-exact in his conversation or writing: he had the Irish love of romancing, and would readily invent in order to gain a point. Sir Henry Newbolt tells the story of how he heard Wilde make a most convincing plea for the lesser Jacobean dramatists, reinforcing it with extremely appropriate quotations which he had made up on the spot. He had a great dislike for those sticklers for exactitude who interrupted his conversational flights to correct some mis-statement of fact, and one of the objects of his paradoxical dialogue *In Defence of Lying* was undoubtedly to defend his own tendencies and defeat the advocates of the literal.

On the other hand, he probably had at least a half-belief in his leadership of the mythical and nonsensical "æsthetic movement." All his life he saw himself as a symbolical figure of artistic and literary rebellion, a specially chosen representative of the *Zeitgeist,* and even in his deepest humility and humiliation, when he was writing *De Profundis* in Reading Gaol, he could still say of himself quite seriously:

> I was a man who stood in symbolic relations to the art and culture of my age. I had realised this for myself at the very dawn of my manhood, and had forced my age to

realise it afterwards. . . . Byron was a symbolic figure, but his relations were to the passion of his age and its weariness of passion. Mine were to something more noble, more permanent, of more vital issue, of larger scope.

This, of course, was the wildest self-delusion. However much Wilde's contemporaries enjoyed him as an entertaining conversationalist and, what was almost the same thing to them, as an amusing dramatist, however keenly a minority appreciated his writing, however violently the majority was irritated by his attitudes and paradoxes, none would have accepted him as symbolic of the period in which he lived. They all regarded him as an exception, an exotic bird in bright plumage which had flown into their grey and brown aviary, and they were right to do so. Wilde's virtues lay in what was untypical and unsymbolic of his age.

But, while it was understandable that in prison he should console himself with such delusions of former acclaim, in youth this lack of vision can only be explained by the assumption that Oscar was at least half-clowning. The humour with which he seemed to regard himself during his American tour is shown by his amusing letters home and by the tolerance with which he accepted and entered into all the jests devised against him by the wilder section of American youth.

The odd guise in which he embarked on his career as an æsthetic lecturer only did him harm with those who were unacquainted with his talents. But his patent earnestness, his considerable scholarship, and the clear intelligence with which he expounded his subjects did not fail to arouse interest and often sympathy, and many people who had gone to his lectures to jeer stayed to listen and learn. He could arouse enthusiasm among American roughnecks; in England a shrewd business man like Richard Le Gallienne's father saw through the overdressed façade and decided that Oscar was "no fool," while the old poet Whitman found him a congenial companion over a bottle of elderberry wine. He started with vast initial difficulties: his agents had billed him as a fantastic showpiece, and the professional humorists united in a solid front against him, which was expressed in newspaper caricatures and endless popular songs like *The Flipperty Flop Young Man,* which ran:

> *I'm a very æsthetic young man,*
> *A non-energetic young man;*
> *I'm a bitter and mildy,*
> *Naturey childy,*
> *Oscary Wildy young man.*

There was much kindred nonsense, often of an even lower type, with which he had to contend, not to speak of the hostile students of Harvard and Yale. Nevertheless, he managed to win much respect, in spite of disadvantages which were largely of his own creation.

The writings of his "æsthetic" period consist mainly of the lectures delivered in America, together with some which were added during his subsequent tours of England and Ireland. Only a few of these works survive in anything like complete form, for in later years Oscar himself thought little of his lectures and made no effort to preserve or publish them. In this he was right, since they are mere apprentice works, gauche in style and clumsy in construction. Nevertheless, they do contain some valuable ideas which should be noted to show that Wilde was by no means wholly a frivolous young poseur.

The English Renaissance in Art, a lecture on the nature and attitudes of the Pre-Raphaelite and the Æsthetic movements, is the most complete and in many ways the most restrained and intelligent of these productions.

It begins on a somewhat familiar note, tracing the birth of the new movement from a union of the mediæval and Hellenistic spirits, set in motion by the French Revolution. The chief characteristic of this movement, Wilde contends, is a return of art to life itself, and a turning away from symbolism and metaphysics, which are alien to true art. The movement had many progenitors, including Byron, Shelley and Blake, "but in the calmness and clearness of his vision, his perfect self-control, his unerring sense of beauty and his recognition of a separate realm for the imagination, Keats was the pure and serene artist, the forerunner of the Pre-Raphaelite school, and so of the great romantic movement of which I am to speak."

As a romantic, Wilde was of course opposed to classical poetry, and he condemns satirical verse—an attitude in which he continued all his life and which made him permanently blind to some of the greatest of English writers, including Pope and Dryden. This gives an added irony to the fact that he himself was, in prose, an inimitable satirist.

A return to nature, which he was later to condemn, and a more close attention to technique and the problems of artistic construction, which he always maintained to be necessary, were the two main ideas of this movement, but to these he added his own theory, later elaborated in *Intentions*, that Art has not any necessary reference to the social problems of an artist's own day:

> There is indeed a poetical attitude to be adopted towards all things, but all things are not fit subjects for poetry. Into the secure and sacred house of Beauty the true artist will admit nothing that is harsh or disturbing, nothing that gives pain, nothing that is debatable, nothing about which men argue. He can steep himself, if he wishes, in the discussion of all the social problems of his day, poorlaws and local taxation, free trade and bimetallic currency, or the like; but when he writes on these subjects it will be, as Milton nobly expressed it, with his left hand, in prose and not in verse, in a pamphlet and not in a lyric.

This was a view Wilde was to abandon radically in his last years, for in *The Ballad of Reading Gaol* he brought vigorously and effectively into art both the harsh and the disturbing, the painful and the debatable. Indeed, throughout his mature life, in spite of all the theory of art for art's sake which he continued to expound, he could never be wholly consistent, but was always leaving his pedestal to enter the struggle of social ideas, and these beneficial lapses into social consciousness characterise, not merely pamphlets like *The Soul of Man Under Socialism,* but also his plays, his poems, his stories, his one novel, and even *Intentions;* everything, in fact, except perhaps *Salome* and the last plays, though even a romantic fragment like *La Sainte Courtisane* carries its moral.

He sees healthy art in a recognition of the limitations of form and material, and points out that, far from art having to harmonise itself with modern society, it is for society to achieve art, and the true rôle of the critic is "to teach the people how to find in the calm of such art the highest expression of their own most stormy passions." He admits that for a wholly great art a noble public is necessary; only the lyricist can sing in a desert; the dramatist needs a great age to succeed. Nevertheless, it is in the love of art that lies the secret of civilisation.

> This devotion to beauty and to the creation of beautiful things is the test of all great civilised nations. . . .
> For beauty is the only thing that time cannot harm. Philosophies fall away like sand, and creeds follow one another like the withered leaves of autumn; but what is beautiful is a joy for all seasons and a possession for eternity.

But, he emphasises, art must not be external to normal life. If it is to have any therapeutic effect on individuals and nations, it must be closely related to common experience, for all the objects we use have their own part in the pattern of our lives and should therefore come as clearly within the province of art as paintings and statues. "For he who does not love art in all things does not love it at all, and he who does not need it in all things does not need it at all."

This movement in art should be valuable alike to those who do and to those who think, and here Wilde makes a distinction, which in later years he was to expand, between these two vital aspects. Incidentally, in expressing it, he brings in more than an echo of those golden words of Pater which were always to inspire him with a desire to live fully and dangerously:

> There are two kinds of men in the world, two great creeds, two different forms of natures: men to whom the end of life is action, and men to whom the end of life is thought. As regards the latter, who seek for experience itself and not for the fruits of experience, who must burn always with one of the passions of this fiery-coloured world, who find life interesting, not for its secret, but for its situations, for its pulsations and not for its purpose; the passion for beauty engendered by the decorative arts will be to them more satisfying than any political or religious enthusiasm, any enthusiasm for humanity, any ecstasy or sorrow for love. For art comes to one professing primarily to give nothing but the highest quality to one's moments, and for those moments' sake. So far for those to whom the end of life is thought. As regards the others, who hold that life is inseparable from labour, to them should this movement be specially dear: for, if our days are barren without industry, industry without art is barbarism.

On this note, which has been echoed in our day by a whole school of critics and industrial designers, led by such men as Herbert Read, Wilde goes on to plead for pleasant surroundings in which men can work, suggesting that the burden of labour can be lightened merely by placing the worker in pleasing and well-decorated surroundings, a fact that has since been proved in practice.

He ends, on a somewhat pontifical note, "We spend our days, each one of us, in looking for the secret of life. Well, the secret of life is in art."

I have quoted this lecture at some length in order to show that, however much Wilde may have played the clown on and off the platform during his æsthetic period, he expressed many sensible ideas, and, while his theories were not completely formed and the influences he had accepted were not wholly assimilated, he was already shaping those characteristic attitudes towards art and life which he later elaborated so brilliantly in conversation and criticism. Indeed, far from being frivolous, this and other lectures showed a vein of solemnity and earnestness which only rarely breaks into the flickering paradox of his later talk. This impression is supported by the words of Dion Boucicault, the old Irish dramatist who happened to be in New York at the time of Wilde's tour, and who was shocked at the way in which the lecture managers were exploiting Oscar's simplicity and honesty.

> He is the easy victim of those who expose him to ridicule and to the censure of the thoughtful. Those who have known him as I have, since he was a child at my knee, know that beneath the fantastic envelope in which his managers are circulating him there is a noble, earnest, kind and lovable man.

For those who are still attracted by the theory of Wilde's inveterate insincerity, it would be well to ponder these words of a very shrewd elder writer, spoken at Oscar's most ridiculous period of exhibitionism.

It might also be well to consider the good sense of some of the ideas contained in other lectures. Talking of house decoration and furniture, Wilde claimed that "art means value to the workman and it means the pleasure which he must necessarily take in making a beautiful thing. . . . Now what you must do is to bring artists and handicraftsmen together. Handicraftsmen cannot live, certainly cannot thrive, without such companionship."

In the same address he asks for the introduction of art and handicrafts into child education. He evidently felt strongly on this subject, for he devoted much time to it, pleading for a beautiful environment in which children could grow up, and criticising strongly the orthodox systems of education. "Give children beauty, not the record of bloody slaughters and barbarous brawls, as they call history, or of the latitude and longitude of places nobody cares to visit as they call geography."

Elsewhere he declared his gratitude for machinery, but gave a warning against its too uncritical acceptance:

> . . . We reverence it when it does its proper work, when it relieves men from ignoble and soulless labour, not when it seeks to do that which is valuable only when wrought by the hands and hearts of men. . . . Let us not mistake the means of civilisation for the end of civilisation. . . .

He pleaded for appropriateness of decoration, attacked the funerary urns on cast-iron stoves and the disappearing perspectives of moonlight scenes at the bottom of soup-plates, and declared it the great heresy of craftsmanship to make any material appear other than it was, to paint steel to look like wood or plaster to look like stone.

The ideal environment for the development of a vigorous art movement he saw in a society where each town would have its own nucleus of culture and not be swamped by metropolitan values. A clean atmosphere and a good standard of health are equally necessary. But, most of all, a sense of individuality, such as could only be found in a society where all men were free and no man king over his neighbours.

Such were Wilde's early views on art, and he held them,

with some variations, all his life. He had taken richly from his masters—Ruskin, Morris, Pater—but he had also considered the matter very thoroughly for himself, and made these ideas his own. One man he took very little from—James McNeill Whistler. I mention this because of the legend, founded and fostered by the American painter, who was jealous of Oscar's reputation as a conversationalist, that Wilde borrowed all his ideas on art from what Whistler had told him. In fact, Wilde's theories were formed long before he had even met the peppery James, and although in his innocence he was once foolish enough to ask Whistler for a few hints to help in an English lecture, he certainly did not base his ideas to any great extent on those which his rival expounded, although his taste in art may have been similar. In any case, Whistler had little real ground for complaint, since we advance theories so that other people may accept them, and cannot justly be annoyed when they do so. Imitation is an unavoidable phenomenon in art and thought, and even Whistler borrowed and imitated far and wide, but never considered himself the worse for it.

The whole test of imitation in art is whether the borrower has made good use of his appropriations. In the case of a man like Shakespeare, success in transmutation is so obvious that nobody seriously thinks of condemning him as a plagiarist. With lesser men the question is more bitterly disputed. But I think we shall find, in applying this simple test, that Wilde certainly made good use of his acquisitions from other artists; very little that he wrote, however many influences can be counted on dissection (and they are usually numerous), was without that flavour of originality which made it, as a whole, a new thing, quite distinct from anything his masters or any other artists had succeeded in creating.

There is a certain truth in Whistler's argument that Wilde could not talk as a real expert on the plastic arts. He was an amusing casual draughtsman, but had no training or ambitions in painting; on the other hand, he had a real eye for design, as was shown by his encouragement of painters like Charles Conder, Ricketts, Shannon and Rothenstein, though he always disliked Beardsley's work. Of music he clearly knew little, and, while he talked occasionally of this art in order to bring it into the scope of his theories, and even at times claimed it was the most perfect of the arts, such phrases as "the deferred resolutions of Beethoven" showed his pretensions in an odd light. He was probably speaking the truth when, being asked whether he liked music, he said to the lady whose daughter was thumping out a Scotch reel on the piano, "No, but I like that!"

He was clearly much better fitted for literary criticism than for expounding the merits of visual art, on which he could only venture into quickly exhausted generalisations. After his American tour, on which he was kept going largely by popular attention and by the oddities of life in a strange country, lecturing on the æsthetic idea soon began to pall, and he quickly abandoned what was becoming the unbearable drudgery of public speaking, and took to the slightly more congenial toil of literary reviewing.

For a period of some years, with the slowness that characterised his general literary development, he perfected himself in this form of criticism. It was often tedious work, and something of the boredom he experienced is conveyed by a passage in *The Critic as Artist*:

> As a rule, the critics—I speak, of course, of the higher class, of those, in fact, who write for the sixpenny papers—are far more cultured than the people whose work they are called upon to review. . . .
> Where there is no style a standard must be impossible. The poor reviewers are apparently reduced to be the reporters of the police-court of literature, the chroniclers of the doings of the habitual criminals of art.

His work led him into the by-paths of nineteenth-century writing, and it is not surprising that many of his reviews are mere journeyman's work, sufficient perhaps for their purpose, but not aspiring to the levels of good or fine literature. What, indeed, astonishes one is how often he managed to produce an entertaining article out of what must have been a very dull book. He had a catholic willingness to handle odd themes, and we find him, in 1885, writing pleasantly on a cookery book, while a long review of Lefebure's history of embroidery gave him the excuse for some pages of decorative writing which he later used, with characteristic economy of energy, to fill out a chapter in *The Picture of Dorian Gray*.

But his reviewing work was not all of this playful kind, and he began to develop sound critical sense and also a mordant yet unmalicious style of comment which steadily developed towards the epigram and paradox of his maturer days. The long pages of notes on forgotten books are studded with lively paragraphs of rapid assessment which show a vivid and sure sense of literary value. Of a dull "Life" he remarked: "Biographies of this kind rob life of much of its dignity and its wonder, add to death itself a new terror, and make one wish that all art were anonymous."

Meredith, a writer whom Wilde admired both for his work and for the personal integrity he had displayed in always refusing to court an unappreciative public, called forth the following remarks, which still remain among the best short opinions on that novelist:

George Meredith's style is chaos illuminated by brilliant flashes of intellect. As a writer he has mastered everything, except language; as a novelist he can do everything, except tell a story; as an artist, he is everything, except articulate. Too strange to be popular, too individual to have imitators, the author of *Richard Feverel* stands absolutely alone. It is easy to disarm criticism, but he has disarmed the disciple. He gives us his philosophy through the medium of wit, and is never so pathetic as when he is humorous. To turn truth into a paradox is not difficult, but George Meredith makes all his paradoxes truths, and no Theseus can thread his labyrinth, no Œdipus solve his secret.

On the face of it, these remarks contain merely that kind of pleasant absurdity which one associates with Wilde's wit. They seem to be superficial jests cracked off like the folds of a jumping firework, with pyrotechnic skill but very little thought. Yet when one examines them closely, when one considers their individual justice, it is seen that each statement contains its undeniable truth, and that the whole paragraph illuminates our view of Meredith with the brilliance of a series of mirrors catching the light from different angles. It is impossible to put one's finger on any of these brisk statements and say that it is untrue. But how disconcerting they appear at first reading! Wilde, like many other and less able writers, learnt early the value of shock in awakening people to realise a truth they would not absorb from the mere repetitions of a literary sermon.

But, quite apart from this kind of occasional virtuosity, he was also building up a sound general critical attitude, which was very soon to be reflected in his creative work; it can be seen in such passages as the following note on the drama, which already shows the standard on which he was later to build his own dramatic productions:

> The aim of social comedy, in Menander no less than in Sheridan, is to mirror the manners, not to reform the morals, of its day, and the censure of the Puritan, whether real or affected, is always out of place in literary criticism, and shows a want of recognition of the essential distinction between art and life.

These reviews were for Wilde not only a means of earning money; they also served to perfect his prose and to elaborate his general critical theories of style, form and subject, which were to be expressed more fully in the long essays and dialogues, most of them collected in his little volume, *Intentions*, and which found a more directly creative expression in his stories and plays.

Intentions is a collection of two dialogues and two essays, all of which have some relation to problems of literary criticism, or art criticism in general. The two essays, *Pen, Pencil and Poison* and *The Truth of Masks*, need not detain us long. The first, a study of the writer and poisoner Wainwright, is of some interest, since Wilde, in his acute psychological study of this strange figure of the Romantic revival, gives us incidentally a most interesting reflection of his own personality, and, as a piece of self-expression, *Pen, Pencil and Poison* is perhaps the one complete example of Wilde's own theories of criticism carried into practice. Creative criticism, he declared, lay in a critic using the work on which he writes as a point of departure for an original expression of his own imagination. While portraying Wainwright with great competence, Wilde brings such light to bear on certain sides of his own character that one often wonders how much of the essay really concerns Wainwright and how much is intended as a portrait of himself. Certainly Wainwright's own attitude towards criticism, as interpreted by Wilde, agrees sufficiently well with that of his expositor for the essay to fit integrally into the pattern of *Intentions* as a whole; there is, for instance, a clear anticipation of *The Critic as Artist* in these lines:

> As an art-critic he concerned himself primarily with the complex impressions produced by a work of art, and certainly the first step in æsthetic criticism is to realise one's own impressions. He cared nothing for abstract discussions on the nature of the Beautiful, and the historical method, which has since yielded such rich fruit, did not belong to his day, but he never lost sight of the great truth that art's

first appeal is neither to the intellect nor to the emotions, but purely to the artistic temperament, and he more than once pointed out that this temperament, this "taste" as he calls it, being unconsciously guided and made perfect by frequent contact with the best work, becomes in the end a form of right judgment.

Wilde did not invent Wainwright. That strange character had already fascinated nineteenth-century writers as varied as De Quincey and Dickens, Bulwer and W. C. Hazlitt. But he sketched him from a new angle and in particularly vivid colours, doubtless because he felt so much in common with Wainwright and therefore put so much of himself into the study.

But, if Wilde largely portrayed his own personality in *Pen, Pencil and Poison,* he put far more of his thoughts and dreams on many subjects into the two dialogues, *The Decay of Lying* and *The Critic as Artist,* the latter of which, for all its manifest faults of style and argument, remains one of the most significant critical works of recent English literature, embodying a whole philosophy of life and art, and, in the process, telling us much of Wilde's intellectual autobiography. Both essays sustain theories which at first sight may seem absurd, but which on examination are found to contain a wide basis of truth in their paradoxical daring, while their author's wit, flickering like sheet-lightning over whole landscapes of thought, reveals many new and unsuspected aspects of life, literature and philosophy.

Through studying them, we reach the conclusion that Wilde was no great critic in the analytical tradition. Here he could not compete with men like Matthew Arnold or Coleridge. But if the faculty of perceiving with almost intuitive rapidity and accuracy the essential nature of a writer's work, and expressing this perception in concise and aphoristic form, is to be regarded as a critical faculty, as it should rightly be, then Wilde in his own way was a critic of high merit, particularly when one takes into account the validity of so many of his generalisations concerning the wider problems of art.

The main theme of *The Decay of Lying* consists of an attack on realism in art. Wilde contends that art, like thought, has an independent existence, that it has direct relation neither to its own time nor to external nature. Its appeal is timeless and, "so far from being the creation of its time, it is usually in direct opposition to it, and the only history that it preserves for us is the history of progress."

Art is essentially imaginative, and therefore, while nature and life may be its raw materials, they can never be its real motives and are of use to it only after they have been converted into terms of artistic convention. "The moment Art surrenders its imaginative medium it surrenders everything. As a method Realism is a complete failure," he remarks justly.

From this he proceeds to his more paradoxical theory, that, far from its being the duty of the artist to imitate life and nature, life itself is necessarily an imitator of art. "This results not merely from Life's imaginative instinct, but from the fact that the self-conscious aim of Life is to find expression, and that Art offers it certain beautiful forms through which it may realise that energy." He then continues in the extravagance of paradoxical fancy, to claim that not merely life, but also nature, is imitative of Art, since: "The only effects she can show us are the effects we have already seen through poetry or in paintings." As a final attack on Philistine moralism, he puts forward the contention that the current form of reverence for the truth is ridiculous and that "Lying, the telling of beautiful untrue things, is the proper aim of Art."

Clearly, taken literally these theories are all somewhat absurd. But Wilde was intent on shocking people out of their complacent faith in the old theories of art, and nowadays there can be few critics who would disagree fundamentally with his basic ideas which, as he claimed, certainly helped people to look with a new insight into the problems of art and paved the way for the justification of most of the artistic revolutions of his time.

No serious critic or artist or writer to-day would contend that the object of art is merely to imitate or represent life as it is. Photographic realism is no longer considered seriously, and the "realism" which makes its appearance in contemporary art is in fact usually an attempt to convey a political teaching by a version of life which seeks to change people's actions by a form of propagandism, a mock realism, that is definitely selective and therefore fundamentally artificial.

The theory of life imitating art, bad art as well as good art, is also a valid one. If we include such manifestations as folk ballads, popular fiction, religious writing and music, the modern film, it is clear that these forms have had an all-pervasive effect on the lives of the people which it is impossible to estimate fully, while on more selective minds the effects of books and visual art are even more profound. The novels of Dickens, the satires of Voltaire, the romantic thoughts of Rousseau, all had a vast influence in changing society subsequent to their appearance, while the impact of such a phenomenon as cinematographic sadism on an impressionable public is terrifying in its magnitude. Painters have helped to change the dress and decoration of an age, poets have contributed to the evolution of political conceptions, and the aims and ideals of the masses have been sapped steadily by the various kinds of *kitsch* art in which they are reflected as in distorting mirrors. Wilde expresses his theme in a fantastic manner and supports it with airy and improbable little stories of the effects of imaginary works of art in changing individual lives; nevertheless, his theory is basically true, and the grim fact is that most of the influence wielded on life by art has been that of bad art. The reign of good art is yet to come, except in the lives of isolated individuals.

There is even some truth, from a subjective point of view, in Wilde's contention that nature imitates art. To the idealist philosopher, the world exists only because we see it. It is the sum of our perceptions, and, if our perceptions of nature are increased or changed by a work of art, then nature, in so far as it exists in our minds, has been changed and enlarged. The impressionist painters, as Wilde points out, gave a new aspect to the natural landscape by their revolutionary technique of reproducing light.

As for Wilde's last contention, of the necessity of lying, it must be remembered that lying was justified by such authorities as Plato and Bacon on much more disreputable grounds than those put forward by Wilde. Plato advocated it on the theory that rulers had a right to tell their subjects falsehoods for the good of the community, and Bacon held similar views on the virtues of lies as a means of "doing good." Wilde, however, did not justify what he called lying from any ulterior motive, and no doubt the propaganda lie of our own age would have aroused his contempt. What he claimed was that objective truth is no concern of the artist, who is ruled by the imagination, and that the products of true art never give an objectively exact view of the world outside the artist's brain. What Wilde called "lying" in Art is merely an acknowledgment of the validity of subjective truths, and of the invalidity of realism.

The Decay of Lying is written very much in the style of Wilde's own conversations, and similar flights of fantasy and epigrammatic brilliance decorate it throughout. The novelists of the late nineteenth century are reviewed in concise and accurate sentences, and it would be difficult to find a better estimate of a writer who is to-day enjoying a revived popularity than this:

> Mr. Henry James writes fiction as if it were a painful duty, and wastes upon mean motives and imperceptible

"points of view" his neat literary style, his felicitous phrases, his swift and caustic satire.

Amusing, provocative, pleasantly argued and fundamentally sound as *The Decay of Lying* certainly is, it does not reach the standard of *The Critic as Artist*, which is one of Wilde's best pieces of writing, and into which he put much of his own personality and his real thoughts.

Wilde's thesis in this essay is that criticism should be creative, and that all great art, since it must be selective, contains the critical as well as the creative element. In another sense, all creative art is a criticism of life. The function of the critic, where he exists as distinct from other creative artists, is not so much to analyse and break down the work of art he is considering, as to probe into its true spirit and, from his own subjective impressions, to create a work of critical art that will live both in its own artistic and imaginative right and also as an extension, through the critic's imagination, of the spirit of the original work. Wilde's category of criticism is therefore a wide one; it includes the musicians who by their playing are creative critics of the composer, and also such writers as Darwin, whom he admiringly calls "the critic of the Book of Nature."

His claims for criticism seem at first sight extravagant indeed.

> The critic occupies the same relation to the work of art that he criticises as the artist does to the visible world of form and colour or to the unseen world of passion and of thought. He does not even require for the perfection of his art the finest materials. Anything will serve its purpose. . . . Treatment is the test. There is nothing that has not in it suggestion or challenge. . . . Indeed, I would call criticism a creation within a creation. . . . Nay, more, I would say that the highest criticism, being the purest form of personal expression, is in its way more creative than creation, as it has least reference to any standard external to itself, and

is, in fact, its own reason for existing, and as the Greeks would put it, in itself, and to itself, an end. It is the only civilised form of autobiography, as it deals, not with the events, but with the thoughts of one's life; not with life's physical accidents of deed or circumstance, but with the spiritual moods and imaginative passions of the mind.

But in all this there is a basis of truth, since, as Wilde shows later, the really great work of art, once it is created, has an independent life and can often convey to other men what the artist never considered when he was creating it. Such impressions the critic can justly express. It is also true that the critic, since he is usually, unlike the specialist artist, a man of wide and varied culture, can relate the work he discusses to realms of thought and imagination beyond its immediate reference. But neither of these facts necessarily makes the critic greater than other artists, though it must be granted that in the development of the tradition of art his work of interpretation is of a high importance. Dryden, whose criticism had such an influence in the creation of modern English prose; Byelinsky, who played such a vital part in the development of Russian literature; Stendhal, whose interpretations of Shakespeare were so important in the French romantic movement—such men were key figures in the art of their age. But it is doubtful whether they were more important than the poets, dramatists and novelists who worked in the same movements, with the possible exception of Dryden, who was so versatile a creative writer in almost every form that he completely dominated the literature of his age. The core of Wilde's theory of the critic's function is taken from Pater, and it is significant that he quotes this author as the great practitioner of imaginative criticism.

In discussing the development of the critic, who should aim always at the perfection of his own personality, Wilde returns to a somewhat escapist praise of art in relation to life. Life is formless, he says. "Its catastrophes happen in· the wrong way and to the wrong people. There is a grotesque horror about its comedies, and its tragedies seem to culminate in farce. One is always wounded when one approaches it." Wilde was always trying to evade life, but it caught him in the end and destroyed him in a tragedy more tawdry than he would have dared to imagine. What he says is true enough; life for most men is a succession of failures, and there is often no failure so bitter as success. But, as Wilde found, it is not to be avoided by indulging in artistic fantasies, by living in Dante's *Paradiso* or trying to resurrect the lives of the Greek poets. The make-believe sorrows of art cannot save us from the real sorrows of life; they can only help us to understand and endure them.

Wilde somewhat illogically connects his advocacy of art as an escape route from life with the philosophy of non-action he shared with the Taoists. "Art is immoral." It differs from social morality, since "emotion for the sake of emotion is the aim of art, and emotion for the sake of action is the aim of life, and of that practical organisation of life which we call society."

Contemplation is the highest end of thought and life, and "the contemplative life, the life that has for its aim not *doing* but *being*, and not *being* merely, but *becoming*—that is what the critical spirit can give us."

Men in ordinary active life, politicians, social reformers and priests, are all incapable of unbiased judgment, for "we live in the age of the over-worked and the under-educated; the age in which people are so industrious that they become absolutely stupid." Therefore the thinker has his necessary function in society, even though he may seem to be opposed to the immediate practical aims of politicians and social reformers, precisely because his lack of personal bias makes him more clear-sighted than the man who is earthbound by practical "common sense." These ideas will be discussed more fully in the next chapter, and here it is sufficient merely to indicate Wilde's argument that the detached eye of the critic may detect more clearly than that of others the real solution to the fundamental problems of society. Thought, nevertheless, like art, is essentially subversive; its acceptance of reason as a criterion militates always against the stability of fixed societies. On the other hand, the spirit of criticism, which is also the spirit of appreciation, can foster the growth of individual men, and build up their necessary cultural atmosphere and acuteness of thought. In this it is superior to orthodox educational methods, with their unhealthy emphasis on facts. "We teach people how to remember, we never teach them how to grow. It has never occurred to us to try and develop in the mind a more subtle quality of apprehension and discernment."

Criticism, Wilde also contends, makes culture possible by distilling "the cumbersome mass of creative work . . . into a finer essence." It can discover the hidden, and reconstruct the dead past from the study of words or stones.

More than this, the critical spirit is a great bond among men, because it insists on the unity of thought.

> If we are tempted to make war upon another nation, we shall remember that we are seeking to destroy an element of our own culture, and possibly its most important element. . . . Intellectual criticism will bind Europe together in bonds far closer than can be forged by shopman or sentimentalist. It will give us the peace that springs from understanding.

Finally, as a return on a higher level to his old preoccupations, Wilde sublimates the immorality of art by declaring the supremacy of Æsthetics as the great rule of the perfect life:

> Ethics, like natural selection, make existence possible. Æsthetics, like sexual selection, make life lovely and wonderful, fill it with new forms, and give it progress and

variety and change. And when we reach the true culture that is our aim, we attain to that perfection of which the saints have dreamed, the perfection of those to whom sin is impossible, not because they make the renunciations of the ascetic, but because they can do everything they wish without hurt to the soul, and can wish for nothing that can do the soul harm, the soul being an entity so divine that it is able to transform into elements of a richer experience, or a finer susceptibility, or a newer mode of thought, acts or passions, that with the common world would be commonplace, or with the uneducated ignoble, or with the shameful vile. Is this dangerous? Yes, it is dangerous—all ideas, as I told you, are so.

Here we have the doctrine of the decadents declared fully and eloquently, with that consistency which drove Wilde steadily on to his doom, because he mistook his own trivial "sins" for the achievements of great experience, and allowed himself to become so preoccupied with petty vice that he descended into vulgarity and grossness instead of rising, as he had hoped, to his æsthetic level of continually heightened consciousness. He proved in his own misfortunes the danger of such ideas. But that does not make them necessarily or wholly invalid, and this last statement, like much more of *The Critic as Artist,* has in it a great deal of truth, since a man's individual judgment can be the *only* ultimate criterion of the value of his acts. But that judgment may not always be used in such a way as to further the man's development, and then we get such unavoidable accidents of freedom as Wilde's temporary degeneration.

The Critic as Artist is at once more and less than a treatise on criticism. Of the technique of criticism, and particularly of that analytic method in criticism which Wilde seems often to disregard, it says very little. But of the aims and scope of criticism it says a great deal, and rapidly widens its field from a discussion of a particular critical form to a much more comprehensive theme, the idea of imaginative and reasoned criticism as a stimulus to culture and thought, and a foundation of the complete life. And undoubtedly, while the claims which Wilde makes may sound ridiculous if we regard criticism merely in the narrow sense, their validity is much greater if they are seen as a vindication of the necessity for the critical spirit in all life.

The Critic as Artist represents one of Wilde's two great confessions of faith—the other was *De Profundis*. Stylistically, it is a curiously erratic piece of writing, a glittering compound of fantasy and acute objectivity, of nonsense and wisdom, of extravagance and insight. In its epigrammatic style it condenses a whole regiment of ideas into an amazingly short space; they follow one another with all the speed and dexterity of a brilliant conversation. Technically the writing seems artificial, yet there is reason to believe that it represents Wilde's own natural style, the style of his talking, greatly influenced by the language of the Bible and Greek ways of thought. The ideas are always daring, and, while sometimes startlingly ridiculous (as Wilde intended), are generally nearer to the truth than they seem when their paradoxical impact first stirs one's attention. Once again, Wilde cannot resist appearing in literary fancy dress. Sometimes his expression descends to a clowning in words not unlike the sartorial performances of the "Professor of Æsthetics." But this time the quality of thought amply counterbalances the apparent fooling that accompanies it, and shows Wilde a deep thinker as well as an effervescent wit.

The Critic as Artist itself contains little practical criticism, though here and there are embedded brief aphoristic comments which tell us almost as much as a whole essay by an academic critic. An example is this paragraph on Kipling:

As one turns the pages of his *Plain Tales from the Hills*, one feels as if one were seated under a palm-tree reading life by superb flashes of vulgarity. The bright colours of the bazaars dazzle one's eyes. The jaded, second-rate Anglo-Indians are in exquisite incongruity with their surroundings. The mere lack of style in the story-teller gives an odd journalistic realism to what he tells us. From the point of view of literature Mr. Kipling is a genius who drops his aspirates. From the point of view of life, he is a reporter who knows vulgarity better than anyone has ever known it. Dickens knew its clothes and its comedy. Mr. Kipling knows its essence and its seriousness. He is our first authority on the second-rate, and has seen marvellous things through key-holes, and his backgrounds are real works of art.

One reads passages of this kind and regrets that Wilde never wrote the epigrammatic literary history of his age. It would have been more amusing, more compact, and infinitely more accurate in its insight than the kind of volumes in which academic scholars inter each literary age so that only its most vigorous figures can ever emerge from their graves and walk in our minds.

Apart from the reviews already considered, Wilde's only important critical work outside the fragments in the two dialogues consists of *Pen, Pencil and Poison* and *The Portrait of Mr. W. H.* The first of these we have already examined. It is a delightful piece of appreciative writing, and reveals much of Wilde himself, but its critical content is very limited. It might be called rather a fragment of imaginative biography —almost an autobiography in a mirror.

The Portrait of Mr. W. H. is a speculation into the character of Shakespeare and the possibly homosexual basis of some of his poems. Here, again, there is a strong autobiographical element, but it is not so considerable as many of Wilde's enemies have maintained, since his theory that the "Mr. W. H." of the sonnets was a young actor Willie Hughes, with whom Shakespeare had a passionate friendship, is at least hinted at by such early Shakespearean critics as Malone and Tyrwhitt. The final, expanded version of *The Portrait of Mr. W. H.* was lost during the chaotic scenes at the sale of Wilde's property after his arrest; but the early, shorter version appeared in *Blackwood's Magazine*. On its first appearance it was regarded as a piece of pleasant scholarly fantasy, but, as the rumours regarding Wilde's perversion began to spread, his critics soon made it a further proof of their accusations. Undoubtedly, at the time of his trials, it did him much harm, though the published form certainly seems a harmless and engagingly written piece of literary speculation. No doubt, according to Wilde's standards, it would pass as a specimen of imaginative criticism, since it certainly enlarges our view of Shakespeare and adds to the mass of heretical opinion on that enigmatic poet. It is pure conjecture, but, as far as I can see, Wilde's evidence for his theory, based partly on internal word analysis of the sonnets, is as good as that of the Baconians or any other school of Shakespearean heterodoxy. Indeed, the fact that he uses the same kind of evidence as the Baconians makes it seem possible that he first conceived it as a satire on their contentions. This is supported by the fact that he was always somewhat contemptuous of Shakespearean controversies, and on one occasion, at a dinner where his fellow guests discussed vehemently the old question of Hamlet's insanity, he solemnly announced his intention of writing a treatise with the title "Are Hamlet's Commentators Really Mad or only Pretending to be?" Also, at least in his heyday, he did not wholly share the general uncritical adulation of Shakespeare and, according to Alfred Douglas, declared that Webster was a better playwright; Webster, indeed, was the only Elizabethan dramatist whom he imitated (in *The Duchess of Padua*), a sure sign of his admiration. It was not until he himself became a tragic figure that he really appreciated the tragedies of Shakespeare. Before that he often contended that the romantic comedies were Shakespeare's greatest works; Yeats records a conversation in which Wilde said: "Give me *The Winter's Tale*, 'Daffodils that come before the swallow dare,' but not *King Lear*. What is *King Lear* but poor life struggling in the fog?"

For these reasons, it seems possible that *Mr. W. H.* was commenced as a skit, and only became a serious study when Wilde found a personal interest in the subject because of the analogy between his own love for men and that which may have inspired Shakespeare.

In general, Wilde's work does not at first sight seem to entitle him to a high position among our critics. His flamboyance, his frequent clowning, the irrepressible fountain of paradoxical wit that springs every now and then from his most seriously considered argument, certainly mark him off from the writers who follow in the tradition of Dryden, Coleridge and Arnold. He was not a great critic in the analytical manner, and was too anxious to surprise and shock people into wakefulness to be scrupulously careful of the accuracy of his contentions. Nor was he capable of the kind of consistent industry that makes a critic of the solid kind. He devoted too much energy to other activities, to his plays and stories, to talking and pleasure, ever to apply himself at all consistently to critical work. Yet his contribution was both unique and important. He expressed in an original manner a theory of critical method and of the critical spirit which, if not wholly new, had never been considered with sufficient application until Wilde set himself to this work. He gave an effective answer to the realistic theory and showed that art is an extension of life, using life as its raw material, but producing something completely different which in its turn has a profound influence on the pattern of life. He pleaded for the expulsion of ugliness and sham from objects of everyday use, and for an education based on æsthetic and critical standards. He declared that art and criticism had no necessary connection with moral or political ideas; on the other hand, he pointed out that æsthetic appreciation and a truly critical way of thought would in themselves teach people to see the world impartially and to lose all that desire for strife, oppression and exploitation which comes from a failure to think clearly and rationally. All these are important contributions; they represent an æsthetic attitude wholly consistent with Wilde's social and philosophical ideals of non-action and individualism.

His criticism of the visual arts is mainly appreciative; he rarely has anything penetrating to say on this subject, and seems to have discussed it partly because of Ruskin's influence, and partly because he felt the arts so clearly bound together that the true connoisseur must be able to pass his opinion in every province. His views on painting were rarely important, and not often original, except for such sallies as his remark on Frith's *Derby Day*, "Is it all done by hand?"

But on writing, and particularly on the writing of his contemporaries, he always produced illuminating comments. In this kind of criticism, and in the quick insight he brought to it, he was certainly unique in English literature. Nowhere else can be found such compact and at the same time accurate judgments of the work of other writers. Wilde had never patience for the laborious toil of ordinary criticism. He sought to say the most he could as briefly as possible, and, without deliberate analyses supported by masses of quotation, to give the gist of his criticisms in a few sentences or, when at his best, in a single phrase. It was a kind of virtuosity, and nobody without Wilde's quick insight could have succeeded so well. But these critical epigrams were more than mere trickery; they really did contribute in a quite outstanding way to the understanding of many authors. The æsthetic clown had perfected his technique to such an extent that almost every trick had its own original significance as a manifestation of the critical spirit.

PERHAPS Wilde's reputation has largely outlived the ridicule earned by his "æsthetic" and sartorial antics, for in general his writings have redeemed the earlier follies in the minds of those who do not remain prejudiced against him on moral grounds.

An accusation that clings more closely is that of social snobbery. Wilde, it is said, was an arrogant snob and an unmitigated social climber. He had no real sympathy for the poor, it is added, and, indeed, insulted them on numerous occasions. The dinner-tables of London society were his stamping ground, the company of lords and diplomats infinitely more important to him than that of the real intellectual, the artistic or manual worker, and he willingly played the jester to the upper-classes, etc., etc.

In these charges, as in many others made against Wilde, there is a portion of truth. He did love high society and certainly enjoyed entertaining a Mayfair table with his conversation. Wealth, and what wealth can buy, had an almost irresistible fascination for him, while he certainly found it pleasant to consort with titled people—he usually made his personal spokesman in play or novel at least a lord!

But did all these things really make Wilde a snob? Snobbery, after all, is not merely a naïve pleasure in associating with the aristocracy and basking in a wealthy environment. It consists in regarding the social position, the inherent qualities, the intellectual predilections of a certain class as of greater value than those of any other class, and of despising all people who do not belong to this elect stratum of society. If one is not of the desirable rank, it consists in endeavouring to climb into it, to absorb all its values and characteristics, to despise one's own origins and to ape those who arouse one's admiration and envy. Snobbery need not necessarily be aristocratic. It is rife among the middle-classes, particularly those who are rising from one sub-class to the next, and it is rabid among those intellectuals who think they hold all the clues to the world's wisdom and are therefore of necessity superior to their less fortunate neighbours. It is frequent among the working-class, where the smallest difference of employment or wages, or the mere fact of living in different streets of the same slum district, may be the reason for one working-woman to despise another. And it finds perhaps its most curious form in that inverted snobbery by which certain types of political radicals, usually themselves of middle-class origin, worship the working-class, confer on it all the highest virtues of mankind, and try to adopt the attitudes and attributes of the labourer with as much ardour and as ludicrous results as the jumped-up shopkeeper trying to ape a lord.

According to these definitions, Wilde, although a case might easily be made for accusing him of intellectual snobbery, was certainly not a social snob. He consorted with the upper-classes, but he did not accept their values and he frequently criticised them in his writings and conversation. His attitude is clarified by some remarks of Yeats, who, coming from a similar background, can perhaps be expected to understand Wilde's outlook. In *The Trembling of the Veil*, Yeats said, "He was a parvenu, but a parvenu whose whole bearing proved that if he did dedicate every story in *The House of Pomegranates* to a lady of title, it was but to show that he was Jack and the social ladder his pantomime bean-stalk. 'Did you ever hear him say *Marquess of Dimmesdale?*' a friend of his once asked me. 'He does not say *The Duke of York* with any pleasure.'" And when Hugh Kingsmill put the direct question whether he considered Wilde a snob, Yeats replied: "No, I would not say that. England is a strange country to the Irish. To Wilde the aristocrats of England were like the nobles of Bagdad."

A certain pleasure in high living, a childish preoccupation with titles, a naïve glee at seeing that Oscar Wilde, the Irish doctor's son, had the nobility of England falling over them-selves to secure his amusing presence at their dinner-parties, were the principal causes of Wilde's preoccupation with the upper-classes. It is, of course, impossible to deny that his suc-cess went rather to his head and made his ideas assume mega-lomaniac proportions, as when he allowed himself to remark, "A man who can dominate a London dinner-table can domi-nate the world." He was soon to find that such power over men's minds as he wielded in the brief hours of his exquisite conversation had a transitory and gossamer effect which did not help to save him when at last the world turned against him and deposed him like a tawdry Saturnalian king.

He admired the code of manners which theoretically ad-hered to the aristocracy, although, in point of fact, many of those with whom he came into close contact, such as the churlish Marquess of Queensberry, had less of this quality than Wilde himself. He saw gentlemanly manners as a neces-sary ingredient of social harmony. As he put it in his rather flamboyant and cynical manner:

> Society, civilised society at least, is never very ready to believe anything to the detriment of those who are both rich and fascinating. It instinctively feels that manners are of more importance than morals, and in its opinion the highest respectability is of much less value than the pos-session of a good chef.

While there was for him a certain glamour about titles and the glitter of social life, what he really saw in polite society was an ideal of good relationships, an ideal which, as he was to find later, had very little behind it. He himself, whatever may have been his failings in other respects, usually behaved towards other people with exemplary consideration and grace. He was, indeed, helped in this by his placid and singularly unmalicious temperament, but the fact remains that he did strive to attain the good aspects of the eighteenth-century ideal of a gentleman. In this he was often more successful than his genuinely aristocratic acquaintances, since, among other things, he would not support racial prejudice, and never indulged in the anti-Semitism which was then fashionable in certain Mayfair circles. Nor did he ever despise a man for his origins, as many of those who have risen into society by the backstairs are liable to do.

Perhaps for these reasons he can be forgiven a certain perverse adoration of titles; after all, the only difference between him and the sturdy revolutionary, William Morris, was that, while Morris was wise enough to write of dead kings and noblemen, Wilde was foolish enough to sentimentalise living ones.

But in the course of two decades as a public figure in the London salons, he found out that the aristocrats did not even justify their wealth and privileges by displaying virtue or serving any social purpose, and he quickly came to despise the majority of them. In his plays they become the most grotesque figures, the Lady Bracknells and Lord Cavershams; upper-class stupidity is pilloried in his elderly parliamentarian aristocrats, and calculating vulgarity in his dowagers and duchesses.

Of the nobility in general he once remarked, "They are nothing but exaggerated farmers." The *Peerage,* he said, was "the best thing in fiction the English have ever done." And in one of his potent social epigrams he epitomised all his con-

tempt for a class—"The English country gentleman gallop-
ing along after a fox—the unspeakable in pursuit of the
uneatable."

For the middle-classes he had a distaste that knew no reser-
vation. He hated their Jingoism, their morality, their generally narrow attitudes. They were "Tartuffe seated in his
shop behind the counter," and their attitude towards life,
"the Bayswater view of life" as he called it, seemed to him
wholly warped and mean.

Like Baudelaire he always set out to *épater les bourgeois,*
and he certainly succeeded in affronting them and making of
them thorough-paced enemies who triumphed relentlessly at
his downfall.

Towards the poor he was sometimes severe, and at times
they, like everybody else, fell victims to his passion for making a good phrase. But, in general, he was careful to point
out the reasons for their failings, to excuse them in a way he
never excused their social "superiors." "There is only one
class in the community," he said, "that thinks more about
money than the rich, and that is the poor. The poor can
think of nothing else. That is the misery of being poor."

He criticised the poor when they accepted their degrada-
tion, and condemned charity because it merely sought to per-
petuate the injustices of poverty. His solution was not, as
some of his critics seem to have thought, that of a leisured
and cultivated rich class and a debased caste of workers. He
explicitly denounced such a form of society as being both
faulty and undesirable, and sought, by the elimination of
private property, to take from men the cares of riches and
poverty alike and to allow everybody to realise himself by
enjoying the advantages which had been available previously
only to the rich.

At times he spoke contemptuously of "the people," but it
was because he saw the dangers of mass prejudices and mass
moralities wielded by a majority to the detriment of individ-

uals. He regarded the common people as individually better than their rulers, and he attacked them only because they sought to follow Pope and Prince by establishing the tyranny of the mass instead of that of the individual despot. "They have marred themselves by imitation of their *inferiors*," he remarks in *The Soul of Man*, meaning by "inferiors" the world's rulers.[1]

Wilde's attitude towards the poor developed as his own experience grew, and in *De Profundis*, even more than in *The Soul of Man*, he became more sympathetic towards them than towards any other social class. We are told that he always mixed well with manual workers, and his popularity with warders and prisoners alike in Reading Gaol rather confirms this. From all accounts, it would seem that he always adopted an attitude of complete equality in his contacts with working-class people.

But Wilde was not merely devoid of what his enemies have chosen to call "snobbery." He also—and this is what their accusations were aimed to disprove—had a genuine concern for social justice and a deep consciousness of the essential corruption of the society in which he moved and lived. In his own way he did what he could to expose that injustice and remedy that corruption by satire and polemic.

In all his writings he subjected the very "social life" in which he was involved to the most acute criticism. As we have seen, the aristocrats of his comedies were made as ridiculous as ever Wycherley made any of his characters, with a light-hearted contempt that was in its way even more devastating than Wycherley's distorting bitterness. I think that even when Wilde was most involved in his clownings at London dinner-parties he realised at least partially the folly of his own con-

[1] It is an interesting point that in some editions of *The Soul of Man Under Socialism*, published since Wilde's death, the word *superiors* has replaced *inferiors*, as if a meddling editor, possibly Ross, felt too puzzled at the literal rendering to let it pass.

duct, the pretences he was acting, and there seems no doubt, from a close and unbiased examination of his writings, that his concern for social justice was completely sincere and forms a really important aspect of his character and thought.

It is a concern that appears early in his career. He was brought up in a home where rebellion was a tradition, and his mother owed her reputation to her revolutionary youth. Morality and authority were concepts whose hold over the members of the Wilde family was extremely tenuous, and an unconventional home, while it sometimes produces a reaction to conformity among the children, equally often perpetuates its own spirit.

But, while this Bohemian environment in childhood naturally tended to mould Wilde's attitude towards society and social conformity, it was not until he reached Oxford and came under the influence of Ruskin that he turned definitely towards social interests.

Nevertheless, in his earliest work, that is to say, his poems, we find the libertarian element strongly marked, although Wilde was still rather confused in his preferences, and tended to temper his revolutionary themes with appeals to the spirit of "Order." For instance, in one poem he says:

> These Christs that die upon the barricades,
> God knows that I am with them, in some things,

but elsewhere in the same collection, while indulging in the Shelleyan emotion of

> . . . liking best that state republican
> Where every man is Kinglike and no man
> Is crowned above his fellows,

he continues:

> I love them not whose hands profane
> Plant the red flag upon the piled-up street.

By the time he reached Paris in 1883, his ideas seem to have changed considerably on these subjects, no doubt owing to the influence of his environment, and when on one occasion Sherard was walking with him beside the ruins of the Tuileries, burnt down during the Commune, Wilde remarked: "There is not there one little blackened stone which is not to me a chapter in the Bible of Democracy."

He also became preoccupied with the Russian terrorists of the 1880's, and this interest undoubtedly prompted his play, *Vera, or the Nihilists.* This work, however, showed an almost complete lack of knowledge of the Nihilists. Its action was fixed at the beginning of the nineteenth century, when no Nihilists in fact existed, while it contained many anachronisms and historical inaccuracies. Nevertheless, in a letter to Marie Prescott, who undertook the unsuccessful production of the play in New York, he showed that it was meant to have some real connection with contemporary events:

> I have tried in it to express within the limits of art that Titan cry of the peoples for liberty, which in Europe of to-day is threatening thrones and making governments unstable from Spain to Russia, and from north to southern seas.

He went on to talk of "modern Nihilistic Russia, with all the terror of its tyranny and the marvel of its martyrdoms."

In England, *Vera,* which was to have been produced at the Adelphi, just after the assassination of Alexander II by the People's Will groups, was withdrawn, and a note in *The World,* on which Willie Wilde worked, hinted that this was due to some kind of political consideration.

Wilde's interest in Russian revolutionary movements was maintained throughout his life, and he seems to have been fascinated by the idealism and self-sacrifice of the conspirators who at this period sacrificed their lives in the effort to rid their country and their people of the Romanoff tyranny. The lives and characters of men like Kropotkin aroused his admiration, and in *The Soul of Man Under Socialism* he said:

> No one who lived in modern Russia could possibly realise his perfection except by pain. . . . A Russian who lives happily under the present system of government in Russia must either believe that man has no soul, or that, if he has, it is not worth developing. A Nihilist who rejects all authority because he knows authority to be evil, and welcomes all pain, because through that he realises his personality, is a real Christian. To him the Christian ideal is a true thing.

He admired Dostoevsky as a man who expressed this spirit in Russia, and years later, when he was himself in a kind of Siberian exile from all the fine world he had once thought to rule by the magic of his words, he remarked to Gide: "Russian writers are extraordinary. What makes their books so great is the pity they put into them."

Wilde began early to display a genuine interest in the difficulties of the poor, although he was careful to avoid any suggestion of philanthropy, which he considered degrading to both sides. But he was always ready to denounce the exploitation of the underdog, and this tendency became very evident in the series of fairy stories which he wrote early in his career.

One of these, *The Young King*, deals with a prince who, after having been brought up by a peasant, is suddenly taken from his environment to become the acknowledged heir to the throne of his country. The richness of his new surroundings overwhelms the unsophisticated boy and, rather like Wilde himself, he sets out with a naïve and thoughtless pleasure to enjoy the beautiful life based on wealth and power. Eventually the old king dies, and the young prince succeeds to the throne. Elaborate and pompous preparations are made for his coronation, but on the eve of the ceremony the young king has three terrible visions of the misery in which those who make his robes and gather the jewels of his regalia are forced to live and work in order to sustain their miserable lives.

In the first dream:

He thought that he was standing in a long, low attic, amidst the whir and clatter of many looms. The meagre daylight peered in through the grated windows, and showed him the gaunt figures of the weavers bending over their cases. Pale, sickly-looking children were crouched on the huge crossbeams. . . . Their faces were pinched with famine, and their thin hands shook and trembled. Some haggard women were seated at a table sewing. A horrible odour filled the place. The air was foul and heavy, and the walls dripped and streamed with damp.

The young king talks to one of the weavers about their life, and the man tells him:

In war the strong make slaves of the weak, and in peace the rich make slaves of the poor. We must work to live, and they give us such mean wages that we die. We toil for them all day long, and they heap up gold in their coffers and our children fade away before their time, and the faces of those we love become hard and evil. We tread out the grapes, and another drinks the wine. We sow the corn, and our own board is empty. We have chains, though no eye beholds them, and we are slaves though men call us free.

Then the young king sees that the shuttle is threaded with a thread of gold. In terror, he asks the weaver, "What robe is this that thou art weaving?" The weaver answers, "It is the robe for the coronation of the young king." And the king cries out and wakes in horror.

This is a parable on the capitalist system of industrial exploitation as severe as anything in William Morris, and it can stand beside the grimmest passages of Marx as an indictment of the kind of horrors which, Wilde was fully aware, were inflicted on the toilers in his world, for the benefit of the people he satirised in his plays.

The young king has two other visions, in which he sees the terrible conditions under which men sacrifice their lives in the search for pearls and for precious stones. When he awakens and the courtiers come to dress him for his coronation, he refuses to assume the robes that have been woven with so much misery or the jewels that have been won with so many deaths. Instead, he goes out in his peasant garb, mocked by the nobility and the people alike. He enters the cathedral alone, and the nobles follow in order to kill him, but at the altar he is miraculously crowned with light and his plain staff breaks into flower. This story, exposing the evils of monarchy, capitalism and imperialism, Wilde dedicated, surely in irony, to a minor ruling princess whose wealth had been derived from colonial exploitation, the Ranee of Sarawak.

In another story, *The Happy Prince,* there is a similar theme of the misery of the people and the callousness of rulers, and even such a heavily jewelled fantasy as *The Birthday of the Infanta* exemplifies the theme of the wicked carelessness of people in power towards those below them.

The growing social consciousness which was expressed in these stories is also to be detected here and there among the many reviews which Wilde wrote during the 1880's. Occasionally it takes a satirical form, and makes fun of the rather foolishly Utopian ideas of some Socialists of the time, as when he says:

> . . . As the coming democracy will, no doubt, insist on feeding us all on penny dinners, it is well that the laws of cookery should be explained; for were the national meal burned, or badly seasoned, or served up with the wrong sauce, a dreadful revolution might follow.

On the other hand, he had many sensible things to say. In discussing a Life of Mary Carpenter, the educational pioneer, in 1887, he remarked:

The poor are not to be fed upon facts. Even Shakespeare and the Pyramids are not sufficient; nor is there much use in giving them the results of culture, unless we also give them those conditions under which culture can be realised. In these cold, crowded cities of the North, the proper basis for morals, using the word in its wide Hellenic signification, is to be found in architecture, not in books.

In editing *The Woman's World,* he spoke continually for the intellectual equality of women, remarking that: "The Apostolic dictum, that women should not be suffered to teach, is no longer applicable to a society such as ours, with its solidarity of interests, its recognition of natural rights, and its universal education. . . ."

From many clues we are led to believe that Wilde's interest in socialism and his sympathy with its libertarian forms were implanted long before the famous lecture by Bernard Shaw which, Shavians claim, set him on that path. Socialism, he said at this early time, "has her poets and her painters, her art lecturers and her cunning designers, her powerful orators and her clever writers. . . . If she fails it is not for lack of expression. If she succeeds her triumph will not be a triumph of mere brute force." And later, praising the "many and multiform natures" of socialism in his time, he made the astute remark: "To make men Socialists is nothing, but to make Socialism human is a great thing."

But perhaps the most interesting of his social writings at this time was the essay on Chuang Tzu which we have mentioned earlier in this book, and whose social implications are fully as interesting as its ethical intentions.

Chuang Tzu, Wilde tells us with an emphasis that leaves no doubt of his own agreement with such ideas, "looked back with a sigh of regret to a certain Golden Age when there were no competitive examinations, no wearisome educational systems, no missionaries, no penny dinners for the poor, no Established Churches, no Humanitarian Societies, no dull lectures about one's duty to one's neighbour, and no tedious sermons about any subject at all."

The great evil of society Chuang Tzu found in government. "There is such a thing," he said, "as leaving mankind alone: there has never been such a thing as governing mankind." And Wilde goes on with enthusiasm to amplify this statement:

> All modes of government are wrong. They are unscientific, because they seek to alter the natural environment of men; they are immoral because, by interfering with the individual, they produce the most aggressive forms of egotism; they are ignorant, because they try to spread education; they are self-destructive, because they engender anarchy.

Not only does the Taoist apostle condemn government, but he also condemns capital and the accumulation of property, and here again he finds an enthusiastic advocate in Wilde, who expounds him in epigrammatic style:

> The accumulation of wealth is to him the origin of evil. It makes the strong violent, and the weak dishonest. . . . The order of nature is rest, repetition and peace. Weariness and war are the results of an artificial society based upon capital; and the richer this society gets, the more thoroughly bankrupt it really is; for it has neither sufficient rewards for the good nor sufficient punishments for the wicked.

Wilde quotes Chuang Tzu in support of his own condemnation of State education, reveals him as an early evolutionist, shows that he established a distinction between spontaneous natural morality and the artificial morality of the theologians, and expounds his doctrine of non-action as the mark of the perfect man. He concludes by showing how far such a doctrine of natural anarchy erodes the very foundations of current political and social forms.

It is clear that the reading of Chuang Tzu's writings had a decisive influence on Wilde's own philosophy, confirming his natural tendencies towards non action and philosophic anarchism. In two of his later works, *The Critic as Artist* and *The Soul of Man Under Socialism*, he makes prominent and appreciative references to the Chinese philosopher, and, as we have already noticed in a previous chapter, his moral outlook came to agree in many respects with Taoist ideas. Undoubtedly, Wilde put much of himself into this study, but he only succeeded in doing so because there was already so much common thought between him and the Chinese sage.

The views expressed in Wilde's essay on Chuang Tzu clearly explode the legend that he wrote *The Soul of Man Under Socialism* from the inspiration of Bernard Shaw. Apart from the fact that his conception of Socialism has almost nothing in common with Shaw's Fabianism, it is clear, from reading his essay on the Taoist apostle, that, years before the actual writing of *The Soul of Man*, he already held the anarchistic and anti-capitalist ideas which are characteristic of his major essay.

But the anti-political bias and the dislike of oppression and exploitation shown in these early stories and reviews are not the only evidence which demonstrates Wilde's development of a real social consciousness at this important stage of his career. We have also the records of a number of acts demonstrating his sympathy towards those revolutionary propagandists of his time whose ideas were not far removed from the libertarian individualism he himself preached.

In 1886, a bomb exploded in the Haymarket of Chicago, killing a number of policemen who were dispersing a demonstration, and this resulted in the wrongful accusation and subsequent hanging of the group of American and German revolutionaries who have since become known to history as "the Chicago Martyrs." These men were uncompromising enemies of the society in which they lived, and the respectable members of British and American society were all too eager to overlook the flagrant injustice of their condemnation (later admitted by the Governor of Illinois) and to applaud their wrongful execution. Hardly a single distinguished voice was raised on their behalf, and such was the pressure of public opinion that, of those who had adopted rebellious attitudes in times of safety, almost none came forward to demand justice. At this time Bernard Shaw embarked on the thankless task of attempting to get the signatures of well-known English writers and other public figures to a petition for the reprieve of the Chicago anarchists. He records that, although the men he approached were "all heroic rebels and sceptics on paper," there was only one of them who had sufficiently the courage of his convictions to make a public gesture on behalf of the anarchists. This was Oscar Wilde. Shaw remarked: "It was a completely disinterested act on his part; and it secured my distinguished consideration for the rest of his life."

His sympathy towards anarchists was shown again when a young poet of the 1890's, John Barlas, who also wrote under the *nom de plume* of Evelyn Douglas, was impelled by his social indignation to an act of "propaganda by deed," which consisted of firing a revolver at the House of Commons. Wilde, although he had been in the past a victim of the somewhat excitable temper of Barlas, went forward to bail him out, and afterwards stood as his security when he was bound over. Barlas was later to write a good essay on Wilde's function as an iconoclast, and in a letter after Wilde's death remarked that he "was and remains my ideal of a man of genius in this generation."

Bearing in mind this close sympathy between Wilde and

the anarchists, demonstrated not merely in his general attitude towards society, but also in his actual relations with the
anarchists he encountered, it is not surprising that his scanty
political writings should have given so libertarian a picture
of socialism. In these writings there are traces, not merely of
his reading of anarchist books, but also of his connection
with William Morris and other libertarian Socialists on the
verge of anarchism. Wilde knew Morris well in his later
years, and it is recorded by Shaw that when the old poet lay
dying there was no visitor whom he welcomed so much as
Wilde, with his kindly wit and good-humoured conversation.

Wilde's only social tract is *The Soul of Man Under Socialism,* but before that pamphlet was written he had already included in *The Critic as Artist* a number of comments on political matters which indicated the general tendency of his
social thought and showed the consistency of his libertarian
views.

In the latter work he contends that it is impossible for the
politician or the social reformer preoccupied with narrow issues to view objectively the realities of social life. "The necessity of a career," as he says, "forces everyone to take sides."

He then goes on to criticise the mere reformism, by which
the socially minded of his age strove to delay a social reorganisation based on entirely new conceptions of justice and morality.

We are trying at present to stave off the coming crisis,
the coming revolution as my friends the Fabianists call it,
by means of doles and alms. Well, when the revolution or
crisis arrives, we shall be powerless, because we shall know
nothing. . . . What we want are unpractical people who
see beyond the moment, and think beyond the day. Those
who try to lead the people can only do so by following the
mob. It is through the voice of one crying in the wilderness
that the ways of the gods must be prepared.

He proceeds to attack the general attitude of the philanthropists who try to change or improve man from without. It is only by developing himself, he states, that a man can be of any use, either to himself or to others.

> For the development of the race depends on the development of the individual, and where self-culture has ceased to be the ideal, the intellectual standard is instantly lowered, and, often, ultimately lost. . . . The real weakness of England lies, not in incomplete armaments or unfortified coasts, not in the poverty that creeps through sunless lanes, or the drunkenness that brawls in loathsome courts, but simply in the fact that her ideas are emotional and not intellectual.

Here is individualist philosophic anarchism of the purest kind, and this theory is expanded and applied to direct social issues in *The Soul of Man Under Socialism*.

This pamphlet cannot be called a really great work, either of literature or of social thought. From a literary point of view it is more sprawling and unpolished than the rest of Wilde's essays. From a social point of view it is sketchy and derivative. On the other hand, it has real virtues, since Wilde's epigrammatic style enables him to convey, in a phrase, a social judgment which a more ponderous thinker might have needed a chapter to build up by solemn argument. His pamphlet also, in its very haste, gives a feeling of sincerity which we do not always gain from his more elaborately finished works.

His plea for Socialism begins on an individualist basis, since he sees the virtue of a social reorganisation in the fact that it "would relieve us from that sordid necessity of living for others which, in the present condition of things, presses so hardly upon almost everybody."

Altruism, Wilde contends, leads more often to the perpetuation of social distress than to its elimination. It neither helps the philanthropist nor his subject, and usually results merely in keeping the poor alive in their misery. "The proper aim is to try to construct society on such a basis that poverty will be impossible, and the altruistic virtues have really prevented the carrying out of this aim." In fact, char ity, far from helping the poor, merely demoralises them.

"Under Socialism," says Wilde, "all this will be altered." But he is very careful to define his meaning of socialism in such a way that it is quite clearly understood to mean libertarian and not authoritarian socialism.

> Socialism, Communism, or whatever one chooses to call it, by converting private property into public wealth, and substituting co-operation for competition, will restore society to its proper condition of a thoroughly healthy organism, and ensure the material well-being of each member of the community. It will, in fact, give Life its proper basis and its proper environment. But, for the full development of Life to its highest mode of perfection, something more is needed. What is needed is Individualism. If the Socialism is Authoritarian; if there are Governments armed with economic power as they are now with political power; if, in a word, we are to have Industrial Tyrannies, then, the last state of man will be worse than the first.

Wilde demands for every man the rights of individual development which up to now only a few scholars and artists have enjoyed. He sees that though in some cases property has allowed individual development, in general it is an institution that corrupts and burdens both the rich and the poor. On the so-called "virtues of the poor" he is particularly eloquent and acute. The best of the poor, he contends, far from being grateful for charity, are "ungrateful, discontented, and rebellious." In this they are quite right, for it would be merely brutal to remain contented with a low mode of life. "Disobedience . . . is man's original virtue. It is through disobedience that progress has been made, through disobedience and through rebellion." Similarly, the poor man who practices thrift is wrong: he should refuse to live "like a badly fed animal" and "should either steal or go on the rates." And Wilde concludes that:

> I can quite understand a man accepting laws that protect private property, and admit of its accumulation as long as he himself is able under those conditions to realise some form of beautiful and intellectual life. But it is almost incredible to me how a man whose life is marred and made hideous by such laws can possibly acquiesce in their continuance.

Wilde goes on to praise the work of agitators who show the poor how they should really live and thus help to provoke social upheavals. Thence he returns to his insistence on the need for a libertarian conception of socialism, since the poor cannot be freed by subjecting the whole community to compulsion.

> Every man must be left quite free to choose his own work. No form of compulsion must be exercised over him. If there is, his work will not be good for him, will not be good in itself, and will not be good for others. And by work I simply mean activity of any kind. . . . All association must be quite voluntary. It is only in voluntary associations that man is fine.

It is then argued that, while private property has enabled individualism to exist, it has not been the right kind of individualism. For property has perverted individualism by making gain its aim rather than growth. It has made men forget that the true perfection does not lie in having, but in being. It has stultified the individualism of the poor by starving them, and that of the rich by burdening them with possessions.

> What a man really has, is what is in him. What is outside of him should be a matter of no importance.

With the abolition of private property, then, we shall have true, beautiful, healthy Individualism. Nobody will waste his time in accumulating things, and the symbols for things. One will live. To live is the rarest thing in the world. Most people exist, that is all.

Later in his essay, Wilde mounts an open attack on the very idea of government, and shows, as thoroughly as Godwin, how every form of government carries its evil within. Despotism, oligarchy, democracy are all shown to have their own faults. All authority, indeed, is degrading, to those who use it as well as to its victims. Authority violently abused has the single virtue that it provokes revolt; authority exercised kindly, by means of rewards, is wholly demoralising to all it affects.

From a condemnation of government, Wilde goes on to an equally anarchistic condemnation of punishment:

As one reads history . . . one is absolutely sickened, not by the crimes which the wicked have committed, but by the punishments which the good have inflicted; and a community is infinitely more brutalised by the habitual employment of punishment, than it is by the occasional occurrence of crime. . . . Starvation, and not sin, is the parent of modern crime. . . . When private property is abolished, there will be no necessity for crime, no demand for it; it will cease to exist. Of course, all crimes are not crimes against property. . . . But though a crime may not be against property, it may spring from the misery and rage and depression produced by our wrong system of property-holding, and so, when the system is abolished, will disappear. When each member of the community has sufficient for his wants, and is not interfered with by his neighbour, it will not be an object of any interest to him to interfere with anyone else.

This attitude to crime is all the more interesting, since at the time when he wrote *The Soul of Man Under Socialism*

Wilde can have had little reason to suppose that circumstances would make him one of the most celebrated among the "criminal classes." It is foreshadowed in his essay on Wainwright, and, naturally enough, it was to find more than an echo in his writings after his own imprisonment among the people whom society chooses to isolate and punish as "criminals."

Wilde sees government replaced by a "State" that will in fact have very little similarity with the institution usually understood by such a term, since he says that it is not to govern, and defines it as "a voluntary association that will organise labour, and be the manufacturer and distributor of necessary commodities."

He has no anti-mechanistic illusions of the dignity of manual labour. Indeed, he sees dull and monotonous labour as degrading, and recognises the function of machinery as a liberator of man from the great mass of such necessary but frustrating toil.

> Is this Utopian? A map of the world that does not include Utopia is not worth even glancing at, for it leaves out the one country at which Humanity is always landing. And when Humanity lands there, it looks out, and, seeing a better country, sets sail. Progress is the realisation of Utopias.

Wilde continues with an elaborate discussion of the application of individualism to art, which is perhaps too long for the balance of his essay. Then he returns in quite definite terms to his revolutionary conclusion, a conclusion which is in complete accord with his manifestations of sympathy towards anarchists, criminals and other social rebels.

> Man has sought to live intensely, fully, perfectly. When he can do so without exercising restraint over others, or suffering it ever, and his activities are all pleasurable to him, he will be saner, healthier, more civilised, more him-

self. Pleasure is nature's test, her sign of approval. When man is happy, he is *in* harmony with himself and his environment.

This essay represented Wilde's real social beliefs. Some of his biographers have tried to show that it was merely the result of a passing enthusiasm inspired by hearing Shaw's lecture on Socialism. But in fact, as Hesketh Pearson has pointed out, "his whole trend of thought was antagonistic to the Webb-Shavian deification of the state," and there is no doubt that *The Soul of Man* really did mirror Wilde's personal discontent with society as he found it, and gave a picture of the kind of world in which he would like men to live.

This pamphlet has never been regarded as important in the English Socialist movement, perhaps because it was so much in opposition to the dominant tendencies, but it had much popularity abroad. If Sherard is to be believed, millions of copies were sold in Central and Eastern Europe, and it gained a great reputation among the discontented classes under the Russian, German and Austrian despotisms of the period. In America large pirated editions were printed and sold by revolutionary groups. In England its most important immediate result was to create feeling against Wilde among the influential and moneyed classes.

In the heyday of Wilde's success, from the writing of *The Picture of Dorian Gray* to his abrupt fall from popularity, he seemed rather to turn away from his social ideals. The success of his plays, with their fabulous earnings, turned his head, and there is no doubt that for a period of at least two years he lived very selfishly, and that then the worst sides of his character came to the surface in arrogance and inconsiderate self-indulgence.

Yet even at this period his writings contain a powerful element of social criticism. The English upper-classes represented in his plays are caricatured with clear hostility, and

Wilde does not hesitate to pillory their corruption, their shallowness, their snobbery, their lack of genuine moral scruples. Here and there, too, he inserts epigrams which show his contempt for their social attitude. In both *The Picture of Dorian Gray* and *A Woman of No Importance*, there appears a statement which reproduces one of the main contentions of *The Soul of Man Under Socialism*. The conversation turns to the problem of the East End. A politician remarks that it is "a very important problem," and the wit (Lord Henry Wootton in the novel and Lord Illingworth in the play) replies: "Quite so. It is the problem of slavery. And we are trying to solve it by amusing the slaves."

A Woman of No Importance has, indeed, a general atmosphere of social protest, not only in the satirical and bitter (as far as Wilde was capable of acrimony) attitude towards the upper-classes, but also in the main plot, which is clearly built around a social problem, already sketched in *Lady Windermere's Fan*, of the inequality of men and women in modern society and the ruthlessness of the conventional social code towards the individual who, deliberately or unwillingly, acts against its arbitrary laws. The theme is partly imbued with that sentimentality which in a character like Wilde's always underlies his more obvious cynicism, but this quality is made less obvious by the sparkling wit with which the dialogue flits lightly over the whole range of social life and the political scene. The theme is presented conventionally, in the differing lives of Lord Illingworth, the successful and ruthless public figure, into whose witty conversation Wilde put much of himself, and Mrs. Arbuthnot, by whom Illingworth had a child many years before. The son of this transitory union, grown into an intelligent youth, attracts Illingworth's interest, so far that he proposes to take him as a secretary. In this way are shown the contrasting fates of the man and the woman: Lord Illingworth, who goes through life gaily and unscathed by his cynical refusal to protect the mother of his child from the hostility of conventional society by marrying her, Mrs. Arbuthnot, enduring a life of lonely guilt and bitterness and now faced by the last humiliation of seeing her son wish to go away with the man who has been the cause of her own lifelong misery. The wicked lord is finally defeated when, for a wager with the equally wicked Mrs. Allonby, he attempts to kiss the prudish young American girl, Hester Worsley, with whom his son is in love. The boy turns against him, and Illingworth, his belated paternal feelings defeated, turns tail and departs, after an unpleasant scene with Mrs. Arbuthnot.

Undoubtedly, in his treatment of this plot, Wilde was largely motivated by a desire to give the Victorians a rather sentimental theme of the kind to which they were accustomed, as a means of transmitting the brilliant verbal wit which was always the most pleasant ingredient of his plays—to the author even more than to the audience. Nevertheless, the particular choice of a plot is always significant, and I have no doubt that Wilde, who edited an intellectual woman's paper for some years, and who often had a high opinion of the capacities of the women he encountered in literary society, deliberately intended to draw attention to sexual equality of rights. I think it is also reasonable to assume that, like most cynics, Wilde had a strongly humane aspect to his character, which appears often in his works; *The Ballad of Reading Gaol* is one example, while in parts of *De Profundis* this quality is shown, almost, at times, to the extent of sentimental atrocity.

Nevertheless, however conventionally conceived may have been the main feminist plot of *A Woman of No Importance*, it is presented with great wit and much reason. Wilde's conclusions can best be summarised in a sound remark he made elsewhere, that he was against the existence of one law for men and one for women, and would prefer to see no law for anybody.

This play also contains a quite severe attack on the contemporary British upper-class. There are many bitter social epigrams, and in one place the American girl, Hester Worsley, becomes the mouthpiece for a really scathing condemnation. Although it is spoken by a character towards whom Wilde might at first seem unsympathetic because of her militant puritanism, this tirade nevertheless appears to represent his own real views on these people for whom, while he was attracted towards the richness of their lives like a moth to the fatal candle, he felt a very great contempt. Among a group of superficial upper-class women, Hester bursts out into this tirade:

> You rich people in England, you don't know how you are living. How could you know? You shut out from your society the gentle and the good. You laugh at the simple and the pure. Living, as you all do, on others and by them, you sneer at self-sacrifice, and if you throw bread to the poor, it is merely to keep them quiet for a season. With all your pomp and wealth and art you don't know how to live —you don't even know that. You have the beauty that you can see and handle, the beauty that you can destroy, and do destroy, but of the unseen beauty of life, of the unseen beauty of a higher life, you know nothing. You have lost life's secret.

The next play, *An Ideal Husband,* represents an even more open attack on the social system, in that its basic theme is the innate corruption of political life. A politician, Sir Robert Chiltern, has begun his career by selling State secrets to an international financier, and from the money he has gained by this initial corruption, rises to the heights of a political career. When he reaches this position, his past is used as a means of blackmail by a woman who wishes him to support a fraudulent canal scheme, and thus assure the success of its promoters. He is saved from this threat, not by his virtues, but by his friend, Lord Goring, applying counter-trickery to

Mrs. Cheveley, the blackmailer. In a circle where all are guilty, Chiltern, who has gained most by his roguery, is able to escape without punishment, and the height of his career is reached in a hypocritical speech wherein he denounces "the whole system of modern political finance," regardless of the fact that he is one of the worst examples of its use. His duplicity gains him universal praise for integrity, and so the political farce is drawn to its usual end.

Wilde has been criticised for not bringing a just retribution to the contemptible Chiltern. But in fact he does not accept the justice of Chiltern's fortune; he merely records the fact that in political life fraud and hypocrisy always win the prizes.

In this connection it should be remarked that Wilde showed a consistently hostile attitude towards politics and politicians, not only in his writings, but also in his personal life. There were those among his friends who regretted that, with his gift for talking, he did not go into parliamentary life; one of these was Yeats who, with his odd idea that Wilde was by nature a man of action, said to O'Sullivan: "He might have had a career like that of Beaconsfield, whose early style resembles his, being meant for crowds, for excitement, for hurried decisions, for immediate triumphs." Anything less calculated for crowd appeal than Wilde's conversational or literary style it is difficult to imagine, and when Oscar was told of the idea that he was a man of action, he remarked, disparagingly, "It is interesting to hear Yeats' opinion about one."

According to Douglas, he professed to be a Liberal, but he mocked the Liberals as much as the Tories, and Douglas thought that he never showed enough interest in either party to vote in an election. When his political friends, admiring his conversational gifts, tried to persuade him to accept a safe seat in Parliament, he turned down the offer without hesitation. He admired Disraeli as a man and a writer, but appeared to regret that he should have spoilt himself by going into politics.

O'Sullivan has said that the main ideas of Wilde's plays are few and simple, and describes them thus: "He disliked hypocrisy in social intercourse, he glorified individualism, he denied the moral right of the community to sacrifice the life of any member of it." But, in *An Ideal Husband* at least, we must add his strongly critical attitude towards political life, which occurs in many quite deliberate statements of opinion in various parts of the play.

For instance, when Robert Chiltern is trying to prepare his wife for a revelation of his predicament, which he knows will shatter the pedestalled ideal she has always made of him, he says to her:

> Gertrude, truth is a very complex thing, and politics is a very complex business. There are wheels within wheels. One may be under certain obligations to people that one must pay. Sooner or later in political life one has to compromise. Everyone does.

Then there is the even more revealing conversation between Chiltern and Goring, in which Chiltern tells how he was corrupted by Arnheim with his philosophy of power. Goring, who acts in this play as Wilde's personal voice, expresses his complete disagreement with this philosophy.

> *Chiltern:* One night after dinner at Lord Radley's the Baron began talking about success in modern life as something that one could reduce to an absolutely definite science. With that wonderfully fascinating quiet voice of his he expounded to us the most terrible of all philosophies, the philosophy of power . . . that power—power over other men, power over the world—was the one thing worth having, the one supreme pleasure worth knowing, the one joy one never tired of, and that in our century only the rich possessed it.

Goring (with great deliberation): A thoroughly shallow creed.

Chiltern (rising): I didn't think so then. I don't think so now. Wealth has given me enormous power. It gave me at the very outset of my life freedom, and freedom is everything. You have never been poor, and never known what ambition is. You cannot understand what a wonderful chance the Baron gave me. Such a chance as few men get.

Lord Goring: Fortunately for them, if one is to judge by results.

This attitude towards politics and the political life is supported by a whole series of epigrams scattered throughout the play. An example is Goring's remark to his father: "My dear father, only people who look dull ever get into the House of Commons, and only people who are dull ever succeed there."

The Importance of Being Earnest stands alone among Wilde's plays in having no explicit social theme, but even that play contains, in Lady Bracknell, a satire on the snobbish values of the upper-classes, while Miss Prism and Doctor Chasuble represent respectively Wilde's contempt for the educational system and the Church of his day.

There are some who have tried to elevate Wilde's homosexual practices and his three trials into a great act of rebellion against society. But here is an evident distortion, for all his actions during this period show the weaker side of his character, and reveal him as the victim rather than the defiant rebel.

To begin, Wilde's homosexual activities, however one may support his liberty to practise them and condemn the monstrous laws that inflicted on him such a terrible punishment, represented nothing particularly revolutionary. Homosexual practices, if not so openly recognised and tolerated as they are to-day, were very widespread in London, and it is said that during the 1890's no less than 20,000 people in that city alone were known to the police for this reason. But the police then, as now, turned as blind an eye as possible to such activities, and did not prosecute homosexuals unless they committed some really flagrant indiscretion which brought their case into publicity.

Wilde was for long so discreet, and so far from drawing public attention to his concealed life, that until the time of his trials many of his intimate friends, including Sherard and Frank Harris, were completely unaware that he had been a practising pederast for nearly a decade. It was only fellow homosexuals like Ross and Reggie Turner who knew this side of his life, and they concealed it in their own interests. His fear of exposure led him into furtive relationships with a despicable set of male prostitutes who were afterwards willing to be cajoled and bribed into betraying him to the law, and, however Wilde may later have dramatised his "sins," they remain a rather sordid story, in which the one really rebellious character is Taylor, the procurer who refused to give evidence against Wilde and chose instead to stand in the dock beside him and share his imprisonment.

Wilde's action against Queensberry was also that of a discreet man who wished to *appear* to conform, and it contained a dishonesty which did not fit his declared attitude of social defiance. For Queensberry's accusation that Wilde *posed* as a "sodomite" [sic] was in fact short of reality. Wilde sued Queensberry in the hope of scotching the rumours that were growing up round his activities, so that he might continue them in more security, and he was also propelled into this course by Alfred Douglas's antagonism towards his father. It is clearly ridiculous to suggest that there was anything of the great rebel in going to law with a man who had said about him something less than the truth, merely in order to preserve a false appearance in the eyes of society. Wilde was hoist on his own petard; the fate he had desired to impose on Queensberry was meted out to him, and in his later days he would have been the last to deny that he had only his own folly and inconsistency to thank for his downfall. In *De Profundis* he commented on the poetic justice of his fate:

> The one disgraceful, unpardonable, and to all time contemptible action of my life was to allow myself to appeal to society for help and protection. To have made such an appeal would have been from the individualist point of view bad enough, but what excuse can there ever be put forward for having made it? Of course once I had put into motion the forces of society, society turned on me and said, "Have you been living all this time in defiance of my laws, and do you now appeal to these laws for protection? You shall have these laws exercised to the full. You shall abide by what you have appealed to." The result is I am in gaol. Certainly no man ever fell so ignobly, and by such ignoble instruments, as I did.

Once Wilde realised he was caught in the toils of a hostile law, he began to fight back and show defiance. There was his famous duel of wit with Carson, and, later, his impassioned defence of love between men from the dock of the Old Bailey, when he cried out:

> The "love that dare not speak its name" in this century is such a great affection of an elder for a younger man as there was between David and Jonathan, such as Plato made the very basis of his philosophy, and such as you will find in the sonnets of Michael Angelo and Shakespeare. It is that deep, spiritual affection which is as pure as it is perfect. It dictates and pervades great works of art like those of Shakespeare and Michael Angelo, and these two letters of mine, such as they are. It is in this century misunderstood, so much misunderstood that it may be described as the "love that dare not speak its name," and on account of it I am placed where I am now. It is beautiful, it is fine, it is the noblest form of affection. There is nothing unnatural about it. It is intellectual, and it repeatedly exists be-

tween an elder and a younger man, when the elder man
has intellect, and the younger man has all the joy, hope,
and glamour of life before him. That it should be so the
world does not understand. The world mocks at it, and
sometimes puts one in the pillory for it.

But the value of such defiance was largely vitiated by the
fact that it was used in defence of an untruth. Of course,
there is no cause to blame Wilde for denying the charges
against him when he was faced with a thoroughly savage and
immoral law, but the fact remains that he did not practise
the defiance of a rebel, who would have admitted what was
attributed to him, and defended himself by attacking the law.

Nor should it be forgotten that Wilde's decision to stay
and face his ruin was hardly motivated by any idea of rebellion, but partly by the pressure of his family, with their foolish ideas of the duties of an Irish gentleman, and partly by
that very strongly fatalistic feeling which we have already
noticed as prominent in his philosophy, and which undoubtedly helped his decision to drift with the rapids of destiny
once he was caught in their tow.

Yet, while in this whole affair Wilde was motivated by no
truly rebellious impulse, his acts unconsciously produced an
important social effect, since the publicity given to homosexuality and the indignation of all thinking men at home
and, even more so, abroad, at the savagery of his sentence,
resulted in a gradual but profound change in the public attitude towards this particular sexual eccentricity. As Laurence Housman has said:

> Always, so long as it stays remembered, the name of
> Oscar Wilde is likely to carry with it a shadowy implica-
> tion of that pathological trouble which caused his down-
> fall. And whatever else may be said for or against the life
> of promiscuous indulgence he appears to have led, his
> downfall did at least this great service to humanity, that,

by the sheer force of notoriety, it made "the unmentionable" mentionable.

Prison broadened Wilde's social outlook in two important ways: firstly, by bringing him into close and equal contact with working-class people, and, secondly, by revealing to him in concrete form the kind of atrocities which society is always prepared to wreak on those who break the moral and criminal codes which are regarded as necessary for its existence. In this condemnation of all the worst evils of an authoritarian society he became more than ever convinced of the need for a change that would humanise social relationships and remove the fearful cruelties always associated with the domination of man by man.

For a number of reasons, including Wilde's own mental condition at the time, and the requirements of the prison regulations, it was the first of these discoveries that appeared most strongly in *De Profundis,* where he expressed something of his appreciation of the kindness and solidarity he found among the poor towards those who were victims of society and its harsh laws.

> The poor are wise, more charitable, more kind, more sensitive than we are. In their eyes prison is a tragedy in a man's life, a casualty, something that calls for sympathy in others. They speak of one who is in prison as of one who is "in trouble" simply. It is the phrase they always use, and the expression has the perfect wisdom of love in it.

Wilde was impressed and pleased at the contrast between this attitude of working-people and that of his literary and upper-class friends, who, with very few exceptions, regarded him as a pariah from the day his action against Queensberry failed. After he left Reading Gaol, he often spoke with affection of the men he had met in prison, and maintained a correspondence with some of the prisoners and the more friendly warders, a few of whom visited him in his exile near

Dieppe. He even went so far as to provide cash out of his own scanty means, so that those he knew to be needy should not come out of prison in complete destitution.

His condemnation of the system that had tortured him and his fellow prisoners was the dominant theme of the only literary works of any importance which he produced during the last phase of his life. These are *The Ballad of Reading Gaol* and the two letters which he wrote to the *Daily Chronicle* on prison conditions soon after his release from gaol.

The first of these letters appeared on May 28th, 1897, and was prompted by the news that Warder Martin, a man who by his repeated kindnesses had helped to soften the last few months of Wilde's imprisonment, had been dismissed from the service for the crime of giving a few biscuits to a hungry child.

In Wilde's day, children were still imprisoned in the ordinary gaols, and this happened even when they were merely on remand. Wilde was profoundly disturbed by the sufferings he saw inflicted on these terrified young boys.

He begins with an attack on the stupidity of the system whose unconscious cruelty produces such evil and brutal results, and returns to his old criticism of the faults inherent in any type of authority.

> It is the result in our own days of stereotyped systems, of hard-and-fast rules, and of stupidity. Wherever there is centralisation there is stupidity. What is inhuman in modern life is officialdom. Authority is as destructive to those who exercise it as it is to those on whom it is exercised. It is the Prison Board, and the system that it carries out, that is the primary source of the cruelty that is exercised on a child in prison.

Wilde then describes in detail what a child endures in prison—the hardships he shares with other inmates, but which react with peculiar severity on his unformed and easily disturbed nature. He ends by saying that, if a child is corrupted by prison life, it is due, not to the prisoners, but to—

> . . . the whole prison system . . . the governor, the chaplain, the warders, the solitary cell, the isolation, the revolting food, the rules of the Prison Commissioners, the mode of discipline, as it is termed, of the life.

He adds some equally pungent remarks on the prison treatment of the mentally unbalanced, describing in detail one particularly shocking case of the persistent punishment of a madman which he had witnessed during his own imprisonment and which had caused him great unhappiness.

His letter aroused much attention, and, if Frank Harris is to be believed, it had some effect in procuring a mitigation of the conditions under which children were imprisoned.

The second letter was occasioned by a proposal of the Home Secretary to reform the prison system by appointing more inspectors. Wilde points out that this would do more harm than good, since the evils of prison life were caused largely by the prison regulations, and it would only make matters worse if the code were more rigorously observed. He adds:

> The necessary reforms are very simple. They concern the needs of the body and the needs of the mind of each unfortunate prisoner.

With regard to the first, there are three permanent punishments authorised by law in English prisons:

1. Hunger.
2. Insomnia.
3. Disease.

He describes in some detail the bad and unhealthy food given in the prisons (food more appallingly inadequate even than that of a modern English prison), the foul sanitary arrangements, the insomnia caused by the barbaric sleeping facilities, the monotonous toil which takes its toll on weak and poorly fed bodies, the illnesses that arise from these abundant contributory causes, and the unjust and unimaginative punishment inflicted on any prisoner who, from weakness or incapacity, fails to fulfil all the requirements of this brutal system.

Nor are the mental consequences of imprisonment, he goes on to show, any less terrible, for deprivation of books and human intercourse brutalise the prisoner and drive him into a mentally unbalanced condition.

But even the reform of these abuses would not be enough without a change in the character of the prison staff. It would be necessary to "humanise the governors of prisons, to civilise the warders, and to Christianise the Chaplains."

This second letter, also, was received with much more friendly interest than might have been expected, and it seems possible that Wilde's protests helped to prepare the very inadequate reforms which have since taken place in the English penal system.

There remained one terrible feature of the penal system, the punishment of hanging, and Wilde's protest against this social enormity formed the main theme of the last and greatest of his poems, *The Ballad of Reading Gaol,* into which he condensed all the bitterness and pity engendered by his own prison life, and all of his renewed sense of indignation at social injustice.

The Ballad of Reading Gaol, as well as being the best and most original of Wilde's own poems, is also one of the few permanently successful propaganda poems written in the English language, an ironical fact when one considers that Wilde has been regarded, and usually regarded himself, as the high-priest of Art for Art's sake. At times it sinks into a rather banal sentimentality, but often it has a bare strength which is quite unlike anything else in Wilde's works.

The poem tells of the execution of a young soldier during Wilde's confinement in Reading Gaol. The story is immaterial; what is important is the way in which Wilde conveys the horror of judicial murder and the dreadful character of the life which prisoners live. There is a unique and terrible intensity in such passages as this, in which, after his famous remark that—

> *Each man kills the thing he loves,*
> *Yet each man does not die,*

he goes on to show those terrors which the common man cannot share with the condemned murderer:

> *He does not feel that sickening thirst*
> *That sands one's throat, before*
> *The hangman with his gardener's gloves*
> *Comes through the padded door,*
> *And binds one with three leathern thongs,*
> *That the throat may thirst no more.*
>
> *He does not bend his head to hear*
> *The Burial Office read,*
> *Nor, while the anguish of his soul*
> *Tells him he is not dead,*
> *Cross his own coffin, as he moves*
> *Into the hideous shed.*

The poem is filled with passages showing equally strongly how Wilde came to identify himself imaginatively with the man who was suffering. Nor are there lacking vivid sketches of the misery to which he and his fellows who endured only a living and temporary death were condemned.

> *We tore the tarry rope to shreds*
> *With blunt and bleeding nails;*
> *We rubbed the doors, and scrubbed the floors,*
> *And cleaned the shining rails:*
> *And, rank by rank, we soaped the plank,*
> *And clattered with the pails.*

> *We sewed the sacks, we broke the stones,*
>   *We turned the dusty drill:*
> *We banged the tins, and bawled the hymns,*
>   *And sweated on the mill,*
> *But in the heart of every man*
>   *Terror was lying still.*

And so the poem continues, in a great Jeremiad of indignation and lamentation, a veritable cry from the heart of despair which is quite unlike anything else that Wilde ever wrote in its fevered outpourings of mingled pity and anger, until he reaches his great indictment of the whole system of which prison is the extreme representation:

> *I know not whether Laws be right,*
>   *Or whether Laws be wrong;*
> *All that we know who lie in gaol*
>   *Is that the wall is strong;*
> *And that each day is like a year,*
>   *A year whose days are long.*
>
> *But this I know, that every Law*
>   *That men have made for Man,*
> *Since first Man took his brother's life,*
>   *And the sad world began,*
> *But straws the wheat and saves the chaff*
>   *With a most evil fan.*
>
> *This too I know—and wise it were*
>   *If each could know the same—*
> *That every prison that men build*
>   *Is built with bricks of shame,*
> *And bound with bars lest Christ should see*
>   *How men their brothers maim.*

Since Wilde's day, two great wars have given two generations of intellectuals some chance to see the inside of prisons as conscientious objectors. But none among them has yet written any attack on the prison system, either in prose or verse, that is quite so damning as *The Ballad of Reading Gaol*. With all its literary faults, it remains unique in the history of penological literature. If Wilde had produced nothing else, this poem alone would have justified him as a writer.

Thus, the last of Wilde's writing was a work in which the whole theme was one of humane protest, and this is not out of keeping with the current of his development. As I have shown, he was much more acutely conscious of the ills of society than his critics would like us to believe. Certainly, his sense of social criticism was far more highly developed than that of the great majority of his literary contemporaries. He believed always and fervently in the intrinsic value of the individual; he denied the right of society to condemn any of its members to misery, or to warp their lives by its demands. He hated authority, cruelty, ugliness, in life as in art. He saw clearly the evils inherent in the twin systems of property and government. He detested oppression and injustice, and would always defend the downtrodden and persecuted. Beneath all his superficial callousness, he was a great humanist, and made the freedom of individual men the first article of his social creed. Wherever else he may have seemed insincere, in these matters he always spoke with a conviction that cannot be held in doubt.

THE MASTER OF CONVERSATION

UNTIL his plays brought him wide literary fame, Wilde was more celebrated and appreciated as a conversationalist than as a writer. Even in our own day his surviving acquaintances have remembered him principally for his conversation; there are many who completely failed to appreciate his writing, yet who retained the most vivid memory of the occasions on which they heard him talk. E. F. Benson and Graham Robertson are examples of men who, while regarding his writing as ephemeral and superficial, have left enthusiastic accounts of the delights of his conversation. Wilfred Scawen Blunt wrote, after Wilde's death, "He was without exception the most brilliant talker I have ever come across, the most ready, the most witty, the most audacious. Nobody could pretend to outshine him, or even to shine at all in his company. Something of his wit is reflected in his plays, but very little." And Shaw remarked to Hesketh Pearson some years ago: ". . . Wilde was incomparably great as a *raconteur,* conversationalist, and a personality," reinforcing this opinion as recently as 1948, when asked by a newspaper what famous person he would care to meet, by saying: "I do not want to talk to anybody, alive or dead; but if I craved for entertaining conversation by a first-class *raconteur,* I should choose Oscar Wilde."

It is difficult to compare Wilde with the great talkers of the past, but certainly, if the almost universal praise he received for this talent is anything on which to base our judgment, none was his superior, while the records which survive of the table talk of men like Coleridge, Lamb and Dr. Johnson, justly celebrated in their time, fall short both in lightness of wit and in spontaneous play of ideas when compared with those fragments and descriptions we retain of the conversation of Wilde.

Undoubtedly, as many of his acquaintances have remarked, his abundant physical charm contributed greatly to his success as a talker. But this was only a minor part of the effect; what he said was of such brilliant wit, of such profound wisdom, or stimulating nonsense, that he could impress people who disliked him and charm even his enemies.

The half-mad Marquess of Queensberry, who had a morbid hatred of Wilde, decided, after a luncheon conversation into which he had been pressed unwillingly, that his enemy was "a wonderful man": unfortunately, the luncheon meetings were not continued, and "Old Q." relapsed into his paranoic resentment. George Moore disliked Wilde with all the venom one Irishman could nurture towards another; he looked forward piously to Oscar's being "eaten by worms," and yet, after he had avoided Wilde for seven years, one dinner party was sufficient to make him admit that his conversation was one of the delightful things of life. W. H. Henley, who despised Wilde as an æsthete and joined heartily in the cry that hounded him from society in 1896, was so impressed on their first meeting that he went away admitting his remarkable qualities. And Sherard has preserved a description of Wilde in his last days, written, we are assured, by a man who was "not a friend."

. . . As he proceeded he was caught by the pathos of his own words, his beautiful voice trembled with emotion, his eyes swam with tears; and then suddenly, by a swift, indescribably brilliant, whimsical touch, a swallow-wing flash on the waters of eloquence, the tone changed and rippled with laughter, bringing with it his audience, relieved, delighted, and bubbling with uncontrollable merriment.

Nor was his wit bound by narrow privacies of class or clique. He talked of literature, but also of life in general; in the Mayfair drawing-room he might make social small talk, but elsewhere he would enter profoundly and with great insight into scientific or philosophical discussion. He could make himself agreeable to politicians, to workmen, to tough country squires, and especially to women, but he always enjoyed best of all the company and conversation of artists and writers, particularly, as he would point out, those second-rate artists and minor poets who, unlike the really great, do not put everything into their work, and enact part of their poetry in their lives.

His adaptability is illustrated by the tragi-comic tale of the Home Office representatives who visited Reading Gaol, where, peering through a spyhole into the hospital ward, they saw Wilde sitting on his bed and keeping his fellow prisoners in paroxysms of laughter with his stories—an incident which unfortunately helped to prevent his gaining an early release. The peasants and coastguard men at Berneval-sur-Mer liked him for the friendly and amusing way he talked to them, and even waiters, we are told, were so charmed by his manner that they did not resent his objecting to the menu or the food they put before him.

Before considering in detail the quality or nature of what Wilde said to the people he charmed so effectively, it is of interest to recall a general description by Frank Harris which, while it may not be wholly correct in detail, at least gives a vividly impressionist picture of Wilde in action. There is reason to believe that Harris over-emphasised the superficiality of the conversation, for, as many writers have told us, Wilde's talk, particularly after his release from prison, tended to become increasingly profound in character, but Harris's description certainly tells us much about the talker's technique.

He was a born improvisatore. At the moment he always dazzled one out of judgment. A phonograph would have discovered the truth; a great part of his charm was physical; much of his talk mere topsy-turvy paradox, the very froth of thought carried off by gleaming, dancing eyes, smiling, happy lips, and a melodious voice.

The entertainment usually started with some humorous play on words. One of the company would say something obvious or trivial, repeat a proverb or a commonplace tag, such as "Genius is born, not made," and Oscar would flash in, smiling, "Not paid, my dear fellow, not paid."

An interesting comment would follow on some doing of the day, a skit on some accepted belief or a parody on some pretentious solemnity, a winged word on a new book or a new author, and when everyone was smiling with amused enjoyment, the fine eyes would become introspective, the beautiful voice would take on a grave music, and Oscar would begin a story with symbolic second meaning, or a glimpse of new thought, and when all were listening enthralled, of a sudden the eyes would dance, the smile would break forth again like sunshine and some sparkling witticism would set everyone laughing.

The spell was broken, but only for a moment. A new clue would soon be given, and at once Oscar was off again with renewed *brio* to finer efforts.

The talking itself warmed and quickened him extraordinarily: he loved to show off and astonish his audience, and usually talked better after an hour or two than at the beginning. His verve was inexhaustible. But always a great part of the fascination lay in the quick changes from grave to gay, from pathos to mockery, from philosophy to fun.

There was but little of the actor in him. When telling a story he never mimicked his personages; his drama seldom lay in clash of character, but in thought; it was the sheer beauty of the words, the melody of the cadenced voice, the glowing eyes which fascinated you and always and above all the scintillating coruscating humour that lifted his monologues into works of art. . . .

He gave the impression of wide intellectual range, yet in reality he was not broad; life was not his study nor the world-drama his field. His talk was all of literature and art and the vanities; the light drawing-room comedy on the edge of farce was his kingdom; there he ruled as a sovereign.

In considering this opinion it must be borne in mind that the main thesis of Harris's *Life of Wilde* is that Wilde was a weak, effeminate character, of no great moral strength or intellectual profundity, and generally inferior to his robust and deep-thinking biographer. It must also be remembered that Harris was one of the few people to whom Wilde spoke severely, and that this no doubt rankled in a man of his inordinately vain nature.

Some of Harris's statements are palpably wrong. He tells of Wilde giving glimpses of new thought, of his telling stories with symbolical second meanings, and he also admits elsewhere that after imprisonment Wilde's talk had "a wider range of thought and intenser stimulus than before," which implies that it already had a breadth of thought that was worthy of notice. But this is quite inconsistent with his other glimpse of Wilde as a superficial frothy talker, an expert in "the light drawing-room comedy on the edge of farce." In any case, as we can see from Wilde's written plays, which reproduced much of his talk and relied greatly on the epigrams that had already been tried out in conversation before they reached the stage, his wit was by no means of the "light drawing-room comedy" type, but contained a really deep vein of satirical philosophy.

If, therefore, we gain from Harris a sound impression of the manner and style of Wilde's conversation, its spontaneity, variety and virtuosity, it is in the descriptions of other writers that we must seek an appreciation of its deeper elements. And the significant thing is that these men often granted Wilde pre-eminence in the spheres where they thought a great deal of their own abilities. Even Bernard Shaw, who in his dramatic technique gained much from studying and imitating Wilde's technique of delivering a whole profound thought in a single phrase, admitted that he could tell stories "better than I could have told them myself." Vincent O'Sullivan tells us that, although there were men of Wilde's acquaintance who were superior to him in intellect, he "never heard that any of these men denied that he was superior to them all as a talker."

Fortunately, in the writings of Wilde's friends there is abundant material for an analysis of his conversation, and I can do little better than illustrate its characteristics as shown by them.

Yeats remarked on Wilde's ability to talk "with perfect sentences, as if he had written them all overnight with labour and yet all spontaneous." He suggested that the apparent artificiality of Oscar's talk came from this "perfect rounding of the sentences and from the deliberation that made it possible," which also enabled him to "pass without incongruity from some unforeseen, swift stroke of wit to elaborate reverie."

He also records an impression which has struck other observers of Wilde's conversation, though usually less emphatically. His manner "had hardened to meet opposition, and at times he allowed one to see an unpardonable insolence." But, in fact, it was only during Oscar's period of arrogant prosperity that this became really evident, and it was certainly very unjust of Yeats to say that "his charm was acquired and systematised, a mask which he wore only when it pleased

him." It was part of Wilde's real nature to behave consider-
ately and courteously.

Another characteristic observed by Yeats, along with many
other witnesses, is that Wilde's language when he talked was
simpler, more exact and more effective than his writing.
"Only when he spoke, or when his writing was the mirror of
his speech, or in some simple fairy tale, had he words exact
enough to hold a subtle ear."

An example of this conversational superiority is to be seen
in the spoken version of *The Doer of Good,* which Yeats reproduces as he remembered it:

> Christ came from a white plain to a purple city, and as
> He passed through the first street, He heard voices over-
> head, and saw a young man lying drunk upon a window-
> sill. "Why do you waste your soul in drunkenness?" he
> said. "Lord, I was a leper and you healed me, what else can
> I do?" A little farther through the town He saw a young
> man following a harlot, and said, "Why do you dissolve
> your soul in debauchery?" and the young man answered,
> "Lord, I was blind, and you healed me, what else can I do?"
> At last in the middle of the city He saw an old man crouch-
> ing, weeping upon the ground, and when He asked why he
> wept, the old man answered, "Lord, I was dead, and you
> raised me into life. What else can I do but weep?"

Told in this manner, the story has, as Yeats remarked, a
"terrible beauty," and is much superior to the written version in *Poems in Prose,* which is more than twice as long, yet
contains no more substance, and is completely spoilt by over-
elaboration. Wilde knew how to handle conversation as a
great musician knows how to handle an instrument; when he
was talking he had to maintain a constant presence of mind,
to catch the spirit of the moment; this induced simplicity,
and the achievement of subtle effects without undue elaboration. When, however, he began to write, the need for prompt
simplicity was removed, and he was too often tempted into a

style "covered with jewels" but lacking in exactitude. Wilde as a master of decorative writing is already dated and negligible. But his writing is still virile and contemporary where, as in the plays and the critical dialogues, he reproduced his own conversational technique, or where he had to face the practical problem of stating some clear argument effectively.

Although Yeats's idea that Wilde switched on his charm to suit the occasion seems to have been inexact, it is nevertheless true that Oscar modulated his conversation in such a way as to please whatever audience he was setting out to entertain. Gide, who incidentally differs from Wilde's English friends in declaring that his French pronunciation was almost perfect, tells us that—

> . . . in his wisdom, or perhaps in his folly, he never betrayed himself into saying anything which he thought would not be to the taste of his hearers, so he doled out food to each according to his appetite. Those who expected nothing from him got nothing, or only a little light froth, and as at first he used to give himself up to the task of amusing, many of those who thought they knew him will have known him only as the amuser.

This characteristic has been exploited by some of Wilde's critics to suggest that he was a hypocrite. In fact, Wilde detested hypocrisy, but he regarded himself as an artist in words and wished to create the best impression by charming his audience into his mood. He was also moved by a genuine and genial desire to please other people, and an equally intense and rather pathetic wish to be liked by all those with whom he came into contact. Out of the power of his words he thought he had built himself a little empire of admiration, but too often in fact he had merely provided an hour of quickly forgotten entertainment, like a rather sophisticated cabaret artist.

His kindly nature became evident in the complete lack of

malice in his conversation. Good-humour and "consideration for the feelings of others, however young and insignificant," was, O'Sullivan tells us, the most memorable characteristic of his talk. "There was nothing trenchant about it, no air of laying down the law without privilege of appeal, of uttering truths undisputable and not to be disputed." Benson says that he was "always genial, he was lambent but not burning, he neither barked nor bit, his gaiety was not barbed for wounding."

This good humour led to his conversation being, not a monologue, but genuine communication. O'Sullivan remarks: "He watched his listener carefully, waited for his replies, studied his mood, and adapted himself to it. There, no doubt, was the weakness of his talk. It lay in his pliancy, his readiness to swerve round."

This last characteristic developed at times to flattery, particularly in his talk with women, whom he regarded as the rulers of society. He also had one kind of conversation which was calculated to impress people for whom he had really a great intellectual contempt. "It was overdone," says O'Sullivan, "loaded with crushing compliments, almost oily. . . . Perhaps it was a variation of his national 'blarney.'"

Octave Mirbeau, in his *Diary of a Chamber Maid,* gave a hostile portrait of Wilde in this shallow and supercilious mood, which also prompted Henry James to call him a "fatuous cad," while the French writer, Jean-Joseph Renaud, describes a dinner-party at which Wilde, who was feeling his way into the mood of his audience, began with the kind of affectations that bewildered and slightly disgusted his hearers. Once he had caught the atmosphere of the gathering, however, he began to discourse on French history with great virtuosity, and passed into his finest style of talk.

Arthur Symons, who also speaks of Wilde assuming "un masque de parade" before certain people in order to "astonish and amuse and exasperate them," says that he was always at his best when one was alone with him. He describes him as always "effective" rather than "reflective," and points out the essential logicality of his conversation:

His mind was eminently reasonable, and if you look closely into his wit, you will find that it has always a basis of logic, though it may indeed most probably be supported by its apex at the instant in which he presents it.

Wilde, says Symons, was a greater personality than an artist, and it was for this reason that his talk was so interesting, and the part of his writing which resembled talk more interesting than the rest. Finally, Symons disagrees rather fundamentally with Harris in emphasising the dramatic quality of Wilde's conversation and the element of acting contained therein:

He had the voice and at times the gestures of a born actor. In fact, he often played his parts too effectively both in private and in public. One never knew what he would say next, no more did he.

This element of inspiration, of spontaneity, of ability to follow any clue with some startling and yet logically apposite remark, is a characteristic of Wilde's conversation which impressed all his listeners, and which was one of the causes of its extraordinary quality. It was a manifestation of that general quickness of apprehension whicn astonished Wilde's friends in many other ways. Related to it was his uncanny ability to read a book with great rapidity, while at the same time retaining its essential contents. Some of his friends have told how he would flick in a few minutes through the pages of a book previously unknown to him, registering their meaning with a kind of immediately photographic apprehension, and then, after closing the book, giving his audience a rapid and accurate synopsis. This faculty may have been perfected during his reviewing days, but, as all professional reviewers will know, it is not the kind of gift that comes from mere practice, and must have been founded on a really remarkable natural aptitude. Undoubtedly it was this ability that enabled Wilde to maintain such a comprehensive and up-to-date literary knowledge, while apparently spending so much of his time in talking, thinking, writing and pleasure. It is a faculty closely linked, not only with his verbal quickness, but also with his ability to give such accurate and condensed assessments of the work of other writers.

Both Rothenstein and Chalmers Mitchell, as we have already noted, remarked on the extraordinarily illuminating intellect and the wide range of knowledge shown in Wilde's conversation, and even Henley praised his scholarship. All these reports directly contradict Harris's accusation of superficiality. Rothenstein, indeed, says categorically: "It is nonsense to say that he talked shallow paradox which dazzled young people; I still recall perfect sayings of his, as perfect now as on the day when he said them."

Pater, his master in prose, spoke of Wilde as an "excellent talker," though at other times he may have felt a certain rather envious contempt for this ephemeral occupation of Oscar's, since he also referred somewhat slightingly to "the strange vulgarity which Mr. Wilde mistakes for cleverness." But, then, Pater himself was so poor a talker that his lectures were almost inaudible, which once led Wilde to remark that he "overheard" him well.

Henri de Régnier brings out another prominent characteristic of Wilde's conversation—his tendency to despise exactitude, to mingle fact and fantasy in such a way that the two became inextricably connected threads of the same complex tapestry. Incidentally, he gives some further hints of Wilde's manner of conversation:

> One might not press M. Wilde too closely for the meaning of his allegories. One had to enjoy their grace and the

unsuspected turns he gave to his narratives, without seeking to raise the veil of his phantasmagoria of the mind which made of his conversation a kind of "Thousand and One Nights" as spoken. . . .

M. Wilde was persuasive and astonishing. He excelled in giving a certificate of truth to what was improbable. The most doubtful statements when uttered by him assumed for the moment the aspect of indisputable truth. Of fable he made a thing which had actually happened, from a thing which had actually happened he drew out a fable. He listened to the Scheherazade that was prompting him from within, and seemed himself first of all to be amazed at his strange and fabulous inventions.

Nothing annoyed Wilde more than to have his talk interrupted by people who wished to correct him on the facts he adapted or to throw doubt on his inventions. He attacked their passion for factual truth with great irony in *The Decay of Lying*. O'Sullivan tells us that—

. . . there was a certain description of man loathed by Wilde. This was the kind of man who insists on precise facts in the most casual of talk. . . . This kind of thing really had the power of exasperating Wilde beyond endurance. He said freely that he abhorred such men.

This tendency to exaggeration and invention found its best expression in the stories he was continually telling. Douglas tells us that " 'I have thought of a story' was an announcement for ever on his lips, and his intimates knew that five times out of six the story would be worth listening to."

His stories were infinite in number and variety. Only a few of them ever found their way into print, usually after he had told them already to a series of audiences and perfected them verbally. *Lord Arthur Savile's Crime*, *The Birthday of the Infanta* and the story which was later dramatised as *La Sainte Courtisane* were among his favourite parlour stories, but all were told in a much simpler form than they later assumed in prose. Telling them, Wilde was completely spontaneous and unself-conscious; writing seemed to impose constraint on him —he admitted to Gide that "writing bores me so"—so that the natural "artificiality" of his conversation was replaced by the stiff and loaded artificiality of his prose. Some of the stories that were never published have survived in the memories of his friends. Yeats, Benson, O'Sullivan and Graham Robertson all record examples, and some others were collected by Mr. Hesketh Pearson from surviving acquaintances and published in his biography of Wilde.

There was no single type that could be called "the Wilde story." They varied according to the talker's mood. Some, like the pleasant story of "Aunt Jane" printed by Graham Robertson in his *Time Was,* were in the vein of a gentle social satire. Some, like that which was later elaborated into *A Florentine Tragedy,* were sensational in an Elizabethan manner, others were delicate in fantasy, and there were many parables in the Biblical style, some of which we have already quoted, used to convey a lesson which could hardly have been pleasing to the orthodox Biblical student. Stories were such a necessary part of Wilde's conversation that he had a little allegory to illustrate every point and theory. Not all of them were long or elaborate, but some of the really slight ones were also some of the most delightful. There is, for instance, this parable in theology, which was later elaborated, lengthened and spoilt in *Poems in Prose:*

And there was a great silence in the House of Judgment; and the soul of the man stood naked before God. And God opened the book of the man's life and said, "Surely thou hast been very evil. Since thou hast done all these things, even into hell will I send thee." And the man cried out, "Thou canst not send me into hell." And God said, "Wherefore can I not send thee into hell?" And the man answered, "Because in hell I have always lived." And there was a great silence in the House of Judgment. And God

said to the man, "Seeing that I may not send thee into
hell, even into heaven will I send thee." And the man said,
"Thou canst not send me into heaven." And God said,
"Wherefore can I not send thee into heaven?" And the
man said, "Because I have never been able to imagine it."
And there was a great silence in the House of Judgment.

These stories all illustrate the essentially concrete operation of Wilde's mind. Abstractions meant little, unless he
could make them live in imagery, and therefore his talk was
filled, not merely with stories which give life to his ideas, but
also with vivid metaphors and illustrations. For instance, a
fragment recorded by Laurence Housman puts forward in a
pleasant manner the very core of the doctrine of philosophical idealism:

> Travellers in South America tell of a bird which, if seen
> by you unawares, flies to hide itself. But if it has seen you
> first, then, by keeping its eye on you, it imagines that it
> remains invisible, and nothing will induce it to retreat.
> The bird-trappers catch it quite easily merely by advanc-
> ing backwards. Now that, surely, is true philosophy. The
> bird, having once made you the object of its contempla-
> tion, has every right to think (as Bishop Berkeley did, I
> believe) that you have no independent existence. You are
> what you are—the bird says, and the Bishop says—merely
> because they have made you a subject of thought; if they
> did not think of you, you would not exist. And who knows?
> —they may be right. For, try as we may, we cannot get be-
> hind the appearance of things to the reality. And the ter-
> rible reason may be that there is no reality in things apart
> from their appearances.

Two qualities which were prominent in Wilde's conversation remain to be noticed. Firstly, although those who took
his talk for mere frothy frivolity were mistaken, or had been
unfortunate enough to encounter him on those occasions
when for some reason he felt he could not give himself freely

to his company, nonsense did indeed play a great and fruitful part in his conversation. It was used partly in order to entertain, to relieve his hearers from too much concern with serious or satirical matters, but it also had a function and life of its own. In his own day it was the element that gave his talk its air of good humour and lightness—Graham Robertson talks of "the boyish good humour, the almost child-like love of fun, the irresponsible gaiety and lightness of touch in which lay his unquestionable charm"—and it remains to-day some of the most delightful reading in the memoirs of his contemporaries. Wilde, who realised the therapeutic value of yielding to temptation, also realised the value of giving way to any spontaneous impulse of fun that came unannounced into his mind. Of this quality E. F. Benson gives us a fairly thorough analysis, in which he says:

> . . . I am not sure whether Oscar Wilde's most individual conversational gift was not that well-spring of nonsense, pure and undefiled, which perennially flowed from him.
> Such nonsense was rich in decoration of phrase: sometimes . . . it was highly dramatic. . . . Sometimes it was sheer nonsense, unharnessable to any idea. He was arranging a symposium and hoped I would come to it. "Everybody nowadays is settled by symposiums," he said, "and this one is to deal finally with the subject of bi-metallism: of bi-metallism between men and women. . . ."
> His witty gaiety never left him in the darkest days, for when the late Lord Haldane, who held very strong views about the brutality of his punishment, went to see him in prison and recommended him, now that he had so much leisure, to embark on some considerable work, he plucked up at once and said he was preparing a small volume of table epigrams.

The volume of table epigrams never materialised, but much of Wilde's conversational nonsense is embedded in his plays. Indeed, towards the end it was developing into their

principal element, displacing the more directly rational wit
of the earlier plays by this fantastic pattern of nonsensical
but pointedly satirical fun. In *An Ideal Husband,* the conversations of Goring with his valet, his father and his fiancée
have all this delightful quality of inverted reason; in *The
Importance of Being Earnest* this wit, tied down by no
bounds of formal logic, has completely taken control, replac-
ing the stock Victorian plots of the earlier plays, their lurk-
ing sentimentality and fan-and-glove Scribeian melodrama,
with a flickering play of lightly satirical folly over the social
manners and personal follies of the characters. The kind of
nonsensical wit which Wilde introduced into the theatre
with *The Importance of Being Earnest* has been a model un-
successfully striven after by playwrights ever since, and has
almost established a convention in current theatrical method.

The other quality of Wilde's conversation that needs to be
mentioned at least briefly is the feeling of well-being experienced by those who listened to him in his best moods. People
who were depressed when they encountered him went away
imbued with a feeling of happy optimism; artists unsure of
their abilities were given confidence by his discussion of their
problems; he had just the right quality of understanding to
make people realise, not only what was in him, but also what
was in themselves. But his abilities went even beyond this,
and one is reminded of his explanation for the stories of
Christ's "healing powers" when one reads some of the accounts of how Wilde's conversation relieved people of severe
nervous pains or charmed the apparently inconsolably be-
reaved back into the state of mind where they could loosen
their sorrows in laughter. This effect was undoubtedly in part
due to Wilde's effervescent good humour and the evident
pleasure he himself gained from exercising his conversational
gifts. It was also in some degree caused by the physical charm
of his eyes and voice which, when he was caught in the tide
of talk, won even those who had gone to him with hatred

or envy in their hearts. But undoubtedly there was also a quality of "inspiration" about Wilde when he talked; he was exalté, lifted on a current of conversation that almost dominated him, and this state of "possession" seems to have given him a kind of psychological dynamism which he transmitted to other people and which caused the peculiarly beneficial mental and nervous effect his presence exercised on them.

There remains the general impression which Wilde's conversation made on some of the more intelligent people who listened to him and who have left a record of their impressions. I have chosen the accounts of two men who knew Wilde during that last period when his conversation is universally recognised to have been at its most profound and humane, the conversation of an acute philosopher as well as a very fine writer.

Laurence Housman was not on intimate terms with Wilde, but the few occasions on which he heard him talk made such an impression that more than twenty years afterwards he wrote down his recollections of one of these conversations, prefacing it with a general comment on the nature of Wilde's talk, in which he said: ". . . The impression left upon me from that occasion is that Oscar Wilde was incomparably the most accomplished talker I had ever met." Housman then went on to describe Wilde's conversation as "the smooth-flowing utterance, sedate and self-possessed, oracular in tone, whimsical in substance, carried on without haste or hesitation, or change of word, with the quiet zest of a man perfect at the game."

The second opinion comes from a man who had known Wilde fairly intimately in the days before his downfall, and who saw him frequently in the years of exile after his release from prison. This is Vincent O'Sullivan, who has left two fairly long discourses on Wilde's conversation, parts of which we have already quoted. On the general character of Wilde's conversation he said:

He was certainly the best talker of his time, and it is hard to believe that there was ever a better at any time. He had all the gifts necessary: an imposing presence, a pleasant voice, a control of language, charm, and an extraordinary tact in choosing subjects which would suit his listeners, and in judging his effects. What De Quincey says excellently of Coleridge as a talker—"In this lay Coleridge's characteristic advantage, that he was a great natural power, and also a great artist"—may in all truth be said of Wilde.

I have devoted much space to analysing the various characteristics of Wilde as a conversationalist, since it is this aspect of his activity that epitomises most completely the characteristic qualities of his genius, and reveals the germs of his thought and of his literary methods.

In conversation his good qualities are reflected—geniality, generosity, tolerance, lack of malice or resentment, open-mindedness and lack of prejudice, desire to please and to be pleased. Nor are his weaknesses hidden—vanity, susceptibility to flattery, naïve love of show and the symbols of show. More than this, however, his conversation reflects the merits of his thought and work—his quick intellectual penetration, his breadth of learning and rapidity of intuitive insight, his love of phrases and verbal embroidery, his delight at shocking in and out of season by epigram and exaggeration. And, behind all this, Wilde, as he talked, revealed continually that duality which exists in all his actions and thought, and which is expressed at its extreme in his favourite conversational device, the paradox. Always there is the alternation of depth and superficiality, the probing revelation and the shallow play on words, and, beyond this even, what at first sight appears an empty jest may in fact contain some real discovery of thought, a humorous story may be an allegory with profound psychological or philosophical significance. Wilde undoubtedly used his conversation as a means of cultivating his thoughts and evolving his writings, and it is perhaps just to say that the most brilliant passages of his plays are merely the reflections of the charm of his conversation at its best. Indeed, as I have said, in many cases where told and written versions of the same story survive, the former is usually superior in style because Wilde was forced by the necessities of conversational effect to use a simplicity he did not always observe in his writing.

Only a few fragments of Wilde's conversation have survived—a mass of detached epigrams, some isolated records of talks by Gide, Housman and the unreliable Harris, and a few stories of which we have already given examples.

The light, spontaneous wit, glittering with paradoxes and aphorisms, which formed the most immediately attractive element of his conversation, was unreproducible: to carry in the memory such feats of conversational virtuosity would have been an impossible feat for any among his hearers, and this type of talk is best reproduced in Wilde's own plays and dialogues, though even here, we are told by many of his contemporaries, the demands of writing had robbed the wit of its pristine vitality.

But there was a deeper side to his conversation, the side reproduced in the gentle solemnity of his tales, or in those meditative passages when he subjected life to the operation of his penetrating and profound thought. As in some of the spoken stories there is a terrible and stark beauty of the kind which was usually lost in the overloaded decoration of his prose, so in the few philosophical fragments that have been left to us, particularly from his last days, there is a richness and depth which we rarely find in his writing, at least in a pure form.

To Laurence Housman, who had asked him whether he really thought no artist were successful, he replied:

> Incidentally; never intentionally. If they are, they remain incomplete. The artist's mission is to live the complete life: success, as an episode (which is all it can be); failure, as the real, the final end. Death, analysed to its resultant atoms—what is it but the vindication of failure: the

getting rid for ever of powers, desires, appetites, which have been a lifelong embarrassment? The poet's noblest verse, the dramatist's greatest scene, deal always with death; because the highest function of the artist is to make perceived the beauty of failure. . . . In my own ruin I have found out this truth. The artist must live the complete life, must accept it as it comes and stands like an angel before him, with its drawn and two-edged sword. Great success, great failure—only so shall the artist see himself as he is, and through himself see others; only so shall he learn (as the artist must learn) the true meaning behind the appearance of things material, of life in general, and—more terrible still—the meaning of his own soul.

Gide has left us some records of observations on the nature of art, which reproduce in a more pleasing and rather different form the contentions raised in *The Critic as Artist*. Once Wilde said:

You must understand that there are two worlds—the one exists and is never talked about; it is called the real world because there is no need to talk about it in order to see it. The other is the world of Art; one must talk about that because otherwise it would never exist.

And later, more profoundly, in discussing the peculiar character of æsthetic beauty, he remarked:

Do you know what makes the work of art, and what makes the work of nature? Do you know what the difference is? For the narcissus is as beautiful as a work of art, so what distinguishes them cannot be merely beauty. Do you know what it is that distinguishes them? A work of art is always unique.

Gide gives a further example of Wilde's conversation in a different vein, when he was describing his experiences in prison, which is interesting in itself because, apart from *De Profundis*, there are few accounts available from Wilde's own lips of his real impressions of prison life.

Yes, afterwards we had a charming prison Governor, oh, quite a charming man, but for the first six months I was dreadfully unhappy. There was a Governor of the prison, a Jew, who was very harsh, because he was entirely lacking in imagination. . . .

He did not know what to imagine in order to make us suffer. Now, you shall see what a lack of imagination he showed. You must know that in prison we are allowed to go out only one hour a day; then, we walk in a courtyard, round and round, one behind the other, and we are absolutely forbidden to say a word. Warders watch us, and there are terrible punishments for anyone caught talking. Those who are in prison for the first time are spotted at once, because they do not know how to speak without moving their lips. I had already been in prison six weeks and I had not spoken a word to anyone—not to a soul.

One evening we were walking as usual, one behind the other, during the hour's exercise, when suddenly behind me I heard my name called. "Oscar Wilde, I pity you, because you must suffer more than we do." Then I made a great effort not to be noticed (I thought I was going to faint), and I said without turning round, "No, my friend, we all suffer alike." And from that day I no longer had a desire to kill myself. We talked in that way for several days. I knew his name and what he had done. His name was P . . .; he was such a good fellow; oh, so good. But I had not yet learned to speak without moving my lips, and one evening—"C.3.3." (C.3.3. was myself), "C.3.3. and A.4.8. step out of the ranks."

Then we stood out, and the warder said, "You will both have to go before the governor." And as pity had already entered into my heart, my only fear was for him; in fact, I was even glad that I might suffer for his sake. But the Governor was quite terrible. He had P . . . in first; he was going to question us both separately, because you must know that the punishment is not the same for the one who speaks first and for the one who answers; the punishment for the one who speaks first is double that of the other. As a rule the first has fifteen days' solitary confinement and the second has eight days only.[1] Then the Governor wanted to know which of us had spoken first, and naturally P . . ., good fellow that he was, said it was he. And afterwards when the Governor had me in to question me, I, of course, said it was I. Then the Governor got very red because he could not understand it. "But P . . . also says that it was he who began it. I cannot understand it. I cannot understand it."

Think of it, my dear fellow, he could *not* understand it. He became very embarrassed, and said, "But I have already given him fifteen days," and then he added, "Anyhow, if that is the case, I shall give you both fifteen days." Is not that extraordinary? That man had not a spark of imagination.

We must allow for the fact that undoubtedly these words have suffered in the recording. No writing can reproduce the laughter and genial good-humour with which Gide tells us they were spoken. But they perhaps show, more effectively than his facile chains of epigrams, the essential humanity and sympathy that supported the glittering external manifestations of Wilde's character.

They also show, like his parables and the recorded fragments of his later conversations, that he was no mere table entertainer. On the contrary, he used his conversation, not only as a means of perfecting his writing, but also as an art in its own right, by which he could express his views on art, on society and on life in general. Like those philosophers whose thought was nearest to his, Lao Tzu and Epicurus, he expressed himself most easily in the spoken word.

So vivd, so exact in its phrasing, so happy in its imagery, and so concrete in its philosophical exposition does his conversation seem from these fragments that have survived in

[1] So far as I can discover, the actual sentences which a governor could impose for talking, even in Wilde's day, were considerably less, but there is no reason to doubt Gide, as Oscar was probably exaggerating for artistic effect.

the writings of various auditors, that we can hardly find any reason to doubt that Wilde was indeed the greatest talker of his age, and, so far as we can tell from the records that have survived, one of the greatest talkers of all time. Individuals recording the conversation of other individuals may add their own genius; undoubtedly in reading the Platonic dialogues we read Socrates transformed by the superb literary genius of Plato and, equally certainly, distorted by his perverse social ideas. But where a great number of accounts, many of them by people who have but scanty literary talents of their own, combine to make a homogeneous picture of a talker, a picture that gives such a uniform impression of greatness as that which we possess of Wilde, there can be no doubt remaining of his genius in this respect. Nor can there be much doubt that he was a greater talker than writer. The only amazing thing is that a man with such qualities of improvisation, of happy imagery, of the ready concretisation of abstractions into hard images, should have been so unoriginal a poet and, with a few exceptions, so undistinguished a fiction writer. As Arthur Symons has remarked, his personality was "certainly more interesting than any of his work."

When Wilde was dying, he awoke once from sleep, and said to a friend who was sitting at his bedside: "I have had an appalling dream. I dreamed I was banqueting with the dead."

His friend replied immediately, "My dear Oscar, I am sure you were the life and soul of the party."

And that summarises justly Wilde's standing as a conversationalist. If we could imagine, as Hazlitt did, a muster of the great talkers of the past, from Socrates down to Coleridge and Whistler, Wilde, we can be sure, would outshine them all in brilliance, the last great exponent of the art of conversation before the iron shutters of a mechanical age came crashing down upon the kind of spontaneous communion among men of which Wilde's superlatively good talk was such a brilliant flowering.

IN THIS chapter I shall discuss a theme which has already been covered, at least partially, in the preceding chapters of this book, but which seems sufficiently important to deserve special consideration on its own account. This is the dual legend of Wilde the playboy and Wilde the prophet; the selfish and corrupt sybarite seen by his enemies, and the martyred visionary seen by too many of his admirers to the exclusion of his most evident faults. Clearly, neither of these portraits is exact; each, indeed, is a somewhat monstrous exaggeration of one side of Wilde's character as shown in his personal life. My object is to demonstrate that, reduced to their just proportions, the two apparently inconsistent personalities are in fact quite compatible, that there is no real conflict between the profligate man about town and the penitent who spoke in the pages of *De Profundis,* and who, after his imprisonment, sent up that great cry of poetic indignation at the world's injustice to individual men in *The Ballad of Reading Gaol.*

It is perhaps impossible to consider Wilde thoroughly in his manhood without reverting to the adolescent emotional attitude which persisted throughout his life. Intellectually mature at an early age, he nevertheless retained, in spite of his superficial sophistication, a remarkably juvenile feeling of wonder at the various and ever-renewed beauty of the earth (a beauty which he held the searching eye could see even in what appeared at first sight foul or ugly), and an almost insatiable greed for satisfaction in every mode of sensation. Mingled with these were a childish love of splendour and extravagance and a typically adolescent and theatrical attitude of defiance towards the world of dull regimentation and humdrum everyday life. Above all, there was a great sense of fun which made play of everything that happened to him, changing even tragedy and sorrow into games that mingled with the general world of make-believe where Wilde always lived. And the world of make-believe is, in reality, only a part of that visionary universe from which the great mystics and the great artists alike have drawn their wisdom and their inspiration. Wilde himself was, after all, no mean artist, and had more than a little of inverted mysticism in his make-up.

Even in his work the element of play is evident to a far greater extent than in most other artists. Writing, like talking, he regarded as a game of virtuosity and inspiration, and he would have been the last to object to some of the present-day critics, like Julian Symons, who contend that the basis of poetry is to be found in play. To Wilde, indeed, it was the greatest of games, and Bernard Shaw, one of the few dramatic critics of the 1890's really to appreciate Wilde's comedies, spoke with unusual discernment when, reviewing *An Ideal Husband,* he said that:

> In a certain sense Mr. Wilde is to me our only thorough playwright. He plays with everything: with wit, with philosophy, with drama, with actors and audience, with the whole theatre.

Oscar more than once acknowledged this openly, saying: "I write plays to amuse myself. After, if people want to act in them, I sometimes allow them to do so." When the young nineties story-writer, Hubert Crackanthorpe, asked what

Wilde thought of his work, he received the casual reply: "Your play, dear boy, your play!"

But life itself was also a wonderful game, and every pose, every gesture of defiance, every new sensation, every mental extravagance or physical excess, added to its fascination. The great Mayfair houses, at whose magnificence Wilde whispered with boyish awe, "This is how a gentleman should live," the enthusiastic audiences who shouted with delight when he solemnly complimented them on *their* success in appreciating *his* plays, the orgies with grooms in the Savoy Hotel and the blackmailers coming to the front door in Tite Street, the American women pelting him with flowers and the romantically sinister crooks he delighted to chat with in the cafés of the Left Bank, were all part of the game, of the great charade of life played around Oscar Wilde, the King of Playboys and the "Lord of Life." Like a child, he imagined the whole world would dance to his tune. When Fate broke up the dance, when his playmates betrayed him or turned away to jeer, the game was ended, and the more responsible and adult part of him assumed control. Or was it perhaps just a new game, this time the solitary game of a child cast out and transforming the sorrows of his defeat into a new and more magnificent play? It is always hard to tell. But in all Wilde's life the two elements were intermingled. In his play he had visionary glimpses of truths that had passed others by; persisting in his folly, he became wise. Yet in his most reflective moods the natural gaiety of his character was never far below the surface, and would burst out at the most unexpected moments.

The conjunction of a fundamentally child-like love of play, an extreme curiosity for sensation, an intense appreciation of the physical enjoyments of life, and a contempt for the society in which he found himself living, was already bound to produce extravagant behaviour.

When there were added a personal charm and an unparalleled power of conversation which gave him entry into every rank of society, combined with the sudden access to almost unlimited money, which he thought only of spending as rapidly as possible, it is not surprising that this extravagance should have reached an insane tempo in a life geared to unrestrained pleasure and sensation and which, if external society and Wilde's own folly had not between them created an arbitrary end to the play, must inevitably have led to physical and perhaps mental breakdown.

Looking back over these years, while he never expressed a regret for what he had done, Wilde admitted that he had acted in a way unworthy of himself. In *De Profundis* he said:

> The gods had given me almost everything. But I let myself be lured into long spells of senseless and sensual ease. I amused myself with being a *flâneur*, a dandy, a man of fashion. I surrounded myself with the smaller natures and the meaner minds. I became the spendthrift of my own genius, and to waste an eternal youth gave me a curious joy. . . .
>
> I used to live entirely for pleasure. I shunned suffering and sorrow of every kind. I resolved to ignore them as far as possible; to treat them, that is to say, as modes of imperfection. They were not part of my scheme of life. They had no place in my philosophy.

This may be regarded as part of the self-dramatisation of repentance that was undoubtedly a prominent element in *De Profundis*. But it is reinforced by a very similar confession in letters to his friends, written after his release from imprisonment, and at a time when he was in a very healthy and equable state of mind.

It was only unfortunate that Wilde was not able to maintain the simplicity of life he had hoped to achieve, that, in however tawdry and unsatisfactory a way, the old game called him back among its players and destroyed so many of his fine resolutions. However, I shall return to this aspect of his later career; for the present I am concerned with his own afterthoughts on the course that led to his downfall.

Wilde, it will be observed, while he realised his own folly, did not accept the world's verdict that he had necessarily been *wrong* in his actions. He regarded them rather as an error in judgment. Certainly, he would never have supported the kind of moral extravagances with which society replied to his own defiance of the moral code.

But, before we pass to a more detailed discussion of the nature of Wilde's "play" and its underlying motives, it may be well to see what his life looked like to those outside it. And for this reason I have chosen to take one example which approximates to the attitude of the average Victorian bourgeois of Wilde's day, and another which represents that of those friends who did not join the cry against him, yet who disapproved of his actions and were able to describe them with a certain objectivity. The first is from an editorial in the *Daily Telegraph*, and it was written by Sir Edwin Arnold, an enthusiastic propagandist for Buddhism who does not appear to have assimilated much of the Buddha's essential tolerance towards human frailty. One of the reasons for Arnold's bitterness, it has been said, was that he nursed a grudge because of a review in which Wilde had made fun of one of his translations from the Hindustani. Arnold said, among other unpleasant things:

> The grave of contemptuous oblivion may rest on his foolish ostentation, his empty paradoxes, his insufferable posturing, his incurable vanity. Nevertheless, when we remember that he enjoyed a certain popularity among some sections of society, and, above all, when we reflect that what was smiled at as an insolent braggadocio was the cover for, or at all events ended in, flagrant immorality, it is well, perhaps, that the lesson of his life should not be passed over without some insistence on the terrible warning of his fate. . . .

We speak sometimes of a school of Decadents and Æsthetes in England, although it may well be doubted
whether at any time its prominent members could not have
been counted on the fingers of one hand; but, quite apart
from any fixed organisation or body such as may or may
not exist in Paris, there has lately shown itself in London a
contemporary bias of thought, an affected manner of expression and style, and a few loudly vaunted ideas which
have had a limited but evil influence on all the better tendencies of art and literature. Of these the prisoner of
Saturday constituted himself a representative. He set an
example, so far as in him lay, to the weaker and the
younger brethren; and, just because he possessed considerable intellectual powers and unbounded assurance, his fugitive success served to dazzle and bewilder those who had
neither experience nor knowledge of the principles which
he travestied, or of that true temple of art of which he was
so unworthy an acolyte. Let us hope that his removal will
serve to clear the poisoned air, and make it cleaner and
purer for all healthy and unvitiated lungs.

This, clearly, was a piece of prejudiced dishonesty; Wilde's
literary success had no relation to his private sexual life and,
in general, his work was singularly lacking in any genuinely
pornographic element, even by the standards of his own age.
The "shocking" views he put forward were in reality little
more extreme than those of Swinburne or Whistler, and he
had a fastidiousness about literature which led him, while
he claimed the absolute right of the artist to use whatever
words or subjects he might choose in making literature, to
show his distaste for any undue coarseness. For instance, he
went so far as to say disapprovingly of George Moore, after
the publication of *Esther Waters,* that "he leads his readers to
the latrine and locks them in." As for his recommendations
to taste experience fully, in this he advanced little farther
than Pater, merely drawing that writer's arguments to their
logical conclusion, while *The Picture of Dorian Gray* carried

such an appearance of moral intention that Robert Buchanan protested against the attacks that had been made on it, on the grounds that it was a book that could show young men the folly of debauchery. Whatever may have been Wilde's personal influence on any of the individuals with whom he came into direct contact, it is certainly unlikely that his literary influence did anything more than widen the appreciation of life and art among those who read him with attention.

A much more humane and understanding view of Wilde's excesses and extravagances is taken by E. F. Benson, who discusses the moneyed and honeyed days when Wilde trod the last stages of his primrose path:

> It was as the man of genius and fashion, careless and gay, witty and elaborate, that he loved to appear in the halcyon days of the early nineties. He envied that particular *insouciance* which he thought to be the habit of those who have been brought up in certain traditions, and he aped the manner of it, without having the instincts to render it natural. There was no more of the flamboyant charlatanism of sunflower and velveteen breeches; a garb of ultra-conventional propriety best fitted the man of the world who happened also to be a consummate artist. He played his part without the slightest touch of pomposity (for the *clue* to it was this care-free gaiety), but with a child-like zest and gusto. . . .
>
> These triumphant and ludicrous progresses with button-holes in a hansom, this life with its gorgings and drinkings, its very various companionships, its luncheon parties and its laughter, its largesses of jewelled sleeve-links and gold cigarette-cases, its Dorian Gray pageantry in which he was the principal figure, sound in the telling of them more like the antics of one dressed up for some preposterous charade than the normal behaviour of a man of fashion leading the delectable life, and they were conducted, it must be remembered, on the smoking sides of a volcano which might

burst into eruption at any moment. He was doubtless the victim of a monstrous megalomania; he thought himself a man apart, exempt from the laws that govern others, and set above the thunder. . . . He believed himself to be the Lord of Life and the Lord of Language, and as such he might order his goings on as he pleased, and the world would only gape at him and applaud his radiant hedonism. Mayfair was his washpot and Piccadilly was glad of him. The desire to appear magnificent is no doubt a quality common to both sexes, but these gewgaws, these glittering trappings and millineries of which he, like Dorian Gray, was so much enamoured, point perhaps to a feminine trait in him, which is not without significance.

The theory that Wilde suffered from some form of mania has often, indeed, been advanced, particularly by those among his friends who were embarrassed by his more unorthodox actions. Sherard, for instance, a man of aggressive sexual normality, could not believe that the friend whom he admired so much and defended so loyally could have fallen into sexual perversions when in his right senses, and suggested that Wilde had a strain of mental unbalance which was so aggravated by alcohol that he sometimes went out of his mind and then performed his perverted deeds. This, however, ignores two facts—firstly, that Oscar Wilde detested immoderate drinking, and, secondly, that he associated with his homosexual acquaintances when he was completely sober, as well as when he had been drinking. Sherard, however, not trusting to one rather weak argument, puts forward the further conjecture that all the actions of Wilde which he (Sherard) considered crazy are to be attributed to the effects of syphilis.

The idea that Wilde suffered from syphilis and that this disease was at least a complicating factor in his death is a persistent one, which I have never seen either satisfactorily confirmed or fully disproved. The immediate cause of death was cerebral meningitis, which can be traced to an ear injury caused by a fall in the prison chapel at Reading, and the course of this last illness was certainly complicated by excessive absinthe and brandy drinking. Wilde also suffered from a severe rash during his last years which he used to attribute to eating mussels, and this may, but equally well may not, have been syphilitic. I have seen no evidence that he actually received treatment for syphilis, either before or during his last illness, nor have Sherard's suggestions of contraction been confirmed, and for this reason I think it is justifiable to leave the question open, while admitting that the recklessness of his actions during the prosperous years is similar in some respects to that of people suffering from syphilitically-induced delusions of grandeur.

On the other hand, syphilitics are by no means the only people who suffer from delusions of grandeur, and Wilde's later realisation of his folly tends rather to diminish the likelihood of his actions springing principally from a condition of physical disease. Moreover, it must be remembered that he was brought up by a mother who herself loved ostentation and had a vastly exaggerated idea of her own importance, and that even before he arrived at Oxford, in his days at Trinity College, he had begun to show a tendency towards studied eccentricity.

Personally, I am inclined to believe that his actions were those which could be expected of any physically healthy person of immature emotional development who is suddenly offered what appears to be unlimited wealth and endless admiration. He was swept off his feet by good fortune, and, like the adolescent he was in so many ways, he set out to enjoy himself without restraint. "In this world," says Dumby in *Lady Windermere's Fan*, "there are only two tragedies. One is not getting what one wants, and the other is getting it. The last is much the worst, the last is a real tragedy!"

As for the lack of emotional development which is evident

in so many of his actions, this might be explained partly by environmental and partly by glandular causes. Undoubtedly, Wilde's belated dependence on his mother—even at the time of his trial his principal anxiety was for her and not for his wife—was a retarding factor. On the other hand, such a continued dependence must in itself have been caused by an original tendency to emotional fixation at an adolescent stage, and the clue to this can perhaps be found in Wilde's peculiar physique. The large fleshy figure, the big flabby hands, and the rather long and massive face with its heavy lips, all give the impression of some kind of glandular disorder. Personally, I think that this explanation of Wilde's eccentric behaviour from environmental and physical causes is quite sufficient, and that there is no need to suppose the existence of a disease which it has not yet been proved conclusively he ever contracted.

But whatever the cause of Wilde's actions, whether it was organic disease, glandular malformation, or family environment, or whether it sprang from a calculated desire for self-advertisement, or a genuine rebellion against a society that filled him with disgust, or merely a boyish feeling of wonder that the Dublin doctor's son should be feted in the salons of the mighty, he was always ready to put up a screen of paradoxical and inverted philosophy to defend his life, and undoubtedly, for the time being at least, he believed implicitly in this self-justification.

He made a cult of joy and pleasure, claiming that through them one could better improve the world than by a preoccupation with its miseries. "One should sympathise with the joy, the beauty, the colour of life," he said. "The less said about life's sores the better." It should not be forgotten that he wanted that joy for everybody, but he also felt quite genuinely that each man must realise it for himself, that even the poor can only be rescued by their own rebellion against ugliness, not by other people renouncing joy and beauty on their behalf. "The modern world," he argued, ". . . aims at an Individualism expressing itself through joy. . . . Pain is not the ultimate mode of perfection. It is merely provisional and a protest. . . . When the wrong, and the disease, and the injustice are removed, it will have no further place." Later, he was to realise that suffering too had its necessary place in life, but in the halcyon days he not only desired to give it no place in his scheme of life, but also wished to shun it as much as he could. In *De Profundis* he admits:

> Failure, disgrace, poverty, sorrow, despair, suffering, tears even, the broken words that come from lips in pain, remorse that makes one walk on thorns, conscience that condemns, self-abasement that punishes, the misery that puts ashes on its head, the anguish that chooses sackcloth for its raiment and in its drink puts gall: all these were things of which I was afraid.

But his desire to avoid pain did not spring from any essential callousness. He was not one of those who could build his happiness on the sufferings of others, and watch their pain with equanimity. On the contrary, he had a really morbid over-sensitivity towards pain, ugliness, and misery. A sordid room set him into almost unbearable agitation, the sight of a woman weeping made him violently unhappy, and physical ugliness or disease revolted him acutely. For instance, though he regarded Verlaine and his poetry with the greatest respect, he felt so disgusted by the Frenchman's appearance that he was able to meet him only on rare occasions. In spite of his denunciation of sympathy, he was in fact so full of sympathy that he could not face the pain which the sight of misfortune caused him. As the cynic almost always cloaks the sentimentalist, so the determined seeker of pleasure is more often than not the man who beneath it all feels the burden of the world's pain too much for him to bear. For a time Wilde even hardened himself against his innate sympathy and assumed a mask of arrogance, but then life itself thrust its sorrows upon him, "And as I had determined to know nothing of them, I was forced to taste each of them in turn, to feed on them, to have for a season, indeed, no other food at all." As he had appreciated the happy things of life, so he came to appreciate and know at their full value the unhappy things, the manifestations of misery and sorrow.

But while, in his periods of extravagant living, Oscar Wilde shunned whatever might arouse his feelings and remind him too much of the great mass of sorrow existing in the world, his life could not justly be called selfish. Apart from the fact that he always shrank from any malicious act or word, or from causing any unnecessary pain to other people, he was possessed of a spirit of unending generosity, and, while he deprecated self-sacrifice as demoralising to both sides, he was never so happy as when he was pleasing or helping others. He gave away money and assistance recklessly, and his continual motto was "Friends always share." Sherard, who, like all his poorer friends, was a frequent beneficiary of Wilde's generosity, argues that this generosity was linked closely with his vast natural enjoyment of the pleasures of living.

> Oscar Wilde was at once a supreme egotist and the least selfish of men—that is to say, that he combined individualism with a large and generous altruism. He had not the masked selfishness of self-sacrifice where his strong nature rebelled against the victimisation of himself.
>
> He could not go against his own nature to oblige another. He would not have divided his last shilling with a friend, but, what is infinitely more rare, he was always ready to give away his superfluity. . . . I have known Oscar Wilde, who never invested a penny, give away hundreds of pounds. His comfort had to be assured, and he made no pretence, as some do, of philanthropy which imposed privation on himself. And no one who knew him,

who had watched his physical life, could expect it of him, or blame as selfishness what was only egotism. In his intense joy of life, asceticism was impossible to his nature. It was a pleasure to watch his enjoyment at table, his delight in comfortable clothes, the bounding gratitude of all his being for all the good things of existence.

But there was nothing coarse or gross in his sensualism. He was a man of too much refinement to overstep the line. I never once saw him drink to excess; and that he always held a whip-hand over his habits was shown by the ease with which he adapted himself to the prison regulations. . . . He was not the helpless slave to his passions that he has been represented to be.

Sherard's testimony in this matter was supported by that of many other friends—by all, indeed, except those like Harris and Douglas, who were too anxious to tell of their own generosity to remember Wilde's virtues in this respect. While Oscar had money in his pocket or a balance in the bank, any friend in need could be sure of receiving whatever he might ask, and there were cases in which Wilde contributed quite substantially to alleviate the distress of men who had acted towards him in a hostile way.

There was in all this more than mere generosity. It showed what is perhaps of even greater significance—a complete lack of the sense of property. Wilde's idea of *meum* and *tuum* was slight in the extreme; he once said to Sherard, as he produced a handful of notes earned on a lecture tour, "You know I have no sense of property," and this was no idle remark. He had nothing of the careful literary worker who builds up a fortune out of his successes. He saved nothing, and the £8,000 a year which he received while his plays were enjoying a vast success in the West End theatres (the equivalent, when one takes into account changed prices and the low income tax of the 1890's, of between £40,000 and £50,000 to-day) was spent and given away as it was earned.

It can be safely assumed that more was distributed in presents or assistance to friends and parasites than was ever spent on Wilde himself.

Thus his denunciation of private property was not wholly incompatible with his great income as a playwright, since the money never stayed in his hands long enough to become property. He saw among his acquaintances the effects of property-owning, the anxiety and mental coarsening it incurred, and took good care that this should never happen to him.

Nor did Wilde restrict his sharing with his friends—and enemies—to the times when he was prosperous. In his not very wealthy youth he gave freely of what little he had, and in the poverty of his last years in France he was still eager to help any person whose need was greater than his own. In Dieppe, when he was devoid of any property and living on credit and the gifts of his friends, he took care of the indigent Dowson, paid his hotel bill, and subsidised him for a considerable period with loans which he must have known would not be repaid for many months.

Having no sense of property, and being always ready to share whatever came his way, Wilde saw no reason why he should not accept and even expect the gifts and loans of others when he was himself in need. He took money from his friends during his last years, completely ingenuously and without any thought of parasitism, since social ostracism prevented him from earning a living by his writing.

Unfortunately, some of these so-called friends were not so generous as they appeared, and experienced regrets, or liked to publicise their munificence in such a way as to make Wilde appear a miserable sponger on their good-will. One of these was Douglas, who went to the extent of adding up the amounts of his gifts and publishing the totals in one of his books, in order to support his picture of himself as the pure young man imposed on by an ungentlemanly cad. Harris, who had once promised Wilde a gift of £500 and then produced a cheque for £50, was another of these benefactors who blazoned their generosity abroad. Harris, indeed, went even farther, for he, the financial adventurer *par excellence* who had made a number of fortunes by the most shady means, also hinted that Wilde's actions were not particularly honest. All this arose out of the scenario of a play which Wilde had prepared and which he was in the habit of offering to writers who wished to make him a discreet gift. Nobody thought of using the plot except Harris, who worked it up into a successful play, thus depriving Wilde of a useful source of income. Some of the other purchasers of the plot remonstrated with Harris, who then proceeded to accuse Wilde of dishonesty. But in fact, it was Harris who had been the rogue, for, out of £175 which he had promised, Wilde only received £25, although Harris himself made a great deal from the play, *Mr. and Mrs. Daventry*. With the surprising confidence which he often showed in the statements of that wholly unreliable witness, Bernard Shaw accepted all Harris's accusations at their face value, and, with apparent inconsistency for a self-conscious critic of the institution of property, went so far as to say that Wilde in his last years declined into a sponger and a swindler. Thus, damned by three such authorities as Douglas, Harris and Shaw, Wilde stands in many people's minds with the unjustified repute as a man who ended his days as a rather despicable crook.

In reality, however, Wilde himself had given away in his life far more than he ever received; it is certainly likely that Douglas, before the debacle, received from him in various gifts at least as much as he ever gave afterwards, while Harris must often have shared Oscar's hospitality in the years up to 1895. As for Shaw, he must clearly be criticised for supporting accusations against a fellow writer without sifting the matter at all thoroughly, thus giving the weight of his vast literary prestige to a thoroughly unjust condemnation.

Quite apart from the folly of judging a writer by his financial activities, these critics also chose to condemn Wilde by a system of monetary ethics which he himself did not admit and therefore cannot be blamed for infringing. If he had upheld private property, if he had been inclined always to take and never to give, they might have been justified. As it was, their accusations are as irrelevant as were similar charges used to discredit other writers lacking in the sense of "mine and thine."

Wilde's financial extravagance was thus, in fact, one way in which he expressed his individualist attitude towards property. It may not have been the best way, but its motives were at least honest.

Many of the other extravagances which he committed as a "playboy" can be attributed, not to any artificial decadentism, but to a natural enjoyment of the good things of life which is evident in all the surviving accounts of his character. He loved talking, drinking, eating, sexual indulgence, all to apparent excess; but one must take always into account his superabundant energy and the great natural zest he brought to life. He sought to break down the inhibitions which restrain men's enjoyment of the natural pleasures. Escaping from the strict moral prison of his age, he naturally reacted excessively, but underlying all this was that respect for natural urges and instincts which he showed so often in his writings. The man who is greedy for life is always preferable to the man who is afraid of it. All Wilde's enjoyment of physical and, equally, of intellectual and emotional pleasures is shown in his celebrated remark that: "Moderation is a fatal thing. Enough is as good as a meal. More than enough is as good as a feast." He himself never admitted moderation in his gestures and actions, though this did not mean that he indulged in personal vulgarity. Indeed, in his dealings with men and women he showed usually a remarkable delicacy, and his conversation, while it went to the dizzy heights of fantasy and imaginative nonsense, never declined into crudity. But in living his life as he felt it should be lived, Wilde would admit no limitations, and went to extremes that would not have been necessary for a man who lived in free surroundings and who therefore had no need to break violently away from convention.

Daring and even rashness he considered necessary, and indeed the only means of impressing one's ideas on society. "Nothing succeeds like excess," he would say, and he built up a whole philosophy of phrases to justify his self-conscious and open defiance of the social conventions. "Nothing," he tells us, "looks so like innocence as an indiscretion"; and elsewhere: "The one advantage of playing with fire . . . is that one never gets even singed. It is the people who do not know how to play with it who get burned up." From Wilde's own career it would seem that these statements were not the whole truth, for he himself certainly got "burned up." Yet it might be said that his downfall came from too little daring, since it emerged from that hidden part of his life where he tried to be discreet and where he played with a fire he was incapable of handling. In the realms where he was sure of himself, his daring certainly brought him success.

Thus beneath all Wilde's playboy follies there lurked a certain basis of reason and meaning. His financial extravagances were mingled with a faultless generosity and were also the expression of an emotional as well as an intellectual revulsion from property values. His physical excesses were the expressions of a desire to free the instincts from the pathological tyranny of Victorian moral restraints which produced mental unbalance and psychological frustration. His rashnesses were the expression of a philosophy of intellectual daring and moral courage not unlike that propounded by Nietzsche and, less forthrightly, by his own master, Pater. Wilde was merely simple enough to put his theories into practice, and too naïve to see all the perils for the unwary.

But perhaps the most controversial of his extravagances was his dandyism, his elevating a cult of sartorial elegance into a symbol of life, of the life of manners which he held to be more important than the life of morals.

It is this symbolism which has proved to many people the most irritating of all Wilde's "perversities." At times it is expressed in forms which on the surface seem to have no virtue beyond their cleverness. "The future belongs to the dandy," says Lord Illingworth, in *A Woman of No Importance*. "It is the exquisites who are going to rule. . . . A well-tied tie is the most serious step in life." The prophecy in this phrase was certainly inexact; sadly enough, since, if we must endure rulers, the dandies would undoubtedly be better than the commissars or the plutocrats. Again, Lord Illingworth's "most serious step in life" at first sight seems merely ridiculous. But these remarks set the tone for Wilde's own dandyism, for his successive affectations, beginning with the "æsthetic garb," and going through the Balzacian and flowered-waistcoat stages, until finally we find him dressing just a little on the florid side of the genteel fashion, and attaching, or pretending to attach, a vast importance to the right coiffure or the appropriate buttonhole.

There was a great deal of fun in all this, and many of the variations he played on the sartorial theme were clearly intended as jokes against both himself and his public. He would appear, for instance, in deep mourning at a luncheon party and, when his friends condoled with him for a supposed bereavement, would remark that it was his birthday and that he was mourning the death of another year of his waning youth. The first night of one of his plays was usually the occasion for some sartorial stroke of fun, in which he would get as many young disciples as possible to co-operate. The most celebrated of these was the great green carnation jest, when, on the first night of *Lady Windermere's Fan*, he persuaded a number of his friends to wear these artificially coloured flowers in public. The explanation he gave to one of these supporters is interesting, since it throws a light on the whole question of his dandyism. He said that he wanted to annoy the public.

"But why annoy the public?"

"It likes to be annoyed. A young man on the stage will wear a green carnation; people will stare at it and wonder. And then they will look round the house and see here and there more and more specks of mystic green. 'This must be some secret symbol,' they will say: 'What on earth can it mean?'"

"And what does it mean?"

"Nothing whatever, but that is just what nobody will guess."

There was indeed much of Wilde's fun that was meant just to mystify his audience and to infuriate those whom he considered to be Philistines. Gide remarks that "skilful in misleading those who are the heralds of earthly fame, Wilde knew how to hide his real personality behind an amusing phantom, with which he humorously deluded the public." He would persist in a joke if he found it good or provocative, and undoubtedly he took a great pleasure in arousing the ire of the public, for he once said, "Praise makes me humble, but when I am abused I know I have touched the stars."

From this point of view the green carnation was certainly a fruitful jest. The very flower itself became in the eyes of Philistia a symbol of all the superficial buffoonery that seemed to characterise Wilde, and it was almost in response to popular mythology that Robert Hichens took it as the title for his anti-Wilde novel. By this time the middle-class public had become so used to Wilde's *blagues* that some of the stuffier critics took the book to be another work of his own in what appeared to them the monstrous tradition of *The Picture of Dorian Gray,* and this gave Oscar the chance to wave his eccentric buttonhole even more defiantly in the faces of Bayswater and Birmingham by writing provocatively to the *Pall Mall Gazette* in 1894:

> Kindly allow me to contradict, in the most emphatic manner, the suggestion, made in your issue of Thursday last, and since then copied in many other newspapers, that I am the author of *The Green Carnation.*
>
> I invented that magnificent flower. But with the middle-class and mediocre book that usurps its strangely beautiful name I have, I need hardly say, nothing whatever to do. The Flower is a work of Art. The book is not.

Clearly, such a letter, however good a jest it may have been to Oscar and those who sympathised with his dislike for bourgeois values, must have seemed ridiculous and deliberately insolent when read at the tea-tables of Westbourne Terrace or by the season-ticket holders of Lewisham and Kew. Perhaps he hoped by this treatment to shock some of his readers from their complacency and arouse sufficient curiosity to lead them out of the Philistine desert. Or perhaps it was merely that he despised them, and considered them worth nothing more than mystification and annoying jokes. Or perhaps, and this seems very likely, he used his nonsense as protective guise. Many of his hearers, as I have already shown, testify that he would always try out the ground with a new audience by talking a little light folly before he began to speak in his real style, and with the middle-class he never got beyond this primary skirmishing of nonsense. They were not admitted behind his carefully prepared defences, and such people, like Watts-Dunton, condemned the "Harlequin" they saw, never imagining there was anything else.

It is also very likely that Wilde's defences were raised partly against himself, that, as Dr. Renier has suggested, he "decided to be a clown, and, like Molière and so many other professional amusers, he made his choice because he shrank from the essential earnestness of his nature." This theory at least accords with the fact that he avoided horror and ugliness because they had such a violent and disturbing effect on his peace of mind. The world he had to face was so horrible that, when he could not find refuge in fantasy, he did his best to repel it with a jest. Although in many ways so self-conscious, he even jested at himself.

Here and there in his writings occur comments on dandyism which tell us not only that to Wilde it may have meant more than appears at first sight, but also that, while it was symbolic of his external, attitude, he did not regard it as by any means the symbol of his deeper self. Firstly, there are two comments on Lord Goring, taken from the stage directions to *An Ideal Husband:*

> He is clever, but would not like to be thought so. A flawless dandy, he would be annoyed if he were considered romantic. He plays with life, and is on perfectly good terms with the world. He is fond of being misunderstood. It gives him a point of vantage. . . .
>
> His are all the delicate fopperies of Fashion. One sees that he stands in immediate relation to modern life, makes it indeed, and so masters it. He is the first well-dressed philosopher in the history of thought.

Here dandyism is clearly intended, partly as a mask to hide his secret, inner world of thought, and partly as the symbol of a philosophy of life involving alike rebellious individualism and the art of manners that civilises human contacts.

Elsewhere in his writings dandyism seems to manifest yet other values. In *The Soul of Man Under Socialism,* for instance, Wilde defends his cult of strange clothes as a manifestation of individualism, a symbol of the independence of each man to realise his personality in his own way, and he links it with that true self-expression in life which is too often stigmatised as mere selfishness.

A man is called affected, nowadays, if he dresses as he likes to dress. But in doing that he is acting in a perfectly natural way. Affectation, in such matters, consists in dressing according to the views of one's neighbours, whose views, as they are the views of the majority, will probably be extremely stupid. Or a man is called selfish if he lives in the manner that seems to him most suitable for the full realisation of his personality. But this is the way in which everyone should live. Selfishness is not living as one wishes to live, it is asking others to live as one wishes to live. And unselfishness is letting other people's lives alone, not interfering with them. Selfishness always aims at creating around it an absolute uniformity of type. Unselfishness recognises infinite variety of type as a delightful thing, accepts it, acquiesces in it, enjoys it.

Here we can see how far Wilde considered his exhibitions as manifestations of his own extreme individualism. Indeed, every man who becomes separated from the mass in intellect or feeling tends to act differently from them, and individuality in dress is one way of showing this difference. Wearing brighter colours, allowing the hair to grow longer, assuming beards in a clean-shaven age, are all ways in which artists, and among them many of the best artists, have marked themselves off from their fellow men, without anybody thinking worse of them. Wilde merely carried this tendency to an extreme, but it could be said that his feeling of rebellion was so great that it needed an extreme manifestation. Every attitude towards life that is manifested in action becomes involved in its own form of exhibitionism. Among artists, the most self-conscious poseur is often the man who tries to appear as unlike an artist as possible, to emulate a stockbroker or a horny-handed worker. As Wilde said elsewhere, "Being natural is simply a pose, and the most irritating pose I know."

In *The Picture of Dorian Gray*, where Wilde set out on the dangerous task of examining and justifying himself in the persons of his two principal characters, Dorian Gray is represented as aiming at the achievement of Wilde's own desire to "combine something of the real culture of the scholar with all the grace and distinction and perfect manner of a citizen of the world." He regards life as the greatest art, for which all other arts seem merely preparations, and there is a further insight into Wilde's theories on dandyism and his illusions concerning his own influence on the world of fashion, in this curious passage:

> Fashion, by which what is merely fantastic becomes for a moment universal, and Dandyism, which, in its own way, is an attempt to assert the absolute modernity of beauty, had, of course, their fascination for him. His mode of dressing, and the particular styles that from time to time he affected, had their marked influence on the young exquisites of the Mayfair balls and Pall Mall club windows, who copied him in everything that he did, and tried to reproduce the accidental charm of his graceful, though to him only half-serious fopperies.

Wilde's own fopperies, in fact, had very little influence on the Pall Mall clubmen, young or old, and in Mayfair, for all the popularity of his conversation, he must always have appeared an overdressed and tastelessly ostentatious near-bounder. If his somewhat florid dandyism had any influence at all, it was mostly among the minor literary figures of the time and those middle-class climbers who were even more *parvenu* than he, and mistook his caricature of gentlemanly elegance for the real thing.

Wilde's justifications of dandyism, like all his expressions of ideas, were characterised by a mixture of jesting and earnestness, of paradox and pathos. To begin, he enjoyed the great game of fashion, and it amused him to arouse envy and annoyance by his extravagances. Certainly in some moods he really saw himself as a guardian of taste, as a dictator of manners, and at such times he regarded his dandyism as a serious occupation, to be justified philosophically, to be given a symbolic significance. Dandyism was an expression of the good manners that formed the basis of a social intercourse which had as its first principle a consideration for the feelings and freedom of others; beyond this, and less justifiably, Wilde saw it as a symbol of individual development, of rebellion, even of beauty.

But he was at once too light-hearted and too serious to maintain this absurdity at all consistently. There were times when he clearly recognised his sartorial and social extravagances as merely part of the great game in which he was the leading playboy, and other times when he justified them as a disguise for the deeper and more permanent intentions of his philosophy. He became a clown, it is true, from the fear of his essential earnestness, but he could never suppress that quality, and always, beneath the maddest extravagance or the wildest paradox, hides the social critic, the serious thinker about life, cleverly inserting his destructive theory, using even his nonsense as a means of eating away that complacency which provides so firm an armour for the social conventions. Once again, in *The Picture of Dorian Gray,* we find him elucidating the deeper motives beneath the "half-serious fopperies." He says of his hero, who was at least partly himself:

> . . . In his inmost heart he desired to be something more than a mere *arbiter elegantiarum,* to be consulted on the wearing of a jewel, or the knotting of a necktie, or the conduct of a cane. He sought to elaborate some new scheme of life that would have its reasoned philosophy and its ordered principles, and find in the spiritualising of the senses its highest realisation.

The "new scheme of life," so far as Oscar himself was concerned, was elaborated everywhere in his writings, showing through the glittering paradox of *Intentions,* implicit in his stories, explicit in *The Soul of Man Under Socialism* and in the plays, as well as, one gathers, in his conversation. The character of this philosophy, its religious, moral, social, and critical aspects, have already been discussed in the preceding chapters. Here we are concerned mainly with the way Wilde manifested them in his life.

And we cannot but admit that, because of Oscar's tardy emotional development and his lack of power to realise where the game ended and the serious business of life began, he was not a highly successful example in life of his own philosophical values. He mingled a childish love of the fantastic and the luxurious with a rational scheme of life which, carried to its logical end, would have recognised the pointlessness of excess. He did violence to his own nature by suppressing the impulsive sympathy he felt for pain and suffering. He prepared his downfall by creating vast illusions about his position and power in the world, by grasping after the very kind of influence his own teachings should have brought him to despise. Instead of using experience as a way to inner development, he became its slave. Where he paraded himself as a prophet, he was a charlatan; those aspects of his philosophy which had real value for the outer world he exhibited under an elaborate camouflage of mummery and paradox. He turned his earnest thoughts into the counters in a trivial game, and tried to elevate his absurdities into the pillars of a new life.

No doubt, in its own way, all this was very amusing, and for Oscar himself it may well have served as a fairly successful defence against the depths of his own nature. But the laughter of others was always fraught with more derision than he dared admit to himself. At the debacle it turned to that sinister glee which the Germans call *Schadenfreude,* and for many years he was remembered as the clown destroyed by his own follies, and forgotten as a writer who had made many important contributions to the philosophy of a balanced life.

Yet human nature is mutable; as Wilde himself said, man

is "a being with myriad lives and myriad sensations, a complex multi-form creature that bore within itself strange legacies of thought and passion. . . ." In different circumstances, other aspects of our natures are shown, and at Wilde's downfall the earnest, sensitive and sympathetic being whose impulses had been dissipated in jests and extravagances came into the open, and, in spite of the later backslidings into a poor caricature of his former life of magnificent excess, in many ways retained the ascendancy in his character.

It must be remembered that even at the height of his "glory," the game he played had not been wholly lighthearted. He was too complex for that, and, like a grim ace of spades, there was always that persistent and highly dramatised feeling of fatality, of driving on to a predestined doom, which made his extravagance all the more violent and his laughter at times almost hysterical.

When the crash came, Wilde did not cease to play; at first there was merely an alteration in the game to fit the new circumstances that had entered in, and Oscar's caprices assumed a graver tone. The first day of his ordeal he took lightheartedly, and his duel of words with Carson in the early cross-examinations showed him on the top of his form, thoroughly enjoying the fun as he showed so capably the evident superiority of the elegant literary gentleman over the Philistine lawyer with the unpleasant face and voice. For a time the court, like the theatre, echoed with appreciative laughter at his easy wit. But, unknown to him, Carson's sleeves were packed with a whole covey of black aces, facts obtained by the most sordid devices of private agents and seedy underworld narks, against which Wilde's joker was of little avail. The great game collapsed, and suddenly came crowding in all those terrible factors of defeat, failure, derision, shame, hatred, abuse, and mental agony which he had feared so bitterly, and so assiduously tried to escape in his frantic grasping after joy. All the pain he had avoided for so long descended on him calamitously. He was locked in a prison cell, deprived of all the luxuries he had been enjoying up to the hour before, even of cigarettes, and subjected to the gloating scrutiny of newspaper men, who were now having their grim revenge for the contempt he had expressed towards them in the past. His beautiful home was seized by creditors, and all the treasured books and paintings which had formed his elegant background were sold for a fraction of their value, while a milling crowd of sightseers trampled through his rooms and stole or destroyed his manuscripts. Publishers removed his books from their lists, and the comedies which had been so successful were abruptly taken off the stage. No downfall had ever been more complete; from fortune and popularity one day, he fell literally to destitution and infamy the next.

There followed the nightmare of his release on bail, when he trailed through London from hotel to hotel, with all doors closed against him and a gang of hired thugs on his heels, until in the end he found unwilling refuge in his mother's house and submitted to the triumph of his drunkenly self-righteous brother.

For a while Oscar seemed wholly crushed. But even in his most bitter hours he was still able to play a feeble shadow of a game, for he would repeat to Sherard, "Robert, why have you brought me no poison from Paris?"

There was perhaps a touch of exhibitionism, as well as a yielding to the crazy family pride and his own sense of fatality, in his decision to stand his trial. Yet at the same time there appeared in his attitude a new element of fortitude. By the time of his last appearance he was able to face his destiny with the bearing of a man fortified by an inner resignation, a philosophy that defied misfortune. Yeats, among others, tells that while many of his so-called friends deserted him at this time, there were others, men who had formerly distrusted or contemned him, who suddenly discovered qualities of "audacity and self-possession" that aroused their respect. One old enemy spoke in praise of Wilde's attitude, and said: "He has made of infamy a new Thermopylæ."

Prison was a desolating experience, particularly in a gaol environment infinitely more harsh than that of modern prisons. There was no work in association; the men were locked in their cells twenty-three hours of the day, and during the one hour of exercise they were not allowed to talk. The food was inadequate and foul, "skilly" being the chief item of the diet, and the medical provisions were crude and primitive. A meagre library was in the charge of a narrow-minded chaplain, and no paper was allowed for writing. Add to this the fact that in the early days of his imprisonment Wilde found himself under hostile governors, and warders who used every breach of the rules as an excuse to punish him, add again the personal humiliation of his position, the misery of the break-up of his family, the bitter knowledge that only a mere handful of his former friends had remained faithful, the certainty that when he left prison he would become a dependent pauper, and one can imagine the depths into which this sensitive and proud man was plunged.

But gradually, after he had contemplated suicide and thought he would become insane, he began to find a kernel of consolation even in such misery. He found among his fellow prisoners a common humanity; in sympathy, in solidarity, he found the strength that supported him. The Cell neighbours who sought to encourage him, the few warders who secretly helped him with kindly words, and even tried with gifts of "Scotch scones, meat-pies and sausage rolls" to allay the hunger of the former habitué of Kettner's and the Café Royal, lent him a new insight into human nature. Without laying aside his individualism, he began to realise the Christian truth of pity, to know that even pain can have its value in personal development, that pleasure is, in fact, only one side of the garden of life and cannot of itself make a man whole. He lived through an ever-renewed terror and at times he felt that the world to which he had to return would be no better—"there are times when the whole world seems to me no larger than my cell and as full of terror for me." But he also came to the belief that "at the beginning God made a world for each separate man, and in that world which is within us we should seek to live." In suffering, his latent mysticism was becoming manifest.

Those who knew him in prison observed the almost saintly patience and fortitude with which he bore his sufferings, and the lack of rancour towards his enemies became steadily more pronounced. It is true that he had lapses, like the section of *De Profundis* where he made a hysterical and exaggerated attack on Douglas. It is also true that in *De Profundis* there is a great deal of self-dramatisation. But when all this is taken into account, there was still evident a sincere humility and a love for mankind which persisted in the days after his release. In the pages of this curious autobiographical letter he tells us how he "passed through every mode of suffering" and had come to learn its necessity. Out of the consciousness of the meaning of suffering he had attained Humility.

> It is the last thing left in me, and the best; the ultimate discovery at which I have arrived, the starting-point for a fresh development. . . . It is the one thing that has in it the elements of life, of a new life, a *Vita Nuova* for me. . . .
> . . . I am far more of an individualist than I ever was. Nothing seems to me of the smallest value except what one gets out of oneself. My nature is seeking a fresh mode of self-realisation. That is all I am concerned with. And the first thing that I have got to do is to free myself from any possible bitterness of feeling against the world.

After saying that he is now penniless and homeless, he says he would rather become a beggar than go out from prison with bitterness in his heart. For "the external things of life seem to me now of no importance at all," and in realising this he has reached a greater intensity of individualism than ever before.

> There is much more before me. I have hills far steeper to climb, valleys much darker to pass through. And I have to get it all out of myself. Neither religion, morality, nor reason can help me at all.

It is clear that, whatever Wilde expected of himself, it was not so much as some of his friends, in their disappointment, seem to have anticipated. The change he perceived was only internally fundamental, and towards the external world it was to be expressed in attitude rather than in action. Action, indeed, was not precluded, but Wilde's main concern seemed to view the world with love and understanding, instead of with the hostility and resentment which come only too easily to a man in his position. Naturally, he hoped to achieve more, but he did not expect too much of himself, for he wrote to Ross from prison, after finishing *De Profundis:*

> Of course I need not remind you how fluid a thing thought is with me—with us all—and of what an evanescent substance are our emotions made. Still, I do see a sort of possible goal towards which, through art, I may progress.

Only a *possible* goal *towards* which he hoped to progress! And that much he at least succeeded in doing, for his inner attainment of personal resignation and the solid achievement of *The Ballad of Reading Gaol* cannot be counted as nothing in striking the balance of his life.

But he refused to delude himself that he could accept a discipline foreign to his nature. In prison he read Stevenson's letters and expressed his disappointment, saying that he found in them—

> . . . the traces of a terrible strain to lead a natural life. To chop wood with any advantage to oneself or profit to others, one should not be able to describe the process. In point of fact the natural life is the unconscious life. Steven-

son merely extended the sphere of the artificial by taking in digging. The whole dreary book has given me a lesson. If I spend my future life reading Baudelaire in a café, I shall be leading a more natural life than if I take up a hedger's work or plant cacao in mud-swamps.

However, his new attitude was not merely negative. He was filled with righteous anger at the injustices he had seen in prison, and regarded himself as obliged to do what he could to aid his fellow prisoners. It is significant that all the work he succeeded in producing after his release was centred round the sufferings of imprisoned men. He also tried to help individually those he had encountered in gaol, and there exists a revealing little note which he wrote surreptitiously to one of the warders at Reading, and which shows the cynic of the 1890's in an unexpectedly tender light.

Please find out for me the name of A.2.11.[1] Also: the names of the children who are in for the rabbits, and the amount of the fine.

Can I pay this and get them out? If so I will get them out to-morrow. Please dear friend do this for me. I must get them out.

Think what a thing it would be for me to be able to help three little children. I wd. be delighted beyond words: if I can do this by paying the fine tell the children that they are to be released to-morrow by a friend, and ask them to be happy and not to tell anyone.

The story of Wilde's exile is sufficiently well known for me merely to trace its outlines. There was the first period of tranquillity and confidence, when he lived simply in the little Norman sea-coast village of Berneval-sur-Mer. Then followed a reconciliation with Douglas and a period of work at Naples, when *The Ballad of Reading Gaol* was written, followed by

[1] A.2.11 was a weak-minded prisoner named Prince who had been persistently punished and even flogged for breaking the prison regulations. Wilde was horrified at the treatment given to this unfortunate man, and after his own release brought the case before the public in one of his letters to the *Daily Chronicle*.

the return to Paris and the gradual lapsing into Bohemian ways, dogged by an implacable social ostracism and a sense of frustration at being unable to return to his old position as a writer. And finally, the fatalistic acceptance of a death that might at least have been postponed if he had not persisted in a deliberately suicidal course of alcoholism.

It all sounds very sordid, and several of Wilde's biographers and former friends have chosen to present this last period in its worst light, in order to show that the promises made in the published sections of *De Profundis* were not in fact kept.

Douglas gives a most malicious picture, saying of Wilde:

> He became a sort of show for the Bohemians of Paris; the sport and mock of the boulevard and the reproach of English letters in the City of Light. He got his dinners on credit, and borrowed money from waiters. His health was on the down grade in consequence of the intensification by alcohol of a terrible disease he had contracted. He took to weeping and cursing at the slightest provocation, and, though his wit would flare out and his learning remained with him to the last, it was a poor wreck and shadow of himself which I saw from time to time when I went to Paris on various occasions in the year 1900.

This is a wholly distorted representation, if we are to judge from the statements of most of the people who knew Wilde at this time. If he had to live on credit, it was the fault of the society that had deprived him of the chance of living by his pen, and if he wept, he had surely been given cause to weep! But, far from Wilde being a shadow of his former self, those who have described these last days objectively agree, as I have already shown, that his conversation was never more profound or expansive, while the accusation of "cursing," presumably meaning recrimination over the past, is contrary to everything we know of Wilde's resignation. It seems more likely that Douglas provoked Wilde beyond endurance with his own petulance, and then put the blame where it did not belong.

Harris's account is less malicious, and seems to contain at least a proportion of truth, though it also deserves criticism:

Oscar's second fall—this time from a height—was fatal and made writing impossible to him. It is all clear enough now in retrospect, though I did not understand it at the time. When he went to live with Bosie Douglas he threw off the Christian attitude, but afterwards had to recognise that De Profundis and The Ballad of Reading Gaol were deeper and better work than any of his earlier writings. He resumed the pagan position; outwardly and for the time being he was the old Oscar again, with his Greek love of beauty and hatred of disease, deformity and ugliness, and wherever he met a kindred spirit, he absolutely revelled in gay paradoxes and brilliant flashes of humour. But he was at war with himself, like Milton's Satan always conscious of his fall, always regretful of his lost estate, and by reason of this division of spirit unable to write. Perhaps because of this he threw himself more than ever into talk.

Although these ideas are at least more just than those of Douglas, they do not give any really satisfactory explanation of Wilde's conduct. To begin, Harris's statement is based on recollection. When he was associating with Wilde during the last years in France, De Profundis had as yet been seen only by Ross and an anonymous typist, and therefore Harris had then no opportunity of comparing Wilde's conduct with the philosophy of the book, and never thought of it in this connection. By the time he wrote his Life, his memory of the whole period had grown dim; as we have seen, he filled out the book with scenes, of which some certainly cannot have taken place, and others seem so romantically Harrisian that their authenticity may justly be doubted.

Nevertheless, it is certainly true that Wilde took to drinking heavily and almost ceased to write, while he also appears to have resumed his homosexual activities, though Sherard's inquiries at the Préfecture of Police showed that his actions had not been sufficiently open to attract the attention of the French authorities.

But it must also be remembered that he had every excuse to drink, for life left him very little but the pleasures of talking and physical satisfaction. Nor had he explicitly renounced such a life. What he had blamed himself for was the complete slavery to sensation and sensuality, in which he had been involved before his downfall. But to that life he never returned. The old ostentation was gone, and he seemed to live far more in his thoughts than he had ever done before. A deeply contemplative vein appears in the records of his last conversations, and his attitude was marked, towards others by tolerance and sympathy, towards his own misfortunes by fortitude and forbearance. If he drank excessively, it was a private way of blunting his sorrows, but in general he was at no time so admirable in his personal life as in these last days when he bore his trials without a word of malice. That he should have lapsed into drink or sexual perversion is irrelevant to the fact that he did maintain much of what he had gained in inward grace.

Nevertheless, in these last days he jested almost as much as ever. The playboy was by no means dead, and in the right company he would take up again the old game of fantasy and nonsense. But it was no longer the light play of the triumphant dandy governing the world through its dining tables. Now it was the sombre game of the great failure, enacted in that city dedicated as much to failure as to success, and it may not be altogether far-fetched to suggest that many of Wilde's relapses at this time were prompted by his consciousness of playing the last round in his great game of life, the last act in the greatest of Oscar Wilde's plays.

But there was one type of game for which he could find little zest. He was no longer able to write with any ease, and it is interesting to speculate on the reason for this, particularly as the legend of Wilde as a broken-down man has been wholly discredited.

Clearly, as we can judge from his letters immediately after release, he intended to resume work as soon as he had found his feet, and he did write one work that was unique in his own record and also in English poetry. But it was to be his last.

Already, before completing *The Ballad of Reading Gaol*, he had said: "I am not in the mood to do the work I want, and I fear I never shall be. The intense energy of creation has been kicked out of me. I don't care to struggle to get back what, when I had it, gave me so little pleasure." He managed to finish his poem, but afterwards he began to feel the labour of writing was beyond him. "Something is killed in me," he said. "I feel no desire to write—I am unconscious of power." And towards the end of his life Sherard found him listlessly trying to work, and drew forth the remark: "One has to do something. I have no taste for it now. It is a penance to me; but, as was said of torture, it always helps one to pass an hour or two."

How had this urge been killed in Wilde? Was it, as Harris suggested, the struggle between paganism and Christianity? Internal struggle is usually productive rather than sterile, and in my opinion the cause of Wilde's failure to write was much more simple.

He was always an artist of the type to whom an audience is necessary. Essentially a talker, he needed the stimulus of listeners, and his books or plays interested him only in so far as they expanded the circle. The actual work of writing had never given him great pleasure; it was merely the recording of conversation for a wider group, and as it became less like conversation it became less good.

But now few people wanted to read his work, and he was not the man to write merely for posterity. The reception of

The Ballad of Reading Gaol had been extremely poor, and his plays, printed courageously by Smithers, an eccentric publisher with a smutty reputation, raised hardly a ripple in the literary world. His reputation as a writer was clearly dormant; it even seemed dead, and he found no object in trying to rebuild it. "I have had my hand on the moon," he said. "What is the use of trying to rise a little way from the ground?"

So he accepted his fortune and, with a philosopher's equanimity, contented himself with the audience that remained. Among a handful of friends, he talked with more eloquence than he had ever done before, and left to a few failing memories that conversation in whose scattered fragments we seem to see the evidence of his finest and most mature work.

Let us return to the original problem. Was Wilde a playboy? Was he a prophet? A playboy he certainly was, but in a far deeper manner than his critics imagined, for all life and literature were included in his game, and he played as often earnestly as he did frivolously. A prophet? Hardly in the true meaning of the word. On the other hand, he came very near to being a seer, for he saw with a remarkable insight into the heart of problems over which other men had pondered long, and flashed off his enlightenment in some smart epigram or graceful parable. A sage he was also, in so far as he found wisdom in folly, and learnt in the end how to accept life and grow mild and mellow in inaction. And there was just enough of the saint in him to make him a noble example of that Christian fortitude which is rarest among those who profess Christianity.

But all these things he was partially and imperfectly; at times the seer, the sage and the saint suddenly found themselves caught up in the game of make-believe, just as at other times the play would shade off into earnestness and wisdom blossom out of paradox and pose.

THE CONTRADICTIONS RESOLVED

WILDE, from whatever aspect we observe him, appears as a man of continual variety and contradiction. On the surface he is all movement and change, shifting fitfully from one mood to another, dispensing an iridescence so patently superficial that those who have never taken the trouble to penetrate below the surface dismiss him as an obvious charlatan. But beneath the glittering ripples there are depths of thought and feeling, stirred by conflicts rising from the same basic impulse towards personal realisation. Thus it is that, among those who knew Wilde personally and also among those who have encountered him only in his writings and his legend, there seems an almost irreconcilable divergence of attitudes.

Some men who knew Wilde saw only the triviality of his social manner and dismissed him as a mere poseur. Others, to whom he revealed himself more fully, were convinced of the essential greatness of his nature. Similarly, of those who have read his writing, some have dismissed it as imitative trash, but others have discovered in it what they regard as the indubitable signs of genius.

He was clearly a greater personality than a writer, and this was perhaps inevitable, since writing was only one of the fields in which his vast energy was involved. Already I have quoted Henley's definition of Wilde as the "sketch of a great man," but here it must be stressed that the sketch was on a large scale, and that, while some parts of it were but roughly drawn, there were others almost superbly finished.

It was, indeed, the very breadth of Wilde's ambitions that prevented him from achieving real greatness in any one sphere, except perhaps as a conversationalist and dramatist. It has been given to only a few men, like Leonardo da Vinci, to become universal geniuses. Wilde was not among them, and perhaps that was his greatest tragedy. But that he did not realise this ambition, that he did not in fact become the perfect manifestation of the spirit of his age, should not blind us to the fact that he approached nearer to this goal than most of his contemporaries. Except in his own fields of conversation and dramatic writing, which was little more than a recording of his conversation, there were men in England then who were his superiors in every single activity he attempted. As poet, critic, novelist, social theoretician, philosopher, revolutionist, he was amply excelled in that age of massive intellects and vigorous characters. But when we consider the energy and talent spread over all the activities in which he engaged, it is doubtful if, as a whole personality, any of them was his real superior. Perhaps the most just of all the brief estimates of Wilde's stature is that of Charles Ricketts: "In intellect and humanity he is the largest type I have come across. Other greater men in my time were great in some one thing, not large in their very texture."

It was this *largeness* that could include all his contradictory trends of thought and action, but it was his inability to reach an external reconciliation of these contradictions, to bring them into a final synthesis in life, that represented his ultimate failure, that made him the sketch rather than the finished picture of greatness.

Arthur Symons has put forward the contention that it was

his attitudes rather than his achievements that were important.

This opinion does not seem wholly just to Wilde, since it tends to minimise all his positive achievements, and to negate the actual importance of his writings, both in their own right and in relation to the literature of his age. Nevertheless, it is true that Wilde was greater in intentions than in attainments, and that in these intentions we can see the real quality of his genius, purged of all the follies and weaknesses into which he fell in his daily life. Never did he find the way to express in his writing all that lay within him, and it is not without significance that the work which contains most of himself should itself be called *Intentions*, for it holds the promise of all that was never achieved.

Yet it might be said that Wilde was more effective in his half-fulfilled ambitions than most other men in their completed acts for, by the very vastness of the ideas he presented so sketchily to his age, he stamped his personality on English literature, and, acting catalytically, initiated many changes in writing and thought that were to be completed by other minds and other hands.

Not only did he leave English literature as a whole different from what he found it, but his influence was evident in almost every field of writing. And this can be admitted without disputing the manifest imperfections of his own work, for his importance was, essentially, that of a forerunner, who breaks down obstacles and makes straight the path that others must tread. Thus he is to be seen most significantly as a critic, though in the orthodox sense he was hardly a critic at all.

For he was not a great creative artist, since he preferred to adapt and appropriate the work of other men. Yet nothing he borrowed failed to assume his character. His poems carry undeniable traces of Swinburne, Rossetti and Matthew Arnold; *Salome* is taken largely from Maeterlinck and Flaubert; *The Picture of Dorian Gray* from Maturin and Balzac, with a garnishing of the French decadents; his fairy stories derive from Hans Andersen; his prose style from Pater; his comedies from Scribe, Dumas *fils* and Sheridan. All this can be admitted readily, and Wilde would probably have attempted no denial. Yet, with the exception of some of his early poems, all of these works have a strongly original strain in them, and, for all their obvious borrowings and undisguised influences, they could not have been written by anyone but Wilde. Taking the styles and ideas of his masters, he transmuted and changed them by the process which he himself would probably have called "creative criticism." His works can stand in their own right, and, while some of them are inferior to their originals, there are others, particularly his comedies, so evidently superior as to make all the reproaches of imitation both pointless and ridiculous.

Admittedly, when we examine them from a purely literary criterion, they are not of a consistent excellence. Stylistically, they are often spoilt by over-elaboration or careless haste. *The Picture of Dorian Gray,* for instance, is in many ways an absurd story, while from a formal point of view it is badly proportioned. In addition, the writing is often slipshod, and at times declines into a melodramatic sensationalism which shows that Wilde had not wholly broken with some of the worst faults of Victorian sentimentality. Moreover, it has an almost adolescent self-consciousness; Wilde plays with his wit and his jewelled language with all the naïve virtuosity of a boy of twenty—a singularly accomplished boy of twenty, it must be granted. Some of the stories he preserved in collections, like *The Sphinx Without a Secret* and *The Model Millionaire,* are no more than good magazine pieces, while much of his fiction suffers from a verbose turgidity which does not appear in his conversational stories. Except for some few lyrics like "Tread softly" and "Hélas," his poems are uninspired, though accomplished, reaching a showy virtuosity in *The Sphinx* and *The Harlot's House,* but only contributing anything of real importance to English poetry in the astonishing *Ballad of Reading Gaol*. His criticism, where he troubled to be accurate, was always good, but here again he sometimes allowed his love of paradox to lead him into absurdities no scholarly critic would have perpetrated. His prose style varied widely between the crisp neatness of his epigrammatic dialogue and the sagging slovenliness of those passages in which he took richness of vocabulary as a substitute for style, or drowned all style under the weight of jewelled affectation. Sometimes, as in *Salome*, his decorative technique was worked into a sufficiently close pattern to produce an impressive effect, but usually it spoilt a work that would have been better for a more ascetic form. The lapses into an ornamental style in an essay whose very nature demanded a direct and simple argument marred a great deal of *The Soul of Man Under Socialism*, while the semi-poetical rhapsodies that mingle with its flashing wit undoubtedly gave to *Intentions* an unnecessary appearance of stylistic affectation.

Wilde was at his best in dialogue, and above all in his comedies. Yet it is only in *The Importance of Being Earnest* that his verbal wit and satirical criticism of manners are allowed free play, unalloyed by sentimentality and unhindered by those melodramatic conventions which he seems to have had difficulty in abandoning. The hackneyed devices of fans and gloves and brooches around which the plots are woven, the tedious Victorian themes of self-sacrificing mothers and injured wives which Wilde retained in all these early comedies, are in themselves banal enough, but when we come to such atrocious fragments as Mrs. Arbuthnot's exclamation in *A Woman of No Importance*, "Child of my shame, be still the child of my shame!" we must believe either that Oscar's ironic fun had run away with him and descended into burlesque, or that he really liked this kind of cheap effect, and that when his sentimental self perpetrated it, his critical self must have been looking the other way. Indeed, Wilde's early comedies, with their curious mingling of naïve sentimentality and sophisticated wit, are clear examples of his essentially schizoid nature.

Wilde's sentimentality perhaps reaches its most irritating depth in *De Profundis*. Yet one cannot deny the quality of some of the thought in this curious book, or claim that, taken in general, it is not a piece of good writing which at times attains both eloquence and directness. It is this peculiar combination of mawkishness and clean wit that gives Wilde's writing its appearance of insincerity, as well as its imperfection of technique. It is impossible not to criticise the overdone phraseology and unbalanced construction; it is also difficult to imagine that a man of acutely satirical wit could really be in earnest when he descended into gross sensationalism, or that a critic who could assess the faults and virtues of his fellow writers with such concise rapidity should have been so lacking in self-criticism as not to see how he had spoilt, for example, his *Poems in Prose* by sheer Birmingham bad taste of over-elaboration.

Yet the impression of insincerity, despite Wilde's own attacks on the cult of sincerity, is illusory. The very cleavage in his personality that was evident in all his other activities occurred also in his style, mingling effervescent wit and the heaviest sentimentality. When he was talking and had to keep within the limits of that art of conversation which he mastered so well, the lack of balance was not evident and the same thing can be said of those recorded conversations, his plays. But where he took pains, and was not subjected to limitations of time and taste imposed by an audience, the dual tendencies of his mind had full play, and one was as genuine as the other.

It was this mutability of nature, this continual swinging between two poles of character, that deprived Wilde of the singleness of mind necessary for a really great writer. Only rarely did some consistent impulse support him through any single work, but on such rare occasions the result was an unadulterated masterpiece, like *The Importance of Being Earnest* or *The Happy Prince*.

Yet this same mutability was the very quality which gave versatility and, more important, power of insight. It was this that made Wilde's work potential, or perhaps intentional, rather than giving the qualities of complete achievement. And this very intentional and tentative character made his writing more suggestive than it would otherwise have been, so that, while the more complete artists of his day, like Meredith and Pater, wield their influence only in a limited circle, the influence of Wilde, who, for all his talk, was never so much an artist as a desultory thinker using or misusing the forms of art, has been wide and pervasive.

In this chapter I have perhaps gone to an extreme in criticising Wilde's writing to counter the undue adulation it has received from his disciples, but at the same time I consider that there are few writers of his time whose work stands out so much from the mass of Victorian literature by its distinctive quality. And certainly in those occasional passages where he rises above his imperfections, he writes as well as any of his contemporaries. Whole sections of *The Critic as Artist*, much of *Salome* and the fairy stories, and most of *The Ballad of Reading Gaol* are enough to give Wilde a permanent position in English literature on their own merits. And his comedies remain some of the best work that has come on the English stage since Sheridan.

The peak of Wilde's dramatic achievement, and the one piece of writing in which he came nearest to artistic perfection, was *The Importance of Being Earnest*, of which the critic A. B. Walkley said, with justice: "It is of nonsense all compact, and better nonsense, I think, our stage has not seen." *The Importance of Being Earnest* is indeed unique in English dramatic literature; so far as it has any ancestors, they are to be found in those last and most whimsical of Restoration wits, Congreve and Vanbrugh, but even *Love for Love,* with all its passages of equally stimulating nonsense, has a sufficiently rational basis to place it in a quite different category.

Sometimes his influence was bad, as when his decorative style, which even in his own hands was not always successful, tempted younger writers to abandon simplicity for a pointless elaboration. But more often it was a liberating one, opening literary forms and ways of thought to new ideas and techniques.

Undoubtedly he was the greatest influence in restoring genuine comedy to the English stage. Shaw was almost as much influenced by him as by Ibsen, and had Wilde lived and continued to write for the theatre, there is no doubt that Shaw's prestige would never have reached its present magnitude. It was Wilde's reintroduction of the comedy of wit and satire that opened the minds of theatrical audiences to the kind of social drama which Shaw produced, but even more effectively it detached the stage from melodrama and brought comedy back to its genuine function of an ironical or satirical commentary on life.

In *Salome* Wilde introduced to the English public that type of poetic drama which Maeterlinck was already popularising in France, and this play, rejected by English religious prejudice, became the occasion for Reinhardt on the Continent to introduce the new stage techniques which started a whole series of revolutionary alterations in the theatrical art.

In his dialogues Wilde broadened the scope of criticism and helped to destroy the Victorian conception of realism and replace it by a renewed idea of the function of imagination in art. At the same time, in *The Ballad of Reading Gaol,* he showed how realism itself could be imaginative, and gave an example of how ideas could be used didactically in a work of art without destroying its formal qualities.

He brought the story back to a balanced use of fantasy and symbol, of idea and form, and, in his conversation at least, gave fiction a new simplicity. His stories have found their echoes in remote places, and writers like D. H. Lawrence and Evelyn Waugh are among those in his debt, while his influence on the English fairy story was radical and lasting.

But in considering this question of Wilde's influence, it must not be forgotten that, until very recent years, the reputation and respect he had enjoyed in European countries has been far greater than in England or America. Whether we regard it as a good thing or not, to the German, French or Italian student of literature Wilde stands among the great English writers, while to the reading and theatre-going public of these countries he is certainly more familiar and more popular than any Anglo-Saxon dramatist except Shakespeare and, in later years, Shaw.

This—as it may seem to us—exaggerated continental reputation is due at least in part to the way in which the scandal of Wilde's case fitted in with Anglophobe feeling at the end of the nineteenth century. To countries where the tradition of the Code Napoleon had left a more tolerant legal and moral attitude towards the sexual acts of the individual, it seemed monstrous that a writer worthy of his country's respect should have been treated so savagely for such an offence, while the hostility felt towards England over the Boer War helped to increase the repute of a man who was regarded by many people as the most distinguished victim of English perfidy. The fact that he ended his life in exile only helped to increase this continental idea of him as a kind of Prometheus figure, and it is significant that the most sensational stories of Wilde's misery and poverty in his last years came from French writers.

But, however much the first impulse towards the Wilde cult on the Continent may have been due to a political accident, it must be admitted that it could not have gained such proportions and permanence from this alone, and that there was something in Wilde's writing that appealed particularly to the continental literary taste. No doubt it was in part the fact that he himself was so imbued with French influences that his work often read like a translation from the French, while his Gothicism may have made some appeal to German readers. But there are two factors which seem to me even more important. Firstly, his style had a certain lush ornateness, a lack of English restraint, which has always been more appreciated abroad than in Britain. And, secondly, in a German public already used to the nihilism of writers like Nietzsche, Wilde's destructive epigrams must have found an appreciative audience.

Whatever other reasons may be adduced, Wilde's continental success was rapid and sweeping. In 1896, while he was still in prison, *Salome*, which had not yet appeared in England, was produced in Paris. During the next decade his works began to be published widely in every country in Europe, and by 1905 his standing was assured by two important events. Already *Salome* had become a popular play in Germany, for Reinhardt made his reputation by producing it at the Kleines Theater in Berlin, but in that year the leading German composer, Richard Strauss, added to his own and Wilde's reputations by using it as the libretto for an opera which was produced in Berlin. So much enthusiasm was aroused over this event, even before the actual production, that the Kaiser attended the rehearsals and is actually said to have made suggestions on technical points of staging. In the same year, through the instrumentality of Dr. Meyerfeld, a critic who assiduously defended Wilde's literary reputation, *De Profundis* was actually published in a German translation before it appeared in England. From that time the sale of Wilde's books on the Continent reached such proportions that in a couple of years all his creditors were paid off by the faithful Ross. It is impossible to reach any kind of true estimate of the literary and philosophical influence of Wilde's writings on the Continent, but it is certain that it has been greater than that of any other contemporary English writer except Shaw.

Perhaps even more than in his writing, Wilde's influence lies in the free play of his ideas and his ability to express provocative thoughts in a brief and stimulating manner. When we glance through his books, or read the fragmentary records of his conversation, we are made aware of a host of ideas which may seem banal in our own day, but which do so precisely because, largely through Wilde's influence, they have become current coin among us. Considered in relation to the Victorian era in which Wilde lived, they show him as a daring and liberal thinker whose propaganda for clear thought and tolerance was accompanied by many fruitful suggestions on particular aspects of life.

When psychology was in its infancy, he anticipated Freud and the neo-Freudians by proclaiming the unhealthy nature of repressed impulses. When Fabianism was the height of political fashion and nobody had yet seen State Socialism at work, Wilde was a Socialist who perceived the danger of authority, and proclaimed that any Socialism which would be beneficial to individual men must be based on voluntary co-operation. In *The Soul of Man Under Socialism* he anticipated the whole of Tolstoy's message in his last pamphlets, and before he himself had ever been in prison he realised that punishment defeated its own end by actually producing crime, while he saw the intimate connection between crime and property. When the enlightened were mostly abject worshippers of the new religion of science, he was able to indicate its great weakness, that it "can never grapple with the irrational," and therefore has no future as a salvation for the world. He exposed the current cant about the dignity of labour, and showed that it was merely a means of excusing class domination; therefore, since men are too good for many of the degrading things they are forced to do, he demanded the increased use of machinery, not for profit, but to release men from toil. In his comments on education he condemned the pedagogic methods current in his time, and indicated the value of art as a means of education, thus anticipating the theories put forward in our own day by Herbert Read. He spoke for the equality of men and women, but did not imagine that any such reform as female suffrage was likely to solve this problem. Instead, he declared that the solution lay in the liberation of both men and women from the chains laid upon them by custom and law.

These are only a few of the ways in which Wilde showed himself conscious of the most vital currents of his time. He did not choose to become an intensive propagandist for any of these causes, for such consistency was not in his nature, until the vast experience of imprisonment united for a while the struggling aspects of his character in a protest against the horrors which those in authority will wreak upon the unfortunate men in their power.

But in these ideas, flung off almost casually, with the slightly grotesque gesture of an intellectual gentleman scattering abroad the largesse of his wisdom, Wilde had a greater influence on his time than many men whose work in some of these individual spheres had been painstaking, but had remained obscure because of their very single-mindedness. Perhaps at times Wilde borrowed from these men, but he dispensed freely and "popularised," in the good sense of that word, many ideas which would otherwise have remained longer in obscurity. To the old he most often proved an irritant and, if this did not lead to their conversion, it at least made it easier to define for the young, to whom he was a liberating influence, the struggle against outworn convention.

His personal follies, his downfall through the supreme inconsistency of claiming protection from a society which he despised, seemed for a while to cover in obloquy and contempt the values he had represented. Yet in this very tomb of infamy he gained the experience that was to impel him to speak once again to the world, this time with all his latent earnestness, in the name of all men crushed under the pitiless heel of authority. It was a voice crying from the depths, that would not be silenced. Unheard in the last years of his life, in the days of his death its message began to spread over the earth, into lands where Wilde had certainly never been known when he was alive. And, crowning irony, out of the grave where his enemies thought they had buried him for ever, arose that strange Brocken spectre into which his fame has grown in the last half-century, that mythical saint with the cloven hooves who has actually become in the minds of men the symbolic figure Wilde was misguided enough to imagine himself in life. Indeed, the Wilde legend has been itself a vindication of his own theory of life imitating art, since it was Wilde himself who first suggested that he was a symbolic figure, and life which afterwards made him one.

Indeed, one very significant result of his influence has been the way in which society itself has made him a curious materialisation of so many of the suppressed hopes of men. Wilde, more than any other writer, represents the sins men dare not commit, the wit they cannot speak. He represents the liberation they are seeking vainly to achieve. And all this, not because he was a man who himself gained liberation, but because his search for it was on so impressive a scale, because his intentions were so vast.

In one way, Wilde is a kind of latter-day representation, on an intellectual plane, of the Till Eulenspiegel myth. There is much in him of the classic fool whose antics are the mask for a biting criticism of established values, and whose vagaries disguise an essential wisdom. It is this element of folly that has caught the imagination, and has helped to give Wilde the influence his achievements as a writer would not have deserved.

In this way, he has become an influence over successive generations of youth. To many thousands of young men and women he has provided a key to at least partial liberation, an opening to new vistas of thought. The very fact that they should pass rapidly beyond "the Wilde stage" is a sign of the stimulating nature of his ideas. And that quality itself arises out of the impulses within his nature which motivated his restless shifting, his apparent inconsistencies and contradictions, all finally united in the search for personal liberation.

For the essential link in Wilde's thought and action, the goal to which all his intentions turn, is to be found in his doctrine and practice of individualism. Around this idea of the individual human being, the autonomous and free personality, all his activities revolve, and from it stem, on one side or the other, his apparently contradictory tendencies. At the height of his pleasure-seeking folly, in the depths of his pitiful suffering, in his arrogance and his humility, he still sought the free development of his own self. In the pagan worship of pleasure and the Christian cult of pain he finds alike an essentially personal salvation; but Jesus and the Greek philosophers are valid for him only in so far as they are prophets of individualism, while in the inaction preached by the Chinese sages he sees the way for each man to become perfect. The impulse of art and thought he seeks within, and to the inner world of the imagination he gives a far deeper importance than to the external world of society, which is merely the background against which the individual acts his drama; criticism is primarily a way in which human consciousness can be extended. The general values of social morals he despises, but the code of manners that smooths the intercourse of equal individuals he values, while in Socialism he sees a means to divest the individual of those burdens of property and power which prevent him from realising his own nature. His very debaucheries and follies are means of individual experience, and therefore, while they may be rejected, should never be regretted. Each man, declares Wilde, should seek to make himself perfect, but he can do this only from within, by living in the personal world that has been given to him and by following his own inner laws and impulses.

To this one belief he held consistently in all his apparent inconsistencies of life. It became the standard by which he measured all life and thought and art; it became his single rule of conduct and determined his philosophy.

And, in the last analysis, when we have considered all his various acts and attitudes, it is here that Wilde's real value remains, in his consistently maintained search for the liberation of the human personality from all the trammels that society and custom have laid upon it. All the rest is intentions, the intentions of a man struggling to realise his own greatness, and finding it completely only in failure.

INTRODUCTION

OSCAR WILDE was born in Dublin in 1854. His father was a celebrated oculist and archæologist, his mother a devoted Irish nationalist who, under her pen name of " Speranza," had caused a major sensation by calling on the Irish people to rise up in arms and drive the alien masters from Dublin Castle.

Of Wilde's subsequent life, his achievements as a writer and a conversational wit, his savage punishment for homosexual activities and his death as an exile in Paris during 1900, there are enough readily available accounts, and in this introduction it will be sufficient to indicate the development of his social attitude.

The real beginnings of Wilde's social consciousness can perhaps be traced to the influence of John Ruskin, whom Wilde encountered as an undergraduate at Oxford. Ruskin was then at the height of his period of political criticism, and showed an intense, if at times somewhat futile, activity in trying to give practical effect to his ideas of social renovation.

Among his schemes was an attempt to use the voluntary labour of undergraduates for building a road over the Hinksey marsh near Oxford. In this abortive effort the road finished in the middle of the swamp ; Wilde was one of the labourers, and, while the experience did not diminish his respect for Ruskin, it made him realise, unlike such Ruskinians as Toynbee, that a fundamentally unjust society could not be reformed by mere philanthropic tinkering.

While he was yet at Oxford, Wilde wrote a number of poems showing sympathy for revolutionary ideas and movements, but perhaps at this time the most solid contribution to his social ideas was the realisation of art's function in everyday life. This formed the basis of a famous lecture tour in America which, in spite of Wilde's " aesthetic " platform affectations, is said to have had some real influence in civilising American furnishing styles.

At this period Wilde showed considerable interest in the Russian revolutionary movements of the time, and actually wrote a play, *Vera, or the Nihilists,* of which he said :

" I have tried in it to express within the limits of art that Titan cry of the peoples for liberty, which in Europe of today is threatening thrones and making governments unstable from Spain to Russia, and from North to Southern seas."

The play was not a success ; it was acted in New York, but its performance in London was shelved owing to the assassination of the Tsar Alexander II.

In subsequent years Wilde showed a steady interest in social matters. He did not take an active part in political affairs, because he saw little object in doing so, but *The Soul of Man under Socialism* is by no means the only work in which he makes acute criticism of the class society of his time or praises rebellion against authority. Some of his stories, like *The Young King,* have a subversive undertone, *The Picture of Dorian Gray*

criticises the attitude of philanthropists who attempt
to mend fundamental defects in society by superficial
reforms, while his four comedies all have strong
elements of social satire, which in *An Ideal Husband*
rise to a general condemnation of the corruption
inevitable in political life. *The Ballad of Reading Gaol*
is, in spite of Wilde's ideas on the self-sufficiency of
art, one of the best didactic poems in our language,
with its vivid exposure of the evils of prisons and
punishment, while the long letters on life in gaol
which Wilde wrote to the *Daily Chronicle* actually
had a deep effect in awakening public consciousness
and changing conditions for the better. When the
Chicago anarchists were "framed" and executed in
1887, Wilde was one of the very few English writers
willing to protest on their behalf, and when a young
revolutionary poet, John Barlas, fired a revolver at the
House of Commons in a moment of exasperation,
Wilde was the only man willing to come forward to
help him with his trial and stand surety for him.

   The Soul of Man under Socialism remains the most
complete expression of Wilde's social attitude. This
pamphlet was first published in 1891 in *The Fortnightly
Review* and later appeared in booklet form. It ran
into many editions in many languages, and gained an
especial popularity among the various revolutionary
movements in America and Eastern Europe at the end
of the last century. It is said to have been inspired by
a lecture of Bernard Shaw, but it is clear that the
Shavian influence on Wilde's ideas was negligible,
and that the uncompromisingly libertarian attitude of

his essay has much more in common with the ideas of William Morris and Peter Kropotkin, for whom he had a great admiration both as thinkers and as men, than with Shaw's Fabian state socialism.

As Mr. Hesketh Pearson has pointed out in his biography of Wilde, there is no doubt that *The Soul of Man under Socialism* contributed greatly to upper-class hostility towards Wilde, and was one of the principal causes of the inhuman outcry against him at the time of his trial.

Today, when many people are coming to doubt the wisdom of authoritarian socialism, this pamphlet, with its insistence on individual freedom and the voluntary principle, has a renewed topicality, while there is a particular interest in its discussion of the relationship between the artist and the state, a subject which is now very much in the minds of all those who are interested in the future of the arts.

G. W.

THE SOUL OF MAN
UNDER SOCIALISM

THE chief advantage that would result from the establishment of Socialism is, undoubtedly, the fact that Socialism would relieve us from that sordid necessity of living for others which, in the present condition of things, presses so hardly upon almost everybody. In fact, scarcely any one at all escapes.

Now and then, in the course of the century, a great man of science, like Darwin ; a great poet, like Keats ; a fine critical spirit like M. Renan ; a supreme artist like Flaubert, has been able to isolate himself, to keep himself out of reach of the clamorous claims of others, to stand, " under the shelter of the wall," as Plato puts it, and so to realise the perfection of what was in him, to his own incomparable gain, and to the incomparable and lasting gain of the whole world. These, however, are exceptions. The majority of people spoil their lives by an unhealthy and exaggerated altruism— are forced, indeed, so to spoil them. They find themselves surrounded by hideous poverty, by hideous ugliness, by hideous starvation. It is inevitable that they should be strongly moved by all this. The emotions of man are stirred more quickly than man's intelligence ; and, as I pointed out some time ago in an article on the function of criticism, it is much more easy to have sympathy with suffering than it is to have

sympathy with thought. Accordingly, with admirable,
though misdirected intentions, they very seriously and
very sentimentally set themselves to the task of remedy-
ing the evils that they see. But their remedies do not
cure the disease : they merely prolong it. Indeed,
their remedies are part of the disease.

They try to solve the problem of poverty, for
instance, by keeping the poor alive ; or, in the case of
a very advanced school, by amusing the poor.

But this is not a solution : it is an aggravation of the
difficulty. The proper aim is to try and reconstruct
society on such a basis that poverty will be impossible.
And the altruistic virtues have really prevented the
carrying out of this aim. Just as the worst slave-
owners were those who were kind to their slaves, and
so prevented the horror of the system being realised
by those who suffered from it, and understood by those
who contemplated it, so, in the present state of things
in England, the people who do most harm are the
people who try to do most good ; and at last we have
had the spectacle of men who have really studied the
problem and know the life—educated men who live
in the East End—coming forward and imploring the
community to restrain its altruistic impulses of charity,
benevolence, and the like. They do so on the ground
that such charity degrades and demoralises. They are
perfectly right. Charity creates a multitude of sins.

There is also this to be said. It is immoral to use
private property in order to alleviate the horrible evils
that result from the institution of private property.
It is both immoral and unfair.

Under Socialism all this will, of course, be altered. There will be no people living in fetid dens and fetid rags, and bringing up unhealthy, hunger-pinched children in the midst of impossible and absolutely repulsive surroundings. The security of society will not depend, as it does now, on the state of the weather. If a frost comes we shall not have a hundred thousand men out of work, tramping about the streets in a state of disgusting misery, or whining to their neighbours for alms, or crowding round the doors of loathsome shelters to try and secure a hunch of bread and a night's unclean lodging. Each member of the society will share in the general prosperity and happiness of the society, and if a frost comes no one will practically be anything the worse.

Upon the other hand, Socialism itself will be of value simply because it will lead to Individualism.

Socialism, Communism, or whatever one chooses to call it, by converting private property into public wealth, and substituting co-operation for competition, will restore society to its proper condition of a thoroughly healthy organism, and ensure the material well-being of each member of the community. It will, in fact, give Life its proper basis and its proper environment. But for the full development of Life to its highest mode of perfection, something more is needed. What is needed is Individualism. If the Socialism is Authoritarian ; if there are Governments armed with economic power as they are now with political power ; if, in a word, we are to have Industrial Tyrannies, then the last state of man will be worse than the first. At present, in consequence of the existence of private property, a great many people are enabled to develop a certain very limited amount of Individualism. They are either under no necessity to work for their living, or are enabled to choose the sphere of activity that is really congenial to them, and gives them pleasure. These are the poets, the philosophers, the men of science, the men of culture— in a word, the real men, the men who have realised themselves, and in whom all Humanity gains a partial realisation. Upon the other hand, there are a great many people who, having no private property of their own, and being always on the brink of sheer starvation, are compelled to do the work of beasts of burden, to do work that is quite uncongenial to them, and to which they are forced by the peremptory, unreasonable, degrading Tyranny of want. These are the poor ; and amongst them there is no grace of manner, or charm of speech, or civilisation, or culture, or refinement in pleasures, or joy of life. From their collective force Humanity gains much in material prosperity. But it is only the material result that it gains, and the man who is poor is in himself absolutely of no importance. He is merely the infinitesimal atom of a force that, so far from regarding him, crushes him : indeed, prefers him crushed, as in that case he is far more obedient.

Of course, it might be said that the Individualism generated under conditions of private property is not always, or even as a rule, of a fine or wonderful type, and that the poor, if they have not culture and charm, have still many virtues. Both these statements would be quite true. The possession of private property is very often extremely demoralising, and that is, of course, one of the reasons why Socialism wants to get rid of the institution. In fact, property is really a nuisance. Some years ago people went about the country saying that property has duties. They said it so often and so tediously that, at last, the Church has begun to say it. One hears it now from every pulpit. It is perfectly true. Property not merely has duties, but has so many duties that its possession to any large extent is a bore. It involves endless claims upon one, endless attention to business, endless bother. If property had simply pleasures, we could stand it; but its duties make it unbearable. In the interest of the rich we must get rid of it. The virtues of the poor may be readily admitted, and are much to be regretted. We are often told that the poor are grateful for charity. Some of them are, no doubt, but the best amongst the poor are never grateful. They are ungrateful, discontented, disobedient, and rebellious. They are quite right to be so. Charity they feel to be a ridiculously inadequate mode of partial restitution, or a sentimental dole, usually accompanied by some impertinent attempt on the part of the sentimentalist to tyrannise over their private lives. Why should they be grateful for the crumbs that fall from the rich man's table? They should be seated at the board, and are beginning to know it. As for being discontented, a man who would not be discontented with such surroundings and such a low mode of life would be a perfect brute. Disobedience, in the eyes of any one

who has read history, is man's original virtue. It is
through disobedience that progress has been made,
through disobedience and through rebellion. Sometimes the poor are praised for being thrifty. But to
recommend thrift to the poor is both grotesque and
insulting. It is like advising a man who is starving to
eat less. For a town or country labourer to practise
thrift would be absolutely immoral. Man should not
be ready to show that he can live like a badly fed
animal. He should decline to live like that, and should
either steal or go on the rates, which is considered by
many to be a form of stealing. As for begging, it is
safer to beg than to take, but it is finer to take than to
beg. No : a poor man who is ungrateful, unthrifty,
discontented, and rebellious, is probably a real
personality, and has much in him. He is at any rate
a healthy protest. As for the virtuous poor, one can
pity them, of course, but one cannot possibly admire
them. They have made private terms with the enemy,
and sold their birthright for very bad pottage. They
must also be extraordinarily stupid. I can quite
understand a man accepting laws that protect private
property, and admit of its accumulation, as long as he
himself is able under those conditions to realise some
form of beautiful and intellectual life. But it is almost
incredible to me how a man whose life is marred and
made hideous by such laws can possibly acquiesce in
their continuance.

However, the explanation is not really difficult to
find. It is simply this. Misery and poverty are so
absolutely degrading, and exercise such a paralysing

effect over the nature of men, that no class is ever really
conscious of its own suffering. They have to be told
of it by other people, and they often entirely disbelieve
them. What is said by great employers of labour
against agitators is unquestionably true. Agitators are
a set of interfering, meddling people, who come down
to some perfectly contented class of the community,
and sow the seeds of discontent amongst them. That
is the reason why agitators are so absolutely necessary.
Without them, in our incomplete state, there would be
no advance towards civilisation. Slavery was put down
in America, not in consequence of any action on the
part of the slaves, or even any expressed desire on their
part that they should be free. It was put down entirely
through the grossly illegal conduct of certain agitators
in Boston and elsewhere, who were not slaves themselves, nor owners of slaves, nor had anything to do
with the question really. It was, undoubtedly, the
Abolitionists who set the torch alight, who began
the whole thing. And it is curious to note that from the
slaves themselves they received, not merely very little
assistance, but hardly any sympathy even ; and when
at the close of the war the slaves found themselves free,
found themselves indeed so absolutely free that they
were free to starve, many of them bitterly regretted the
new state of things. To the thinker, the most tragic
fact in the whole of the French Revolution is not that
Marie Antoinette was killed for being a queen, but
that the starved peasant of the Vendée voluntarily went
out to die for the hideous cause of feudalism.

It is clear, then, that no Authoritarian Socialism will

do. For while under the present system a very large
number of people can lead lives of a certain amount of
freedom and expression and happiness, under an
industrial-barrack system, or a system of economic
tyranny, nobody would be able to have any such
freedom at all. It is to be regretted that a portion of
our community should be practically in slavery, but to
propose to solve the problem by enslaving the entire
community is childish. Every man must be left quite
free to choose his own work. No form of compulsion
must be exercised over him. If there is, his work will
not be good for him, will not be good in itself, and
will not be good for others. And by work I simply
mean activity of any kind.

I hardly think that any Socialist, nowadays, would
seriously propose that an inspector should call every
morning at each house to see that each citizen rose up
and did manual labour for eight hours. Humanity has
got beyond that stage, and reserves such a form of life
for the people whom, in a very arbitrary manner, it
chooses to call criminals. But I confess that many of
the socialistic views that I have come across seem to me
to be tainted with ideas of authority, if not of actual
compulsion. Of course, authority and compulsion are
out of the question. All association must be quite
voluntary. It is only in voluntary associations that man
is fine.

But it may be asked how Individualism, which is
now more or less dependent on the existence of private
property for its development, will benefit by the
abolition of such private property. The answer is very

simple. It is true that, under existing conditions, a few
men who have had private means of their own, such as
Byron, Shelley, Browning, Victor Hugo, Baudelaire,
and others, have been able to realise their personality
more or less completely. Not one of these men ever
did a single day's work for hire. They were relieved
from poverty. They had an immense advantage.
The question is whether it would be for the good of
Individualism that such an advantage should be taken
away. Let us suppose that it is taken away. What
happens then to Individualism ? How will it benefit ?

It will benefit in this way. Under the new conditions
Individualism will be far freer, far finer, and far more
intensified than it is now. I am not talking of the great
imaginatively realised Individualism of such poets as
I have mentioned, but of the great actual Individualism
latent and potential in mankind generally. For the
recognition of private property has really harmed
Individualism, and obscured it, by confusing a man
with what he possesses. It has led Individualism
entirely astray. It has made gain, not growth, its aim.
So that man thought that the important thing was to
have, and did not know that the important thing is to
be. The true perfection of man lies, not in what man
has, but in what man is. Private property has crushed
true Individualism, and set up an Individualism that
is false. It has debarred one part of the community
from being individual by starving them. It has
debarred the other part of the community from being
individual by putting them on the wrong road, and
encumbering them. Indeed, so completely has man's

personality been absorbed by his possessions that the
English law has always treated offences against a man's
property with far more severity than offences against
his person, and property is still the test of complete
citizenship. The industry necessary for the making of
money is also very demoralising. In a community like
ours, where property confers immense distinction,
social position, honour, respect, titles, and other
pleasant things of the kind, man, being naturally
ambitious, makes it his aim to accumulate this property,
and goes on wearily and tediously accumulating it long
after he has got far more than he wants, or can use, or
enjoy, or perhaps even know of. Man will kill himself
by overwork in order to secure property, and really,
considering the enormous advantages that property
brings, one is hardly surprised. One's regret is that
society should be constructed on such a basis that man
has been forced into a groove in which he cannot freely
develop what is wonderful, and fascinating, and
delightful in him—in which, in fact, he misses the true
pleasure and joy of living. He is also, under existing
conditions, very insecure. An enormously wealthy
merchant may be—often is—at every moment of his
life at the mercy of things that are not under his
control. If the wind blows an extra point or so, or the
weather suddenly changes, or some trivial thing
happens, his ship may go down, his speculations may
go wrong, and he finds himself a poor man, with his
social position quite gone. Now, nothing should be
able to harm a man except himself. Nothing should
be able to rob a man at all. What a man really has, is

what is in him. What is outside of him should be a
matter of no importance.

With the abolition of private property, then, we
shall have true, beautiful, healthy Individualism.
Nobody will waste his life in accumulating things, and
the symbols for things. One will live. To live is the
rarest thing in the world. Most people exist, that is all.

It is a question whether we have ever seen the full
expression of a personality, except on the imaginative
plane of art. In action, we never have. Cæsar, says
Mommsen, was the complete and perfect man. But
how tragically insecure was Cæsar ! Wherever there
is a man who exercises authority, there is a man who
resists authority. Cæsar was very perfect, but his
perfection travelled by too dangerous a road. Marcus
Aurelius was the perfect man, says Renan. Yes ; the
great emperor was a perfect man. But how intolerable
were the endless claims upon him ! He staggered
under the burden of the empire. He was conscious
how inadequate one man was to bear the weight of
that Titan and too vast orb. What I mean by a perfect
man is one who develops under perfect conditions ;
one who is not wounded, or worried, or maimed, or in
danger. Most personalities have been obliged to be
rebels. Half their strength has been wasted in friction.
Byron's personality, for instance, was terribly wasted
in its battle with the stupidity, and hypocrisy, and
Philistinism of the English. Such battles do not
always intensify strength ; they often exaggerate weakness. Byron was never able to give us what he might
have given us. Shelley escaped better. Like Byron, he

got out of England as soon as possible. But he was not so well known. If the English had had any idea of what a great poet he really was, they would have fallen on him with tooth and nail, and made his life as unbearable to him as they possibly could. But he was not a remarkable figure in society, and consequently he escaped, to a certain degree. Still, even in Shelley the note of rebellion is sometimes too strong. The note of the perfect personality is not rebellion, but peace.

It will be a marvellous thing—the true personality of man—when we see it. It will grow naturally and simply, flower-like, or as a tree grows. It will not be at discord. It will never argue or dispute. It will not prove things. It will know everything. And yet it will not busy itself about knowledge. It will have wisdom. Its value will not be measured by material things. It will have nothing. And yet it will have everything, and whatever one takes from it, it will still have, so rich will it be. It will not be always meddling with others, or asking them to be like itself. It will love them because they will be different. And yet while it will not meddle with others, it will help all, as a beautiful thing helps us, by being what it is. The personality of man will be very wonderful. It will be as wonderful as the personality of a child.

In its development it will be assisted by Christianity, if men desire that ; but if men do not desire that, it will develop none the less surely. For it will not worry itself about the past, nor care whether things happened or did not happen. Nor will it admit any laws but its own laws ; nor any authority but its own authority. Yet it will love those who sought to intensify it, and speak often of them. And of these Christ was one.

" Know thyself " was written over the portal of the antique world. Over the portal of the new world, " Be thyself " shall be written. And the message of Christ to man was simply " Be thyself." That is the secret of Christ.

When Jesus talks about the poor he simply means personalities, just as when he talks about the rich he simply means people who have not developed their personalities. Jesus moved in a community that allowed the accumulation of private property just as ours does, and the gospel that he preached was not that in such a community it is an advantage for a man to live on scanty, unwholesome food, to wear ragged, unwholesome clothes, to sleep in horrid, unwholesome dwellings, and a disadvantage for a man to live under healthy, pleasant, and decent conditions. Such a view would have been wrong there and then, and would, of course, be still more wrong now and in England ; for as man moves northward the material necessities of life become of more vital importance, and our society is infinitely more complex, and displays far greater extremes of luxury and pauperism than any society of the antique world. What Jesus meant, was this. He said to man, " You have a wonderful personality. Develop it. Be yourself. Don't imagine that your perfection lies in accumulating or possessing external things. Your perfection is inside of you. If only you could realise that, you would not want to be rich.

Ordinary riches can be stolen from a man. Real riches
cannot. In the treasury-house of your soul, there are
infinitely precious things, that may not be taken from
you. And so, try to so shape your life that external
things will not harm you. And try also to get rid of
personal property. It involves sordid preoccupation,
endless industry, continual wrong. Personal property
hinders Individualism at every step." It is to be noted
that Jesus never says that impoverished people are
necessarily good, or wealthy people necessarily bad.
That would not have been true. Wealthy people are,
as a class, better than impoverished people, more
moral, more intellectual, more well-behaved. There is
only one class in the community that thinks more about
money than the rich, and that is the poor. The poor
can think of nothing else. That is the misery of being
poor. What Jesus does say, is that man reaches his
perfection, not through what he has, not even through
what he does, but entirely through what he is. And so
the wealthy young man who comes to Jesus is represented as a thoroughly good citizen, who has broken
none of the laws of his state, none of the commandments
of his religion. He is quite respectable, in the ordinary
sense of that extraordinary word. Jesus says to him,
"You should give up private property. It hinders
you from realising your perfection. It is a drag upon
you. It is a burden. Your personality does not need
it. It is within you, and not outside of you, that you
will find what you really are, and what you really
want." To his own friends he says the same thing.
He tells them to be themselves, and not to be always

worrying about other things. What do other things matter? Man is complete in himself. When they go into the world, the world will disagree with them. That is inevitable. The world hates Individualism. But that is not to trouble them. They are to be calm and self-centred. If a man takes their cloak, they are to give him their coat, just to show that material things are of no importance. If people abuse them, they are not to answer back. What does it signify? The things people say of a man do not alter a man. He is what he is. Public opinion is of no value whatsoever. Even if people employ actual violence, they are not to be violent in turn. That would be to fall to the same low level. After all, even in prison, a man can be quite free. His soul can be free. His personality can be untroubled. He can be at peace. And, above all things, they are not to interfere with other people or judge them in any way. Personality is a very mysterious thing. A man cannot always be estimated by what he does. He may keep the law, and yet be worthless. He may break the law, and yet be fine. He may be bad, without ever doing anything bad. He may commit a sin against society, and yet realise through that sin his true perfection.

There was a woman who was taken in adultery. We are not told the history of her love, but that love must have been very great; for Jesus said that her sins were forgiven her, not because she repented, but because her love was so intense and wonderful. Later on, a short time before his death, as he sat at a feast, the woman came in and poured costly perfumes on his

hair. His friends tried to interfere with her, and said
that it was an extravagance, and that the money that the
perfume cost should have been expended on charitable
relief of people in want, or something of that kind.
Jesus did not accept that view. He pointed out that
the material needs of Man were great and very
permanent, but that the spiritual needs of Man were
greater still, and that in one divine moment, and by
selecting its own mode of expression, a personality
might make itself perfect. The world worships the
woman, even now, as a saint.

Yes; there are suggestive things in Individualism.
Socialism annihilates family life, for instance. With
the abolition of private property, marriage in its
present form must disappear. This is part of the
programme. Individualism accepts this and makes it
fine. It converts the abolition of legal restraint into
a form of freedom that will help the full development
of personality, and make the love of man and woman
more wonderful, more beautiful, and more ennobling.
Jesus knew this. He rejected the claims of family life,
although they existed in his day and community in a
very marked form. " Who is my mother? Who are
my brothers? " he said, when he was told that they
wished to speak to him. When one of his followers
asked leave to go and bury his father, " Let the dead
bury the dead," was his terrible answer. He would
allow no claim whatsoever to be made on personality.

And so he who would lead a Christ-like life is he
who is perfectly and absolutely himself. He may be
a great poet, or a great man of science; or a young

student at a University, or one who watches sheep
upon a moor ; or a maker of dramas, like Shakespeare,
or a thinker about God, like Spinoza ; or a child who
plays in a garden, or a fisherman who throws his net
into the sea. It does not matter what he is, as long as
he realises the perfection of the soul that is within him.
All imitation in morals and in life is wrong. Through
the streets of Jerusalem at the present day crawls one
who is mad and carries a wooden cross on his shoulders.
He is a symbol of the lives that are marred by imitation.
Father Damien was Christ-like when he went out to
live with the lepers, because in such service he realised
fully what was best in him. But he was not more
Christ-like than Wagner when he realised his soul in
music ; or than Shelley, when he realised his soul in
song. There is no one type for man. There are as
many perfections as there are imperfect men. And
while to the claims of charity a man may yield and yet
be free, to the claims of conformity no man may yield
and remain free at all.

Individualism, then, is what through Socialism we
are to attain to. As a natural result the State must give
up all idea of government. It must give it up because,
as a wise man once said many centuries before Christ,
there is such a thing as leaving mankind alone ; there
is no such thing as governing mankind. All modes
of government are failures. Despotism is unjust to
everybody, including the despot, who was probably
made for better things. Oligarchies are unjust to the
many, and ochlocracies are unjust to the few. High
hopes were once formed of democracy ; but democracy

means simply the bludgeoning of the people by the
people for the people. It has been found out. I must
say that it was high time, for all authority is quite
degrading. It degrades those who exercise it, and
degrades those over whom it is exercised. When it is
violently, grossly, and cruelly used, it produces a good
effect, by creating, or at any rate bringing out, the
spirit of revolt and Individualism that is to kill it.
When it is used with a certain amount of kindness,
and accompanied by prizes and rewards, it is dreadfully
demoralising. People, in that case, are less conscious
of the horrible pressure that is being put on them, and
so go through their lives in a sort of coarse comfort,
like petted animals, without ever realising that they
are probably thinking other people's thoughts, living
by other people's standards, wearing practically what
one may call other people's second-hand clothes, and
never being themselves for a single moment. " He
who would be free," says a fine thinker, " must not
conform." And authority, by bribing people to
conform, produces a very gross kind of over-fed
barbarism amongst us.

With authority, punishment will pass away. This
will be a great gain—a gain, in fact, of incalculable
value. As one reads history, not in the expurgated
editions written for schoolboys and passmen, but in
the original authorities of each time, one is absolutely
sickened, not by the crimes that the wicked have
committed, but by the punishments that the good have
inflicted ; and a community is infinitely more brutalised
by the habitual employment of punishment, than it is

by the occasional occurrence of crime. It obviously
follows that the more punishment is inflicted the more
crime is produced, and most modern legislation has
clearly recognised this, and has made it its task to
diminish punishment as far as it thinks it can.
Wherever it has really diminished it, the results have
always been extremely good. The less punishment,
the less crime. When there is no punishment at all,
crime will either cease to exist, or, if it occurs, will be
treated by physicians as a very distressing form of
dementia, to be cured by care and kindness. For what
are called criminals nowadays are not criminals at all.
Starvation, and not sin, is the parent of modern crime.
That indeed is the reason why our criminals are, as
a class, so absolutely uninteresting from any psychological point of view. They are not marvellous
Macbeths and terrible Vautrins. They are merely
what ordinary, respectable, commonplace people would
be if they had not got enough to eat. When private
property is abolished there will be no necessity for
crime, no demand for it ; it will cease to exist. Of
course, all crimes are not crimes against property,
though such are the crimes that the English law,
valuing what a man has more than what a man is,
punishes with the harshest and most horrible severity,
if we except the crime of murder, and regard death
as worse than penal servitude, a point on which our
criminals, I believe, disagree. But though a crime
may not be against property, it may spring from the
misery and rage and depression produced by our
wrong system of property-holding, and so, when that

system is abolished, will disappear. When each member of the community has sufficient for his wants, and is not interfered with by his neighbour, it will not be an object of any interest to him to interfere with any one else. Jealousy, which is an extraordinary source of crime in modern life, is an emotion closely bound up with our conceptions of property, and under Socialism and Individualism will die out. It is remarkable that in communistic tribes jealousy is entirely unknown.

Now as the State is not to govern, it may be asked what the State is to do. The State is to be a voluntary association that will organise labour, and be the manufacturer and distributor of necessary commodities. The State is to make what is useful. The individual is to make what is beautiful. And as I have mentioned the word labour, I cannot help saying that a great deal of nonsense is being written and talked nowadays about the dignity of manual labour. There is nothing necessarily dignified about manual labour at all, and most of it is absolutely degrading. It is mentally and morally injurious to man to do anything in which he does not find pleasure, and many forms of labour are quite pleasureless activities, and should be regarded as such. To sweep a slushy crossing for eight hours on a day when the east wind is blowing is a disgusting occupation. To sweep it with mental, moral, or physical dignity seems to me to be impossible. To sweep it with joy would be appalling. Man is made for something better than disturbing dirt. All work of that kind should be done by a machine.

And I have no doubt that it will be so. Up to the present, man has been, to a certain extent, the slave of machinery, and there is something tragic in the fact that as soon as man had invented a machine to do his work he began to starve. This, however, is, of course, the result of our property system and our system of competition. One man owns a machine which does the work of five hundred men. Five hundred men are, in consequence, thrown out of employment, and, having no work to do, become hungry and take to thieving. The one man secures the produce of the machine and keeps it, and has five hundred times as much as he should have, and probably, which is of much more importance, a great deal more than he really wants. Were that machine the property of all, everyone would benefit by it. It would be an immense advantage to the community. All unintellectual labour, all monotonous, dull labour, all labour that deals with dreadful things, and involves unpleasant conditions, must be done by machinery. Machinery must work for us in coal mines, and do all sanitary services, and be the stoker of steamers, and clean the streets, and run messages on wet days, and do anything that is tedious or distressing. At present machinery competes against man. Under proper conditions machinery will serve man. There is no doubt at all that this is the future of machinery ; and just as trees grow while the country gentleman is asleep, so while Humanity will be amusing itself, or enjoying cultivated leisure— which, and not labour, is the aim of man—or making beautiful things, or reading beautiful things, or simply contemplating the world with admiration and delight, machinery will be doing all the necessary and unpleasant work. The fact is, that civilisation requires slaves. The Greeks were quite right there. Unless there are slaves to do the ugly, horrible, uninteresting work, culture and contemplation become almost impossible. Human slavery is wrong, insecure, and demoralising. On mechanical slavery, on the slavery of the machine, the future of the world depends. And when scientific men are no longer called upon to go down to a depressing East End and distribute bad cocoa and worse blankets to starving people, they will have delightful leisure in which to devise wonderful and marvellous things for their own joy and the joy of every one else. There will be great storages of force for every city, and for every house if required, and this force man will convert into heat, light, or motion, according to his needs. Is this Utopian ? A map of the world that does not include Utopia is not worth even glancing at, for it leaves out the one country at which Humanity is always landing. And when Humanity lands there, it looks out, and, seeing a better country, sets sail. Progress is the realisation of Utopias.

Now, I have said that the community by means of organisation of machinery will supply the useful things, and that the beautiful things will be made by the individual. This is not merely necessary, but it is the only possible way by which we can get either the one or the other. An individual who has to make things for the use of others, and with reference to their wants and their wishes, does not work with interest, and consequently cannot put into his work what is best in him. Upon the other hand, whenever a community or a powerful section of a community, or a government of any kind, attempts to dictate to the artist what he is to do, Art either entirely vanishes, or becomes stereotyped, or degenerates into a low and ignoble form of craft. A work of art is the unique result of a unique temperament. Its beauty comes from the fact that the author is what he is. It has nothing to do with the fact that other people want what they want. Indeed, the moment that an artist takes notice of what other people want, and tries to supply the demand, he ceases to be an artist, and becomes a dull or an amusing craftsman, an honest or a dishonest tradesman. He has no further claim to be considered as an artist. Art is the most intense mode of Individualism that the world has known. I am inclined to say that it is the only real mode of Individualism that the world has known. Crime, which, under certain conditions, may seem to have created Individualism, must take cognizance of other people and interfere with them. It belongs to the sphere of action. But alone, without any reference to his neighbours, without any interference, the artist can fashion a beautiful thing ; and if he does not do it solely for his own pleasure, he is not an artist at all.

And it is to be noted that it is the fact that Art is this intense form of Individualism that makes the public try to exercise over it an authority that is as immoral as it is ridiculous, and as corrupting as it is contemptible. It is not quite their fault. The public

has always, and in every age, been badly brought up.
They are continually asking Art to be popular, to
please their want of taste, to flatter their absurd vanity,
to tell them what they have been told before, to show
them what they ought to be tired of seeing, to amuse
them when they feel heavy after eating too much,
and to distract their thoughts when they are wearied
of their own stupidity. Now Art should never try to
be popular. The public should try to make itself
artistic. There is a very wide difference. If a man of
science were told that the results of his experiments,
and the conclusions that he arrived at, should be of
such a character that they would not upset the received
popular notions on the subject, or disturb popular
prejudice, or hurt the sensibilities of people who knew
nothing about science ; if a philosopher were told
that he had a perfect right to speculate in the highest
spheres of thought, provided that he arrived at the
same conclusions as were held by those who had never
thought in any sphere at all—well, nowadays the man
of science and the philosopher would be considerably
amused. Yet it is really a very few years since both
philosophy and science were subjected to brutal
popular control, to authority in fact—the authority of
either the general ignorance of the community, or the
terror and greed for power of an ecclesiastical or
governmental class. Of course, we have to a very
great extent got rid of any attempt on the part of the
community, or the Church, or the Government, to
interfere with the individualism of speculative thought,
but the attempt to interfere with the individualism of

imaginative art still lingers. In fact, it does more than linger ; it is aggressive, offensive, and brutalising.

In England, the arts that have escaped best are the arts in which the public take no interest. Poetry is an instance of what I mean. We have been able to have fine poetry in England because the public do not read it, and consequently do not influence it. The public like to insult poets because they are individual, but once they have insulted them, they leave them alone. In the case of the novel and the drama, arts in which the public do take an interest, the result of the exercise of popular authority has been absolutely ridiculous. No country produces such badly written fiction, such tedious, common work in the novel form, such silly, vulgar plays as England. It must necessarily be so. The popular standard is of such a character that no artist can get to it. It is at once too easy and too difficult to be a popular novelist. It is too easy, because the requirements of the public as far as plot, style, psychology, treatment of life, and treatment of literature are concerned are within the reach of the very meanest capacity and the most uncultivated mind. It is too difficult, because to meet such requirements the artist would have to do violence to his temperament, would have to write not for the artistic joy of writing, but for the amusement of half-educated people, and so would have to suppress his individualism, forget his culture, annihilate his style, and surrender everything that is valuable in him. In the case of the drama, things are a little better : the theatre-going public like the obvious, it is true, but they do not like the tedious ; and burlesque and farcical comedy, the two most popular forms, are distinct forms of art. Delightful work may be produced under burlesque and farcical conditions, and in work of this kind the artist in England is allowed very great freedom. It is when one comes to the higher forms of the drama that the result of popular control is seen. The one thing that the public dislike is novelty. Any attempt to extend the subject-matter of art is extremely distasteful to the public ; and yet the vitality and progress of art depend in a large measure on the continual extension of subject-matter. The public dislike novelty because they are afraid of it. It represents to them a mode of Individualism, an assertion on the part of the artist that he selects his own subject, and treats it as he chooses. The public are quite right in their attitude. Art is Individualism, and Individualism is a disturbing and disintegrating force. Therein lies its immense value. For what it seeks to disturb is monotony of type, slavery of custom, tyranny of habit, and the reduction of man to the level of a machine. In Art, the public accept what has been, because they cannot alter it, not because they appreciate it. They swallow their classics whole, and never taste them. They endure them as the inevitable, and as they cannot mar them, they mouth about them. Strangely enough, or not strangely, according to one's own views, this accept- ance of the classics does a great deal of harm. The uncritical admiration of the Bible and Shakespeare in England is an instance of what I mean. With regard to the Bible, considerations of ecclesiastical authority enter into the matter, so that I need not dwell upon the point.

But in the case of Shakespeare it is quite obvious that the public really see neither the beauties nor the defects of his plays. If they saw the beauties, they would not object to the development of the drama ; and if they saw the defects, they would not object to the development of the drama either. The fact is, the public make use of the classics of a country as a means of checking the progress of Art. They degrade the classics into authorities. They use them as bludgeons for preventing the free expression of Beauty in new forms. They are always asking a writer why he does not write like somebody else, or a painter why he does not paint like somebody else, quite oblivious of the fact that if either of them did anything of the kind he would cease to be an artist. A fresh mode of Beauty is absolutely distasteful to them, and whenever it appears they get so angry and bewildered that they always use two stupid expressions—one is that the work of art is grossly unintelligible ; the other, that the work of art is grossly immoral. What they mean by these words seems to me to be this. When they say a work is grossly unintelligible, they mean that the artist has said or made a beautiful thing that is new ; when they describe a work as grossly immoral, they mean that the artist has said or made a beautiful thing that is true. The former expression has reference to style ; the latter to subject-matter. But they probably use the words very vaguely, as an ordinary mob will use ready-made paving-stones. There is not a single real poet or prose-writer of this century, for instance, on whom the British public have not solemnly conferred diplomas of immorality, and these diplomas practically take the place, with us, of what in France is the formal recognition of an Academy of Letters, and fortunately make the establishment of such an institution quite unnecessary in England. Of course, the public are very reckless in their use of the word. That they should have called Wordsworth an immoral poet, was only to be expected. Wordsworth was a poet. But that they should have called Charles Kingsley an immoral novelist is extraordinary. Kingsley's prose was not of a very fine quality. Still, there is the word, and they use it as best they can. An artist is, of course, not disturbed by it. The true artist is a man who believes absolutely in himself, because he is absolutely himself. But I can fancy that if an artist produced a work of art in England that immediately on its appearance was recognised by the public, through their medium, which is the public Press, as a work that was quite intelligible and highly moral, he would begin seriously to question whether in its creation he had really been himself at all, and consequently whether the work was not quite unworthy of him, and either of a thoroughly second-rate order, or of no artistic value whatsoever.

Perhaps, however, I have wronged the public in limiting them to such words as " immoral," " unintelligible," " exotic," and " unhealthy." There is one other word that they use. That word is " morbid." They do not use it often. The meaning of the word is so simple that they are afraid of using it. Still, they use it sometimes and, now and then, one comes across it in popular newspapers. It is, of course, a ridiculous word to apply to a work of art. For what is morbidity but a mood of emotion or a mode of thought that one cannot express ? The public are all morbid, because the public can never find expression for anything. The artist is never morbid. He expresses everything. He stands outside his subject, and through its medium produces incomparable and artistic effects. To call an artist morbid because he deals with morbidity as his subject-matter is as silly as if one called Shakespeare mad because he wrote *King Lear*.

On the whole, an artist in England gains something by being attacked. His individuality is intensified. He becomes more completely himself. Of course, the attacks are very gross, very impertinent, and very contemptible. But then no artist expects grace from the vulgar mind, or style from the suburban intellect. Vulgarity and stupidity are two very vivid facts in modern life. One regrets them, naturally. But there they are. They are subjects for study, like everything else. And it is only fair to state, with regard to modern journalists, that they always apologise to one in private for what they have written against one in public.

Within the last few years two other adjectives, it may be mentioned, have been added to the very limited vocabulary of art-abuse that is at the disposal of the public. One is the word " unhealthy," the other is the word " exotic." The latter merely expresses the rage of the momentary mushroom against the im-

mortal, entrancing, and exquisitely lovely orchid. It is
a tribute, but a tribute of no importance. The word
" unhealthy," however, admits of analysis. It is a
rather interesting word. In fact, it is so interesting
that the people who use it do not know what it
means.

What does it mean ? What is a healthy or an unhealthy work of art ? All terms that one applies to a
work of art, provided that one applies them rationally,
have reference to either its style or its subject, or to
both together. From the point of view of style, a
healthy work of art is one whose style recognises the
beauty of the material it employs, be that material one
of words or of bronze, of colour or of ivory, and uses
that beauty as a factor in producing the æsthetic effect.
From the point of view of subject, a healthy work of
art is one the choice of whose subject is conditioned by
the temperament of the artist, and comes directly out
of it. In fine, a healthy work of art is one that has both
perfection and personality. Of course, form and
substance cannot be separated in a work of art ; they
are always one. But for purposes of analysis, and
setting the wholeness of æsthetic impression aside for
a moment, we can intellectually so separate them. An
unhealthy work of art, on the other hand, is a work
whose style is obvious, old-fashioned, and common,
and whose subject is deliberately chosen, not because
the artist has any pleasure in it, but because he thinks
that the public will pay him for it. In fact, the popular
novel that the public call healthy is always a thoroughly
unhealthy production ; and what the public call an

unhealthy novel is always a beautiful and healthy work
of art.

I need hardly say that I am not, for a single moment,
complaining that the public and the public Press misuse these words. I do not see how, with their lack of
comprehension of what Art is, they could possibly use
them in the proper sense. I am merely pointing out
the misuse ; and as for the origin of the misuse and the
meaning that lies behind it all, the explanation is very
simple. It comes from the barbarous conception of
authority. It comes from the natural inability of a
community corrupted by authority to understand or
appreciate Individualism. In a word, it comes from
that monstrous and ignorant thing that is called Public
Opinion, which, bad and well-meaning as it is when it
tries to control action, is infamous and of evil meaning
when it tries to control Thought or Art.

Indeed, there is much more to be said in favour of
the physical force of the public than there is in favour
of the public's opinion. The former may be fine. The
latter must be foolish. It is often said that force is no
argument. That, however, entirely depends on what
one wants to prove. Many of the most important
problems of the last few centuries, such as the continuance of personal government in England, or of
feudalism in France, have been solved entirely by
means of physical force. The very violence of a
revolution may make the public grand and splendid for
a moment. It was a fatal day when the public discovered that the pen is mightier than the paving-stone,
and can be made as offensive as the brickbat. They at

once sought for the journalist, found him, developed
him, and made him their industrious and well-paid
servant.   It is greatly to be regretted, for both their
sakes.   Behind the barricade there may be much that
is noble and heroic.   But what is there behind the
leading-article but prejudice, stupidity, cant, and
twaddle ?   And when these four are joined together
they make a terrible force, and constitute the new
authority.

In old days men had the rack.   Now they have the
Press.   That is an improvement certainly.   But still it
is very bad, and wrong, and demoralising.   Somebody
—was it Burke ?—called journalism the fourth estate.
That was true at the time, no doubt.   But at the
present moment it really is the only estate.   It has
eaten up the other three.   The Lords Temporal say
nothing, the Lords Spiritual have nothing to say, and
the House of Commons has nothing to say and says it.
We are dominated by Journalism.   In America the
President reigns for four years, and Journalism
governs for ever and ever.   Fortunately, in America,
Journalism has carried its authority to the grossest
and most brutal extreme.   As a natural consequence it
has begun to create a spirit of revolt.   People are
amused by it, or disgusted by it, according to their
temperaments.   But it is no longer the real force it was.
It is not seriously treated.   In England, Journalism,
except in a few well-known instances, not having been
carried to such excesses of brutality, is still a great
factor, a really remarkable power.   The tyranny that
it proposes to exercise over people's private lives seems

to me to be quite extraordinary. The fact is, that the
public have an insatiable curiosity to know everything,
except what is worth knowing. Journalism, conscious
of this, and having tradesman-like habits, supplies their
demands. In centuries before ours the public nailed
the ears of journalists to the pump. That was quite
hideous. In this century journalists have nailed their
own ears to the keyhole. That is much worse. And
what aggravates the mischief is that the journalists who
are most to blame are not the amusing journalists who
write for what are called Society papers. The harm is
done by the serious, thoughtful, earnest journalists,
who solemnly, as they are doing at present, will drag
before the eyes of the public some incident in the
private life of a great statesman, of a man who is a
leader of political thought as he is a creator of political
force, and invite the public to discuss the incident, to
exercise authority in the matter, to give their views :
and not merely to give their views, but to carry them
into action, to dictate to the man upon all other points,
to dictate to his party, to dictate to his country ; in fact,
to make themselves ridiculous, offensive, and harmful.
The private lives of men and women should not be
told to the public. The public have nothing to do
with them at all.

In France they manage these things better. There
they do not allow the details of the trials that take place
in the divorce courts to be published for the amusement
or criticism of the public. All that the public are
allowed to know is that the divorce has taken place
and was granted on petition of one or other or both of

the married parties concerned. In France, in fact, they limit the journalist, and allow the artist almost perfect freedom. Here we allow absolute freedom to the journalist, and entirely limit the artist. English public opinion, that is to say, tries to constrain and impede and warp the man who makes things that are beautiful in effect, and compels the journalist to retail things that are ugly, or disgusting, or revolting in fact, so that we have the most serious journalists in the world and the most indecent newspapers. It is no exaggeration to talk of compulsion. There are possibly some journalists who take a real pleasure in publishing horrible things, or who, being poor, look to scandals as forming a sort of permanent basis for an income. But there are other journalists, I feel certain, men of education and cultivation, who really dislike publishing these things, who know that it is wrong to do so, and only do it because the unhealthy conditions under which their occupation is carried on, oblige them to supply the public with what the public wants, and to compete with other journalists in making that supply as full and satisfying to the gross popular appetite as possible. It is a very degrading position for any body of educated men to be placed in, and I have no doubt that most of them feel it acutely.

However, let us leave what is really a very sordid side of the subject, and return to the question of popular control in the matter of Art, by which I mean Public Opinion dictating to the artist the form which he is to use, the mode in which he is to use it, and the materials with which he is to work. I have pointed out that the arts which had escaped best in England are the arts in which the public have not been interested. They are, however, interested in the drama, and as a certain advance has been made in the drama within the last ten or fifteen years, it is important to point out that this advance is entirely due to a few individual artists refusing to accept the popular want of taste as their standard, and refusing to regard Art as a mere matter of demand and supply. With his marvellous and vivid personality, with a style that has really a true colour-element in it, with his extraordinary power, not over mere mimicry but over imaginative and intellectual creation, Mr. Irving, had his sole object been to give the public what they wanted, could have produced the commonest plays in the commonest manner, and made as much success and money as a man could possibly desire. But his object was not that. His object was to realise his own perfection as an artist, under certain conditions and in certain forms of Art. At first he appealed to the few : now he has educated the many. He has created in the public both taste and temperament. The public appreciate his artistic success immensely. I often wonder, however, whether the public understand that that success is entirely due to the fact that he did not accept their standard, but realised his own. With their standard the Lyceum would have been a sort of second-rate booth, as some of the popular theatres in London are at present. Whether they understand it or not, the fact however remains, that taste and temperament have, to a certain extent, been created in the public, and that the public is capable of developing these qualities. The problem then is, why do not the public become more civilised ? They have the capacity. What stops them ?

The thing that stops them, it must be said again, is their desire to exercise authority over the artists and over works of art. To certain theatres, such as the Lyceum and the Haymarket, the public seem to come in a proper mood. In both of these theatres there have been individual artists, who have succeeded in creating in their audiences—and every theatre in London has its own audience—the temperament to which Art appeals. And what is that temperament ? It is the temperament of receptivity. That is all.

If a man approaches a work of art with any desire to exercise authority over it and the artist, he approaches it in such a spirit that he cannot receive any artistic impression from it at all. The work of art is to dominate the spectator : the spectator is not to dominate the work of art. The spectator is to be receptive. He is to be the violin on which the master is to play. And the more completely he can suppress his own silly views, his own foolish prejudices, his own absurd ideas of what Art should be, or should not be, the more likely he is to understand and appreciate the work of art in question. This is, of course, quite obvious in the case of the vulgar theatre-going public of English men and women. But it is equally true of what are called educated people. For an educated person's ideas of Art are drawn naturally from what Art has been, whereas the new work of art is beautiful by being what Art has never been ; and to measure it

by the standard of the past is to measure it by a
standard on the rejection of which its real perfection
depends. A temperament capable of receiving,
through an imaginative medium, and under imaginative
conditions, new and beautiful impressions, is the only
temperament that can appreciate a work of art. And
true as this is in a case of the appreciation of sculpture
and painting, it is still more true of the appreciation of
such arts as the drama. For a picture and a statue are
not at war with Time. They take no account of its
succession. In one moment their unity may be
apprehended. In the case of literature it is different.
Time must be traversed before the unity of effect is
realised. And so, in the drama, there may occur in the
first act of the play something whose real artistic value
may not be evident to the spectator till the third or
fourth act is reached. Is the silly fellow to get angry
and call out, and disturb the play, and annoy the
artists ? No. The honest man is to sit quietly, and
know the delightful emotions of wonder, curiosity,
and suspense. He is not to go to the play to lose a
vulgar temper. He is to go to the play to realise an
artistic temperament. He is to go to the play to gain
an artistic temperament. He is not the arbiter of the
work of art. He is one who is admitted to contemplate
the work of art, and if the work be fine, to forget in its
contemplation all the egotism that mars him—the
egotism of his ignorance, or the egotism of his information. This point about the drama is hardly, I think,
sufficiently recognised. I can quite understand that
were *Macbeth* produced for the first time before a

modern London audience, many of the people present
would strongly and vigorously object to the introduction of the witches in the first act, with their
grotesque phrases and their ridiculous words. But
when the play is over one realises that the laughter of
the witches in *Macbeth* is as terrible as the laughter
of madness in *Lear*, more terrible than the laughter of
Iago in the tragedy of the Moor. No spectator of art
needs a more perfect mood of receptivity than the
spectator of a play. The moment he seeks to exercise
authority he becomes the avowed enemy of Art, and of
himself. Art does not mind. It is he who suffers.

With the novel it is the same thing. Popular
authority and the recognition of popular authority are
fatal. Thackeray's *Esmond* is a beautiful work of art
because he wrote it to please himself. In his other
novels, in *Pendennis*, in *Philip*, in *Vanity Fair* even, at
times, he is too conscious of the public, and spoils his
work by appealing directly to the sympathies of the
public, or by directly mocking at them. A true artist
takes no notice whatever of the public. The public
are to him non-existent. He has no poppied or
honeyed cakes through which to give the monster sleep
or sustenance. He leaves that to the popular novelist.
One incomparable novelist we have now in England,
Mr. George Meredith. There are better artists in
France, but France has no one whose view of life is so
large, so varied, so imaginatively true. There are
tellers of stories in Russia who have a more vivid
sense of what pain in fiction may be. But to him
belongs philosophy in fiction. His people not merely

live, but they live in thought. One can see them from myriad points of view. They are suggestive. There is soul in them and around them. They are interpretative and symbolic. And he who made them, those wonderful, quickly moving figures, made them for his own pleasure, and has never asked the public what they wanted, has never cared to know what they wanted, has never allowed the public to dictate to him or influence him in any way, but has gone on intensifying his own personality, and producing his own individual work. At first none came to him. That did not matter. Then the few came to him. That did not change him. The many have come now. He is still the same. He is an incomparable novelist.

With the decorative arts it is not different. The public clung with really pathetic tenacity to what I believe were the direct traditions of the Great Exhibition of international vulgarity, traditions that were so appalling that the houses in which people lived were only fit for blind people to live in. Beautiful things began to be made, beautiful colours came from the dyer's hand, beautiful patterns from the artist's brain, and the use of beautiful things and their value and importance were set forth. The public were really very indignant. They lost their temper. They said silly things. No one minded. No one was a whit the worse. No one accepted the authority of public opinion. And now it is almost impossible to enter any modern house without seeing some recognition of good taste, some recognition of the value of lovely surroundings, some sign of appreciation of beauty.

In fact, people's houses are, as a rule, quite charming nowadays. People have been to a very great extent civilised. It is only fair to state, however, that the extraordinary success of the revolution in house-decoration and furniture and the like has not really been due to the majority of the public developing a very fine taste in such matters. It has been chiefly due to the fact that the craftsmen of things so appreciated the pleasure of making what was beautiful, and woke to such a vivid consciousness of the hideousness and vulgarity of what the public had previously wanted, that they simply starved the public out. It would be quite impossible at the present moment to furnish a room as rooms were furnished a few years ago, without going for everything to an auction of second-hand furniture from some third-rate lodging-house. The things are no longer made. However they may object to it, people must nowadays have something charming in their surroundings. Fortunately for them, their assumption of authority in these art-matters came to entire grief.

It is evident, then, that all authority in such things is bad. People sometimes inquire what form of government is most suitable for an artist to live under. To this question there is only one answer. The form of government that is most suitable to the artist is no government at all. Authority over him and his art is ridiculous. It has been stated that under despotisms artists have produced lovely work. This is not quite so. Artists have visited despots, not as subjects to be tyrannised over, but as wandering wonder-makers, as fascinating vagrant personalities, to be entertained and charmed and suffered to be at peace, and allowed to create. There is this to be said in favour of the despot, that he, being an individual, may have culture, while the mob, being a monster, has none. One who is an Emperor and King may stoop down to pick up a brush for a painter, but when the democracy stoops down it is merely to throw mud. And yet the democracy have not so far to stoop as the emperor. In fact, when they want to throw mud they have not to stoop at all. But there is no necessity to separate the monarch from the mob ; all authority is equally bad.

There are three kinds of despots. There is the despot who tyrannises over the body. There is the despot who tyrannises over the soul. There is the despot who tyrannises over the soul and body alike. The first is called the Prince. The second is called the Pope. The third is called the People. The Prince may be cultivated. Many Princes have been. Yet in the Prince there is danger. One thinks of Dante at the bitter feast in Verona, of Tasso in Ferrara's madman's cell. It is better for the artist not to live with Princes. The Pope may be cultivated. Many Popes have been ; the bad Popes have been. The bad Popes loved Beauty, almost as passionately, nay, with as much passion as the good Popes hated Thought. To the wickedness of the Papacy humanity owes much. The goodness of the Papacy owes a terrible debt to humanity. Yet, though the Vatican has kept the rhetoric of its thunders, and lost the rod of its lightning, it is better for the artist not to live with Popes. It was a Pope who said of Cellini to a conclave of Cardinals that common laws and common authority were not made for men such as he ; but it was a Pope who thrust Cellini into prison, and kept him there till he sickened with rage, and created unreal visions for himself, and saw the gilded sun enter his room, and grew so enamoured of it that he sought to escape, and crept out from tower to tower, and falling through dizzy air at dawn, maimed himself, and was by a vinedresser covered with vine leaves, and carried in a cart to one who, loving beautiful things, had care of him. There is danger in Popes. And as for the People, what of them and their authority ? Perhaps of them and their authority one has spoken enough. Their authority is a thing blind, deaf, hideous, grotesque, tragic, amusing, serious, and obscene. It is impossible for the artist to live with the People. All despots bribe. The People bribe and brutalise. Who told them to exercise authority ? They were made to live, to listen, and to love. Some one has done them a great wrong. They have marred themselves by imitation of their inferiors. They have taken the sceptre of the Prince. How should they use it ? They have taken the triple tiara of the Pope. How should they carry its burden ? They are as a clown whose heart is broken. They are as a priest whose soul is not yet born. Let all who love Beauty pity them. Though they themselves love not Beauty, yet let them pity themselves. Who taught them the trick of tyranny ?

There are many other things that one might point out. One might point out how the Renaissance was great, because it sought to solve no social problem, and busied itself not about such things, but suffered the individual to develop freely, beautifully, and naturally, and so had great and individual artists, and great and individual men. One might point out how Louis XIV, by creating the modern state, destroyed the individualism of the artist, and made things monstrous in their monotony of repetition, and contemptible in their conformity to rule, and destroyed throughout all France all those fine freedoms of expression that had made tradition new in beauty, and new modes one with antique form. But the past is of no importance. The present is of no importance. It is with the future that we have to deal. For the past is what man should not have been. The present is what man ought not to be. The future is what artists are.

It will, of course, be said that such a scheme as is set forth here is quite unpractical, and goes against human nature. This is perfectly true. It is unpractical, and it goes against human nature. This is why it is worth carrying out, and that is why one proposes it. For what is a practical scheme ? A practical scheme is either a scheme that is already in existence, or a scheme that could be carried out under existing conditions. But it is exactly the existing conditions that one objects to ; and any scheme that could accept these conditions is wrong and foolish. The conditions will be done away with, and human nature will change. The only thing that one really knows about human nature is that it changes. Change is the one quality we can predicate of it. The systems that fail are those that rely on the permanency of human nature, and not on its growth and development. The error of Louis XIV was that he thought human nature would always be the same. The result of his error was the French Revolution. It was an admirable result. All the results of the mistakes of governments are quite admirable.

It is to be noted also that Individualism does not come to man with any sickly cant about duty, which merely means doing what other people want because they want it ; or any hideous cant about self-sacrifice, which is merely a survival of savage mutilation. In fact, it does not come to man with any claims upon him at all. It comes naturally and inevitably out of man. It is the point to which all development tends. It is the differentiation to which all organisms grow. It is the perfection that is inherent in every mode of life, and towards which every mode of life quickens. And so Individualism exercises no compulsion over man. On the contrary, it says to man that he should suffer no compulsion to be exercised over him. It does not try to force people to be good. It knows that people are good when they are let alone. Man will develop Individualism out of himself. Man is now so developing Individualism. To ask whether Individualism is practical is like asking whether Evolution is practical. Evolution is the law of life, and there is no evolution except towards Individualism. Where this tendency is not expressed, it is a case of artificially arrested growth, or of disease, or of death.

Individualism will also be unselfish and unaffected. It has been pointed out that one of the results of the extraordinary tyranny of authority is that words are absolutely distorted from their proper and simple meaning, and are used to express the obverse of their right signification. What is true about Art is true about Life. A man is called affected, nowadays, if he dresses as he likes to dress. But in doing that he is acting in a perfectly natural manner. Affectation, in such matters, consists in dressing according to the views of one's neighbour, whose views, as they are the views of the majority, will probably be extremely stupid. Or a man is called selfish if he lives in the manner that seems to him most suitable for the full realisation of his own personality; if, in fact, the primary aim of his life is self-development. But this is the way in which everyone should live. Selfishness is not living as one wishes to live, it is asking others to live as one wishes to live. And unselfishness is letting other people's lives alone, not interfering with them. Selfishness always aims at creating around it an absolute uniformity of type. Unselfishness recognises infinite variety of type as a delightful thing, accepts it, acquiesces in it, enjoys it. It is not selfish to think for oneself. A man who does not think for himself does not think at all. It is grossly selfish to require of one's neighbour that he should think in the same way, and hold the same opinions. Why should he ? If he can think, he will probably think differently. If he cannot think, it is monstrous to require thought of any kind from him. A red rose is not selfish because it wants to be a red rose. It would be horribly selfish if it wanted all the other flowers in the garden to be both red and roses. Under Individualism people will be quite natural and absolutely unselfish, and will know the meanings of the words, and realise them in their free, beautiful lives. Nor will men be egotistic as they are now. For the egotist is he who makes claims upon others, and the Individualist will not desire to do that. It will not give him pleasure. When man has realised Individualism, he will also realise sympathy and exercise it freely and spontaneously. Up to the present man has hardly cultivated sympathy at all. He has merely sympathy with pain, and sympathy with pain is not the highest form of sympathy. All sympathy is fine, but sympathy with suffering is the least fine mode. It is tainted with egotism. It is apt to become morbid. There is in it a certain element of terror for our own safety. We become afraid that we ourselves might be as the leper or as the blind, and that no man would have care of us. It is curiously limiting, too. One should sympathise with the entirety of life, not with life's sores and maladies merely, but with life's joy and beauty and energy and health and freedom. The wider sympathy is, of course, the more difficult. It requires more unselfishness. Anybody can sympathise with the sufferings of a friend, but it requires a very fine nature—it requires, in fact, the nature of a true Individualist—to sympathise with a friend's success.

In the modern stress of competition and struggle for place, such sympathy is naturally rare, and is also very much stifled by the immoral ideal of uniformity of

type and conformity to rule which is so prevalent everywhere, and is perhaps most obnoxious in England.

Sympathy with pain there will, of course, always be.
It is one of the first instincts of man. The animals
which are individual, the higher animals, that is to say,
share it with us. But it must be remembered that
while sympathy with joy intensifies the sum of joy in the
world, sympathy with pain does not really diminish
the amount of pain. It may make man better able to
endure evil, but the evil remains. Sympathy with
consumption does not cure consumption ; that is what
Science does. And when Socialism has solved the
problem of poverty, and Science solved the problem of
disease, the area of the sentimentalists will be lessened,
and the sympathy of man will be large, healthy and
spontaneous. Man will have joy in the contemplation
of the joyous lives of others.

For it is through joy that the Individualism of the
future will develop itself. Christ made no attempt to
reconstruct society, and consequently the Individualism
that he preached to man could be realised only through
pain or in solitude. The ideals that we owe to Christ
are the ideals of the man who abandons society entirely,
or of the man who resists society absolutely. But man
is naturally social. Even the Thebaid became peopled
at last. And though the cenobite realises his personality, it is often an impoverished personality that he so
realises. Upon the other hand, the terrible truth that
pain is a mode through which man may realise himself
exercises a wonderful fascination over the world.
Shallow speakers and shallow thinkers in pulpits and

on platforms often talk about the world's worship of pleasure, and whine against it. But it is rarely in the world's history that its ideal has been one of joy and beauty. The worship of pain has far more often dominated the world. Medievalism, with its saints and martyrs, its love of self-torture, its wild passion for wounding itself, its gashing with knives, and its whipping with rods—Medievalism is real Christianity, and the medieval Christ is the real Christ. When the Renaissance dawned upon the world, and brought with it the new ideals of the beauty of life and the joy of living, men could not understand Christ. Even Art shows us that. The painters of the Renaissance drew Christ as a little boy playing with another boy in a palace or a garden, or lying back in his mother's arms, smiling at her, or at a flower, or at a bright bird ; or as a noble, stately figure moving nobly through the world ; or as a wonderful figure rising in a sort of ecstasy from death to life. Even when they drew him crucified they drew him as a beautiful God on whom evil men had inflicted suffering. But he did not preoccupy them much. What delighted them was to paint the men and women whom they admired, and to show the loveliness of this lovely earth. They painted many religious pictures—in fact, they painted far too many, and the monotony of type and motive is wearisome, and was bad for art. It was the result of the authority of the public in art-matters, and is to be deplored. But their soul was not in the subject. Raphael was a great artist when he painted his portrait of the Pope. When he painted his Madonnas and infant Christs, he was not a great artist at all. Christ had no message for the Renaissance, which was wonderful because it brought an ideal at variance with his, and to find the presentation of the real Christ we must go to medieval art. There he is one maimed and marred ; one who is not comely to look on, because Beauty is a joy ; one who is not in fair raiment, because that may be a joy also : he is a beggar who has a marvellous soul ; he is a leper whose soul is divine ; he needs neither property nor health ; he is a God realising his perfection through pain.

The evolution of man is slow. The injustice of men is great. It was necessary that pain should be put forward as a mode of self-realisation. Even now, in some places in the world, the message of Christ is necessary. No one who lived in modern Russia could possibly realise his perfection except by pain. A few Russian artists have realised themselves in Art ; in a fiction that is medieval in character, because its dominant note is the realisation of men through suffering. But for those who are not artists, and to whom there is no mode of life but the actual life of fact, pain is the only door to perfection. A Russian who lives happily under the present system of government in Russia must either believe that man has no soul, or that, if he has, it is not worth developing. A Nihilist who rejects all authority, because he knows authority to be evil, and welcomes all pain, because through that he realises his personality, is a real Christian. To him the Christian ideal is a true thing.

And yet, Christ did not revolt against authority. He accepted the imperial authority of the Roman

Empire and paid tribute. He endured the ecclesiastical authority of the Jewish Church, and would not
repel its violence by any violence of his own. He had,
as I said before, no scheme for the reconstruction of
society. But the modern world has schemes. It
proposes to do away with poverty and the suffering
that it entails. It desires to get rid of pain, and the
suffering that pain entails. It trusts to Socialism and
to Science as its methods. What it aims at is an
Individualism expressing itself through joy. This
Individualism will be larger, fuller, lovelier than
any Individualism has ever been. Pain is not the
ultimate mode of perfection. It is merely provisional
and a protest. It has reference to wrong, unhealthy,
unjust surroundings. When the wrong, and the
disease, and the injustice are removed, it will have no
further place. It will have done its work. It was a
great work, but it is almost over. Its sphere lessens
every day.

Nor will man miss it. For what man has sought for
is, indeed, neither pain nor pleasure, but simply Life.
Man has sought to live intensely, fully, perfectly.
When he can do so without exercising restraint on
others, or suffering it ever, and his activities are all
pleasurable to him, he will be saner, healthier, more
civilised, more himself. Pleasure is Nature's test, her
sign of approval. When man is happy, he is in harmony with himself and his environment. The new
Individualism, for whose service Socialism, whether it
wills it or not, is working, will be perfect harmony. It
will be what the Greeks sought for, but could not,

except in Thought, realise completely, because they had slaves, and fed them ; it will be what the Renaissance sought for, but could not realise completely except in Art, because they had slaves, and starved them. It will be complete, and through it each man will attain to his perfection. The new Individualism is the new Hellenism.

Page 9   " As I pointed out . . . in an article on the function of criticism," *viz.*: *The Critic as Artist.*   After discussing the follies of philanthropy and showing the necessity of the Utopian thinker, Wilde says:

" I do not deny that the intellectual ideal is difficult of attainment, still less that it is, and perhaps will be for years to come, unpopular with the crowd.   It is so easy for people to have sympathy with suffering.   It is so difficult for them to have sympathy with thought.   Indeed, so little do ordinary people understand what thought really is, that they seem to imagine that, when they have said that a theory is dangerous, they have pronounced its condemnation, whereas it is only such theories that have any true intellectual value.   An idea that is not dangerous is unworthy of being called an idea at all."

Page 19   " Cæsar, says Mommsen, was the complete and perfect man."   Theodor Mommsen, whose *History of Rome* can be regarded as a classic work on the Roman republic, was greatly impressed with the character of Julius Cæsar, and devoted considerable space to an eulogistic and, it would seem, rather overdone appreciation of Cæsar as man and statesman, which culminates in the following passage of adulation, to which Wilde is referring:

" In his character as a man as well as in his place in history, Cæsar occupies a position where the great contrasts of existence meet and balance each other.   Of the mightiest creative power and yet at the same time of the most penetrating judgment; no longer a youth and not yet an old man; of the highest energy of will and the highest capacity of execution; filled with republican ideals and at the same time born to be a king; a Roman in the deepest essence of his nature, and yet called to reconcile and combine in himself, as well as in the outer world, the Roman and the Hellenic types of culture—Cæsar was the entire and perfect man."

Page 25   " As a wise man once said many centuries before Christ."   Chuang Tzu (Chiangtse), the Taoist philosopher who recorded many of the sayings and deeds of Lao Tzu (Laotse). Wilde reviewed at length, and with much sympathy, in *The Speaker* (February 8, 1890), a selection of Chuang Tzu's writings translated by Herbert A. Giles. Chuang Tzu preached an early libertarian philosophy that had much in common with Wilde's version of Socialism.

Page 40   " Was it Burke ? "   No, it was Lord Macaulay, in his review of Hallam's *Constitutional History*, contributed to *The Edinburgh Review*, September, 1828.

Page 43   " Mr. Irving."   Wilde was always a great defender of Irving, who was often accused of putting on inferior plays merely because they gave him an opportunity to display his own acting. Wilde held that a great artist like Irving was perfectly justified in this, since his art as an actor was great enough to stand by itself, without the assistance of a good play.

Page 53   " A man is called affected, nowadays, if he dresses as he likes to dress."   This passage is no doubt intended partly as a self-justification of Wilde's own period of " aesthetic " dress, when he wore velvet jackets, knee-breeches and flowing cravats, and was duly caricatured by W. S. Gilbert in the comic opera *Patience* and by George du Maurier in *Punch*, as well as being castigated by Max Nordau in an eassy on the " decadent " movement. In later years he became a " dandy," and his green carnation buttonholes, initiated on the first night of *Lady Windermere's Fan*, provided the title for a novel in which Robert Hichens satirised Wilde as Esme Araminth.

Page 57   Russia. Wilde always showed much interest in Russian literature and revolutionary movements. His early play, *Vera*, concerned the Nihilists ; he was an admirer of Kropotkin, and he wrote a long and appreciative review of Dostoevsky's *The Insulted and Injured*. When the Russian revolution came, there was a struggle between the authoritarian type of socialism, represented by the Bolsheviks, and the libertarian type, represented by the Social Revolutionaries and the Anarchists, philosophical heirs of the Nihilists. The authoritarians won, and the result has gone to prove the justice of Wilde's warnings against authoritarian socialism.

THE COMING OF WORLD WAR THREE
VOL. 1
From Protest to Resistance/The International War System
by Dimitrios I. Roussopoulos

This profound and timely work analyses the various forces which bring us ever closer to nuclear annihilation. It also takes the reader on a tour of the numerous anti-nuclear and disarmament organisations worldwide and identifies the myriad political issues contributing to international tension.

Since the works of British historian E.P. Thompson are not widely read in North America, Roussopoulos serves some purpose in presenting similar views.
Choice

The author's discussion of the causes and possible prevention of World War Three are penetrating and provocative.
Vancouver Sun

An extremely important book.
Ottawa Citizen

Offers a detailed description of the activities of the anti-nuclear campaign of the 1980's...provides an information resource not readily available elsewhere.
Canadian Book Review Annual

...a penetrating study of the factors leading to a very probable disaster...goes well beyond analysis and warning, to an inquiry into what is being done and what should be done to compel a reversal of course.
Noam Chomsky

299 pages
Paperback ISBN: 0-920057-02-0 $14.95
Hardcover ISBN: 0-920057-03-9 $29.95
International Politics/Sociology

BLACK ROSE BOOKS
has published the following books of related interests

Peter Kropotkin, Memoirs of a Revolutionist, introduction by George Woodcock
Peter Kropotkin, Mutual Aid, introduction by George Woodcock
Peter Kropotkin, The Great French Revolution, introduction by George Woodcock
Peter Kropotkin, The Conquest of Bread, introduction by George Woodcock
    other books by Peter Kropotkin are forthcoming in this series
Marie Fleming, The Geography of Freedom: The Odyssey of Elisée Reclus,
    introduction by George Woodcock
William R. McKercher, Freedom and Authority
Noam Chomsky, Language and Politics, edited by C.P. Otero
Noam Chomsky, Radical Priorities, edited by C.P. Otero
George Woodcock, Pierre-Joseph Proudhon, a biography
Murray Bookchin, Remaking Society
Murray Bookchin, Toward an Ecological Society
Murray Bookchin, Post-Scarcity Anarchism
Murray Bookchin, The Limits of the City
Murray Bookchin, The Modern Crisis
Edith Thomas, Louise Michel, a biography
Walter Johnson, Trade Unions and the State
John Clark, The Anarchist Moment: Reflections on Culture, Nature and Power
Sam Dolgoff, Bakunin on Anarchism
Sam Dolgoff, The Anarchist Collectives in Spain, 1936-39
Sam Dolgoff, The Cuban Revolution: A critical perspective
Thom Holterman, Law and Anarchism
Etienne de la Boétie, The Politics of Obedience
Stephen Schecter, The Politics of Urban Liberation
Abel Paz, Durruti, the people armed
Juan Gomez Casas, Anarchist Organisation, the history of the F.A.I.
Voline, The Unknown Revolution
Dimitrios Roussopoulos, The Anarchist Papers
Dimitrios Roussopoulos, The Anarchist Papers 2

send for a complete catalogue of books
mailed out free
BLACK ROSE BOOKS
3981 boul. St-Laurent, #444
Montréal H2W 1Y5, Québec, Canada

Printed by
the workers of
Editions Marquis, Montmagny, Québec
for
Black Rose Books Ltd.